WITHDRAWN

LIBERTY AND JUSTICE

LIBERTY AND JUSTICE

Essays in Political Theory 2

BRIAN BARRY

CLARENDON PRESS · OXFORD

1991

Oxford University Press, Walton Street, Oxford OX2 6DP

Oxford New York Toronto
Delhi Bombay Calcutta Madras Karachi
Petaling Jaya Singapore Hong Kong Tokyo
Nairobi Dar es Salaam Cape Town
Melbourne Auckland
and associated companies in
Berlin Ibadan

Oxford is a trade mark of Oxford University Press

Published in the United States
by Oxford University Press, New York

Democracy, Power, and Justice: Essays in Political Theory, first published as a hardback 1989
First issued in Clarendon Paperbacks in 2 volumes with new material 1991

British Library Cataloguing in Publication Data
Barry, Brian
Liberty and justice: essays in political theory 2.
1. Politics. Theories
I. Title
320.01
ISBN 0-19-827299-5

Library of Congress Cataloging in Publication Data
Barry, Brian M.
Essays in political theory/Brian Barry.
p.   cm.
Includes bibliographical references and index.
Contents: 1. Democracy and power —   2. Justice and liberty.
1. Political science.   I. Title.
JA71.B347 1991   321.8—dc20   90–21341
ISBN 0-19-827297-9 (v. 1)
ISBN 0-19-827299-5 (v. 2)

Typeset by Wyvern Typesetting Ltd, Bristol
Printed in Great Britain by
Courier International Ltd, Tiptree, Essex

For Anni
and for Dammy and Julian
who brought us together

ACKNOWLEDGEMENTS

Most of the pieces reprinted here originally contained expressions of thanks for helpful comments on drafts. Consolidating these, I should like to thank the following for pointing out mistakes or forcing me to think harder about what I was saying: Bruce Ackerman, James Andrews, Chris Archibald, Benjamin Barber, Charles Beitz, Peter Brown, G. A. Cohen, Hans Daalder, David Donaldson, Patrick Dunleavy, Jon Elster, John Ferejohn, James Fishkin, Bruno Frey, Robert Fullinwider, Allan Gibbard, Robert Goodin, Kenneth Goodpaster, John Gray, Russell Hardin, Albert Hirschman, Keith Hope, Samuel Huntington, Aanund Hylland, Peter Jones, Julian Le Grand, Robin Lovin, Douglas MacLean, John Maguire, Jane Mansbridge, Derek Parfit, Carole Pateman, Douglas Rae, Ronald Rogowski, Jim Sharpe, Charles Silver, Robert Simon, Miller Spangler, Arthur Stinchcombe, Albert Weale, and Aristide Zolberg.

I should also like to thank Claire Wilkinson for obtaining the permissions to reprint and helping with revisions for this volume, and Anni Parker for making proof-reading as near to being a pleasure as is humanly possible.

I am grateful for permission to include the following in this collection:

'Social Criticism and Political Philosophy', originally published in *Philosophy & Public Affairs* 19 (1990), 360–73, © 1990 by Princeton University Press.

'How Not to Defend Liberal Institutions', originally published in *British Journal of Political Science*, 20 (1989), 1–14, and in *Liberalism and the Good*, ed. R. Bruce Douglass, Gerald M. Mara, and Henry S. Richardson (New York and London: Routledge, 1990), 44–58.

'And Who is my Neighbour?', originally published as a review article in the *Yale Law Journal*, 88 (1979), 629–58, reprinted by permission of The Yale Law Journal Company and Fred B. Rothman & Company.

'Lady Chatterley's Lover and Doctor Fischer's Bomb Party: Liberalism, Pareto Optimality, and the Problem of Objectionable Preferences', originally published in Jon Elster and Aanund Hylland (eds.), *Foundations of Social Choice Theory* (Cambridge: Cambridge University Press, 1986), 11–43.

'The Light that Failed?', originally published in *Ethics*, 100 (1989), 160–8, © 1989 by the University of Chicago, all rights reserved.

'Tragic Choices', originally published as a review article in *Ethics*, 94 (1984), 303–18, © 1984 by The University of Chicago; all rights reserved.

'Chance, Choice, and Justice', first published in this volume.

'Can States be Moral? International Morality and the Compliance Problem' has been published in two forms: in Anthony Ellis (ed.), *Ethics and International Relations* (Manchester: Manchester University Press, 1986, for the Centre for Philosophy and Public Affairs, University of St Andrews), and under the title 'Justice in International Society', in Robert J. Myers (ed.), *International Ethics in the Nuclear Age* (Ethics and Foreign Policy Series 4; Lanham, Md.: University Press of America, 1987, for the Carnegie Council on Ethics and International Affairs).

'Humanity and Justice in Global Perspective', originally published in J. Roland Pennock and John W. Chapman (eds.) *Ethics, Economics, and the Law* (Nomos, 24; New York and London: New York University Press, 1982), 219–52, copyright © 1982 by New York University.

'Justice as Reciprocity', originally published in Eugene Kamenka and Alice Erh-Soon Tay (eds.), *Justice* (London: Edward Arnold, 1979), 50–78, © Edward Arnold (Publishers) Ltd., 1979.

'Justice Between Generations', originally published in P. M. S. Hacker and J. Raz (eds.), *Law, Morality, and Society: Essays in Honour of H. L. A. Hart* (Oxford: Clarendon Press, 1977), 268–84.

'The Ethics of Resource Depletion', originally published as 'Intergenerational Justice in Energy Policy', in Douglas MacLean and Peter G. Brown (eds.) *Energy and the Future* (Totowa, NJ: Rowman and Littlefield, 1983), 15–30.

'The Continuing Relevance of Socialism', published in Robert Skidelsky (ed.), *Thatcherism* (London: Chatto & Windus, 1988), 143–58.

CONTENTS

INTRODUCTION

This is the second of two volumes containing articles written in the past fifteen years and originally published in roughly equal proportions in a variety of journals spanning several disciplines and in multi-authored books—a notoriously hit-and-miss way of disseminating one's work. I am therefore pleased to have these pieces appearing in a more accessible form. Volume I contains what might be called analytical political theory, with primary attention paid to questions about the theory and practice of democracy and about the analysis and study of power. Volume II falls within the sphere of normative political philosophy. It focuses especially on justice and its application in a variety of contexts and on some central issues within liberal political theory.

The first chapter, 'Social Criticism and Political Philosophy', differs from the others in not being addressed to a substantive issue within political philosophy. Rather, it is concerned with the nature of political philosophy itself. Although I have to confess to finding most methodological pieces (whether written by me or other people) fairly boring, I hope that this one is saved from the customary aridity by taking the form of an attack on somebody else's views. It also has the advantage of referring to a number of actual writers, from the prophet Amos to the prophet Orwell.

Michael Walzer, the object of the attack, has for a number of years set himself up as the scourge of Anglo-American political philosophy. According to Walzer, this whole body of work suffers from self-defeating aspirations towards detachment and delusive claims to universality. In its place Walzer commends something altogether more cosy which he calls social criticism. This consists in articulating for one's own society the values that its members already share in an inarticulate way.

There is something faintly incongruous in this performance coming from Walzer, who occupies a chair at the Institute for Advanced Study at Princeton—the nearest thing to an ivory tower existing in the contemporary academic world. I cannot claim to know how far Walzer makes up for this disability by frequenting the bars of New Brunswick (the nearest place to Princeton where one can count on finding people uncontaminated by abstract thought), but there is no need to pursue that here, since the accuracy of Walzer's claims for his own interpretations of American values are not at issue. The point that I hope to establish in the chapter is that Waltzer's picture of political philosophy is a travesty, and that the real thing is a good deal more robust and sensible than he admits.

The following four chapters are all concerned in one way or another with the justification of a system of liberal rights and with the limitations that societies can legitimately place upon their citizens' freedom to do what pleases or profits them. The first, 'How Not to Defend Liberal Institutions', confronts head-on a question which is highly relevant in western societies, while in other countries such as India it has unlimited potential for creating political convulsions. This is: can the characteristic institutions of a liberal society, such as freedom of speech and enquiry and freedom of religious worship, be presented to those who do not start from liberal premisses (normally though not invariably because they hold religious beliefs incompatible with liberal values) as worthy of their support? The conclusion reached is that the traditional defences of liberal institutions going back to the seventeenth and eighteenth centuries continue to have validity where the conditions for their applicability obtain, but that there can be no completely general justification of liberal institutions that does not itself invoke liberal values.

I should perhaps say that this chapter was already in draft before Salman Rushdie became the object of threats to his life as the author of *The Satanic Verses*. The implications of my argument are, however, clear though uncomfortable. There is, if I am right, no way of creating a rational conviction favouring toleration in anyone who believes that the Koran is incompatible with toleration and that its precepts are to be followed strictly. The only long-run solution short of mass defection lies in Muslims either accepting a more liberal interpretation of the Koran or taking the view that it is to be followed selectively. Judging by the time it has taken Christianity to move from burning at the stake for heresy to the widespread (though far from universal) incorpora-tion of liberal values, the long run must be measured in centuries rather than decades — and even then it may well be that Islam is, by the very nature of its doctrine, less susceptible to liberalization than Christianity.

Pending the domestication of Islam along the lines of the mainstream Christian churches, what should those societies fortunate enough to enjoy liberal institutions do about Muslim minorities in their midst? There are, I suggest, three lines to be pursued. The first is to do everything compatible with liberal principles to encourage liberal tendencies within Islam. This includes refusing to recognize or deal with hardline leaders and providing public funding for liberal groups and liberal writers within the Muslim community.

The second line is to remove the legitimate grievances of *all* ethnic minorities: the pervasive discrimination against them in the labour market; their lack of representation in institutions such as the police, the judiciary, and management; and the racially motivated harassment that they suffer both at work and at home. Measures such as these obviously ought to be taken anyway but there is an additional reason for doing so if it is true that among Muslims attraction to intransigent religious positions is stimulated by a feeling of alienation from the rest of the society.

Thirdly, while there is every reason for showing sympathy and understanding towards those whose sincere beliefs bring them into collision with the working practices of a liberal society, this should not be used as an excuse for fudging. There is no guarantee that liberal institutions are anything more than a passing phase in human history, but if that is so let them go down fighting. Unprincipled compromise with those whose values are antithetical to liberalism will not gain any credit with them—it will simply be interpreted as weakness—and will make it harder subsequently to make a principled stand anywhere else.

In chapter 3, 'And Who is my Neighbour?', the problem posed in the previous chapter is turned round. The question here is what demands the members of a society can legitimately make on one another. If we subscribe to the ideal of a society with liberal institutions, can we consistently draw a halt to the process of extending rights to people anywhere short of merely prohibiting them from injuring one another?

Critics of liberalism from both the right and the left have united in the claim that a society which gives its members substantial rights is doomed to degenerate into a 'dust of individuals'. I do not, however, see any logical reason why rights must become inordinate in this kind of way. On the contrary, I argue that, within broad limits, societies can legitimately draw the social bonds more or less tightly according to the trade-offs that their members wish to make between the attractions of individual liberty and the attractions of belonging to a system of assured mutual aid. 'And Who is my Neighbour?' proceeds by holding up to critical scrutiny a book which is useful in presenting in an unvarnished way the view that in a just society nobody should be regarded as owing the others anything except refraining from harming them. This is Charles Fried's book, *Right and Wrong*.

One of the themes running through this chapter is the supposed conflict between utilitarianism and rights—a conflict that it has become fashionable (as in the case of Fried) to resolve in favour of rights. I argue that there is no conflict between utilitarianism understood (as it was by the classical utilitarians) as a criterion for a good state of affairs and rights understood as permissions for individuals to act at their own discretion in certain matters. There is indeed a conflict between rights and consequentialism, if this is taken to be the doctrine that each person has at every moment a duty to perform that act which can be expected to do the greatest amount of good. For then there is no moral freedom except in the trivial case where two courses of action have consequences of exactly equal expected value. But there are, I argue, many positions intermediate between consequentialism and Fried's theory of solely negative duties to others, and each of the extreme positions gains plausibility only by being presented as the unavoidable alternative to the other.

Chapter 4 pursues the same issue into the rather more arcane sphere of social choice theory. By 'social choice theory' is meant here a body of formal theory that purports to elicit 'social preferences' over states of affairs from collections of individual preferences over those same states of affairs. In as far as it seeks to form a judgement about the value of alternative states of affairs it is, obviously, in the same line of business as classical utilitarianism. And modern welfare economics (with which social choice theory is largely identified) is indeed the lineal descendent of utilitarianism. Where it differs is in eschewing any appeal to interpersonal comparisons of utility, so it cannot appeal to the utilitarian criterion of maximizing aggregate utility. Instead, it makes do, parsimoniously, with information about preference orderings—that state of affairs x is preferred to state of affairs y and so on.

Fortunately, there is no need here to enter into the travails of those who have tried to get a consistent 'social preference' ordering out of individual ones. All we need to note is that one criterion that has widely been thought of as uncontroversial is the Pareto principle: that if at least one person prefers x to y and nobody prefers y to x then x is better than y. Although it is plain that this criterion will not normally be enough by itself to generate a complete ordering of states of affairs, it has at any rate been thought apparent that any ordering should respect it.

The first part of chapter 4 discusses the claim made by Amartya Sen that the Pareto principle is questionable because it conflicts with the basic liberal principle that each person has a 'protected sphere' within which he should have discretion to act as he thinks fit. The reason for this is that the Pareto principle may require people to do things that a liberal would say they should have a right not to do. However, what is doing the work in creating this alleged conflict is not the Pareto principle for ranking states of affairs but the consequentialist doctrine (smuggled in without a word) that each person has at every moment a duty to produce the best state of affairs that he can attain by taking any of the actions open to him. It is trivial that the Pareto principle, as a criterion for a good state of affairs, will conflict with individual discretion, because *any* principle will do so—as long as we add a universal duty to pursue the best possible state of affairs.

Once we withdraw the consequentialist addition, the conflict disappears because then it becomes clear that the Pareto principle is about one thing—what makes one state of affairs better than another—while individual rights are about the quite different matter of what choices people should have discretion over. We normally have no difficulty in recognizing that people should have a right to act in ways that can be foreseen to produce less than socially optimal results—on the Pareto criterion or any other. This is enough to show that, once we penetrate the flimflam of social choice theory, Sen's supposed paradox is empty.

Having disposed of a meretricious argument against the Pareto principle, I turn in the second part of chapter 4 to the most interesting question that the principle gives rise to. This is the moral status of offers that are freely, perhaps gratefully, accepted by the recipients, but are somehow suspect as degrading or corrupting. Its title is taken from Graham Greene's novel *Doctor Fischer of Geneva or The Bomb Party*, in which the eponymous doctor gives parties at which the guests, who are already quite wealthy, undertake degrading performances in order to receive large prizes.

This group of chapters devoted to the justification of liberal institutions is brought to an end by a review of Alasdair MacIntyre's *Whose Justice? Which Rationality?* MacIntyre is a root-and-branch critic of the entire liberal enterprise, which he takes to be grounded in the 'Enlightenment project'. Hence my borrowing of the title of a Rudyard Kipling story for the review: 'The Light that Failed?' Although MacIntyre's book makes unusually stimulating reading for a work of philosophy, his case against liberalism is deeply flawed, I believe, because there is no reason for supposing that it depends on the feasibility of the 'Enlightenment project' as MacIntyre defines it.

Chapter 6 provides a break from the rather abstract nature of the preceding chapters. It is concerned primarily with the hard choices that societies have to make in allocating scarce resources such as expensive lifesaving therapies and in allocating burdens such as that of military service. This chapter is in the form of a review of an original and influential book, *Tragic Choices*, by Guido Calabresi and Philip Bobbitt. Although I am critical of the authors' conception of a 'tragic choice' and of some of the details of their analysis, I believe that their discussion of alternative mechanisms for distributing benefits and burdens has much to offer, and I endeavour in this chapter to refine it and extend it in various directions.

With chapter 7 there begins a run of six chapters all concerned in one way or another with the idea of social or distributive justice. The first of these, 'Chance, Choice, and Justice', is the most general. In it I suggest two principles: that bad luck should be compensated and that the outcomes of voluntary choices should be left with the chooser. I then show that these seemingly innocent propositions open up many difficulties, and try to deal with them as best I can.

The next five chapters are all concerned with the implications of distributive justice outside its usual sphere of relations among contemporary members of a single society. The first two of them focus on international justice, the last two on justice between different generations, while the one between discusses problems common to both. 'Can States Be Moral?' is devoted to the most basic issue that arises in international ethics, namely, the very possibility of holding states to account for their actions in the international arena. While conceding the strength of the case mounted by those who argue that international conditions preclude binding moral obligations on states, I maintain that there is nevertheless a good deal of room for such obligations. 'Humanity and Justice in Global Perspective' analyses two basic grounds for holding that rich countries have a moral obligation to transfer resources to poor ones: humanity and justice. The argument is made that both humanity and justice provide a grounding for obligations, but different ones in each case.

Much of everyday morality is concerned with reciprocity; in one way or another, one's obligations often arise from the requirement of repaying a benefit received or anticipating one expected. One of the features that makes moral relations between states (and even more between generations) problematic is the relative or absolute lack of reciprocity. 'Justice as Reciprocity' analyses the place of reciprocity in morality and asks what happens when it is weak or absent.

Chapters 11 and 12 are devoted to the peculiar problems that arise in the relations between different generations. Principles that we are familiar with and that work well enough among contemporaries are liable to have bizarre implications when applied to the obligations that one generation has to its successors. 'Justice between Generations' is a general survey of the problems that arise. Although much has been written on the topic (some of it by me) since this piece was originally published, I think that it still stands up as a useful introduction to a mind-bending topic.

'The Ethics of Resource Depletion' provides a sharp contrast with the preceding chapter in that it takes up just one issue concerning obligations to future generations. This is the question raised by the existence of non-renewable resources such as minerals and fossil fuels. To say that future generations should have the same stock of them as we have is a recipe for their never being used at all. But is there any alternative that is just between different generations? In this chapter I offer a general answer to the question, which has found favour with some other writers on the subject. I am well aware, however, of the difficulty of determining what its concrete implications are for a just policy on non-renewable resources.

The piece that I have chosen to be the final one in the collection stands a little apart from the others. It is based upon the text of a public lecture, and in preparing it for publication I have fought off the temptation to retrofit it with the usual scholarly armoury. I have not therefore added the qualifications that one would expect to find in a paper designed to anticipate all possible objections, nor indulged in the citation of authorities to back up my assertions.

'The Continuing Relevance of Socialism' was given as part of a series of public lectures on the theme of 'Thatcherism'. But I should say that, with the exception of the opening section, that lecture largely followed the text of the inaugural lecture that I gave (under the title 'Socialism Today') at the London School of Economics in December 1987 upon taking up the Chair of Political Science first held there by Graham Wallas. The Department of Government at the LSE has the reputation (completely justified) of being the most conservative in the United Kingdom. In trying to decide what to speak about, I reached the conclusion that it would be worth making it apparent that, at any rate as far as this chair was concerned, the pendulum that swung to the right when Michael Oakeshott succeeded Harold Laski had swung back again. A professor may be allowed once in a lifetime, I hope, to take the opportunity of professing. 'The Continuing Relevance of Socialism' is the result.

Readers of this volume are entitled to know how far what appears here has been altered from the form in which it originally appeared. A number of cross-references have been added. Spelling and punctuation have been brought into line with British usage wherever the original source was American. Such matters as italicization of words in foreign languages have been made uniform. So have symbolic conventions: actors are always A, B, and C, actions x, y, and z. Minor changes have been made throughout in the interests of euphony and clarity. In some cases new introductory or concluding material has been added in order to head off, as far as possible, misreadings that the pieces attracted in their originally published form. Various bits of academic shorthand acceptable in a learned journal have been expanded so as to make the pieces printed here accessible to non-professionals. I have also deleted a few paragraphs that, on rereading, seemed to me to hold up the argument rather than advance it. I have not, however, made any attempt to update anything, either to take account of later political events or later publications on the subject.[1] Doing this thoroughly would involve creating a quite different kind of book, and doing it sporadically would, I feel, reduce the value of the collection by leaving the reader unsure whether some successful prediction was a lucky shot or the result of an addition made with the benefit of hindsight. In place of such updating in the text, I have sought in this Introduction to offer a current view of the topics, taking account of later political developments and contributions to the literature.

---

[1] I have, however, on occasion substituted later and more accessible versions or reprints for articles originally published in obscure places or books that are now out of print.

I

SOCIAL CRITICISM AND POLITICAL PHILOSOPHY

I

In two recent books, Michael Walzer has pondered on the practice of social criticism, an activity that he contrasts with academic political philosophy of the kind exemplified by the work of John Rawls. Walzer regards himself as a practitioner of social criticism in such books as *Spheres of Justice*[1] (which began with an attack on Rawls), and is concerned in the two books to be discussed here to defend the approach that he takes to be common to himself and his fellow social critics.

Social criticism, Walzer tells us, is 'connected': the social critic identifies himself with his society. Social criticism is also particularistic: the social critic is concerned to criticize his own society. From these two features of social criticism flow its characteristic techniques: the social critic seeks to convince his audience that the moral beliefs they already have ought to lead them to agree with his criticisms. Political philosophy is different in every way, according to Walzer. Instead of valuing connectedness, the political philosopher prides himself on achieving a state of detachment. Instead of addressing the members of his own society, the political philosopher's cogitations are addressed to human beings everywhere. And instead of starting from, and staying close to, the particular beliefs of the members of a certain community, the political philosopher seeks universal enlightenment.

How good is Walzer's case for social criticism and against political philosophy? Walzer is an attractive and persuasive writer. Nevertheless, I believe that at the core his argument is profoundly and dangerously wrong. His contrast between social criticism and political philosophy is misconceived. The account of the work of political philosophers such as Rawls is a gross caricature. And the commitments of the best of Walzer's social critics are systematically misrepresented in order to lend spurious support to his theses.

[1] Michael Walzer, *Spheres of Justice: A Defense of Pluralism and Equality* (New York: Basic Books, 1983).

The first of the two books, which is entitled *Interpretation and Social Criticism*,[2] is very short. The first two chapters, which began life as a pair of lectures, are together devoted to the defence of social criticism, with fairly extensive invidious comparisons between social criticism and political philosophy. The third chapter, added later, discusses the Hebrew prophets (Amos in particular) as paradigmatic social critics. For convenience I shall refer to this book as *ISC* in what follows.

The other book has a quite different format. Entitled *The Company of Critics* (hereafter *CC*),[3] the bulk of it is taken up with accounts of eleven twentieth-century critics. The eleven chapters devoted to these social critics are preceded by an introductory one that covers much of the same ground as *ISC* and a concluding chapter that reflects on and draws implications from the preceding studies.

I want to focus here on the general issues raised by these two books. I shall therefore eschew the temptation to engage with Walzer's individual accounts of his social critics except where some point he makes about them is relevant to these general issues. But this will be often enough that I must, for the sake of later intelligibility, begin by introducing Walzer's company of critics. All except one wrote their social criticism after the First World War. The exception is Randolph Bourne, a radical journalist who opposed American participation in the war and died immediately after it ended. The others, treated in roughly chronological order, are Martin Buber, Antonio Gramsci, Ignazio Silone, George Orwell, Albert Camus, Simone de Beauvoir, Herbert Marcuse, Michel Foucault, and Breyten Breytenbach (an exiled South African poet and essayist who is, incidentally, the only member of the company still living).

I have mentioned ten names so far. The remaining one is Julien Benda, whose well-known book *La Trahison des clercs* was published in 1927. He is discussed before the other ten, and this is quite appropriate because he is not himself a social critic. Rather, he was engaged in that book in the same kind of second-order activity as is Walzer. And he is in fact not even sympathetic to social criticism as Walzer understands it. Benda is praised for his insistence that a critic must resist the temptation to become the creature of a party or a government. But Walzer rejects Benda's central claim: that to be true

---

[2] Michael Walzer, *Interpretation and Social Criticism* (Cambridge, Mass.: Harvard University Press, 1987).

[3] *The Company of Critics: Social Criticism and Political Commitment in the Twentieth Century* (New York: Basic Books, 1988; London: Peter Halban, 1989).

to his calling a critic must cultivate detachment from the society that he is criticizing. Walzer, on the contrary, might have taken for his motto E. M. Forster's 'Only connect.'

An interesting feature of this line-up is that there are no Americans after Bourne, whose work was already over before the rest had got going. Marcuse was, of course, a European transplant, but one that did not take (a case of the transplant rejecting the host): 'he makes no effort to identify the dominant concepts of American life; he is not committed to a dialogue with ordinary Americans' (*CC*, p. 188). Walzer does not comment on the absence of satisfactory American social critics after 1918, but the implication might be drawn that the United States (especially since the Progressive era) is infertile ground for social criticism as Walzer understands it. I shall come back to this point later.

Walzer himself offers some necessary conditions for inclusion in his company of critics. All of his subjects are, he says, 'working social critics rather than philosophers of criticism' and 'mainstream critics rather than sectarians' (*CC*, p. 27). He does not help us with these distinctions except to tell us that Sartre is ruled out under the first because, although he produced 'one of the most important theories of social criticism in the twentieth century, . . . he was not a first-rate practitioner' (*CC*, p. 27 n.) . This is a bit puzzling since Walzer does not by any means believe that everybody on his list of critics is a first-rate practitioner. Indeed, the words in which he dismisses Sartre would equally well have expressed his view of Marcuse: that 'though he disliked the everyday life of his contemporaries, he was not really interested in it; he held with great consistency a highly stereotyped view of the institutions that give it shape' (*CC*, p. 27 n.). But we can at any rate get the point that the criterion for inclusion is criticizing rather than writing about criticism, though this seems to leave the presence of Benda unaccounted for.

Another feature shared by Walzer's chosen critics is, he says, that they are 'general intellectuals', an expression which he glosses by claiming that 'they all have something to say about the whole society and also about the critical enterprise itself' (*CC*, p. 27). We are not told what the complementary set is but it is noticeable that academics are very thin on the ground. No R. H. Tawney, no C. Wright Mills, and no J. K. Galbraith, for example. And of the two academics who are included, Buber's academic writings are dismissed as 'obscure and portentous' (*CC*, p. 64), the focus being on his occasional writings about Jewish/Palestinian relations, while Marcuse is, as we have seen, regarded by Walzer as a thoroughly unsatisfactory specimen of a social critic.

A further common factor to which Walzer draws attention is that all of his subjects are on the left in relation to their own societies — though this, of course, means different substantive things in each case. (In relation to contemporary Afrikanerdom, for example, it simply means espousing some ideas about equal rights that would have been pretty uncontentious two centuries ago in France.) But even within the left there is a division between sheep and goats to be made. Rejected are those who regard the critics as the 'head' and the proletariat as the 'body'. Rather, for Walzer's critics, 'the revolt of the masses is the mobilization of common complaint'. Thus, 'given the existence of the people as critical subjects, [critics] are newly connected to popular movements and aspirations' (*CC*, p. 26). It should, however, be said that on this criterion it is doubtful whether Gramsci belongs in the company. 'Where would he have stood when Ignazio Silone rejected party discipline and communist orthodoxy in 1929?' (*CC*, pp. 80–1). Imprisonment and premature death saved him from having to decide, but 'he is committed to a doctrine, an integrated set of "scientific" arguments' and to the belief that the Communist party possesses the truth (*CC*, p. 81). We cannot be sure which way Gramsci would have jumped, Walzer says. But with these ideas it seems likely he would have gone the wrong way.[4]

By now we have an implicit definition of 'social criticism'. In *ISC* Walzer offers a useful stipulation of its meaning that runs as follows: 'Social criticism is a social activity. "Social" has a prenominal and reflexive function, rather like "self" in "self-criticism," which names subject and object at the same time. No doubt societies do not criticize themselves; social critics are individuals, but they are also, most of the time, members, speaking in public to other members who join in the speaking and whose speech constitutes a collective reflection upon the conditions of collective life' (p. 35). This rules out critics who address only other critics (perhaps within a vanguard party), or confine their activities to offering advice to those in power. Does it imply, then, that all social criticism must by definition be on the left? Elitist criticism of the Ortega y Gasset variety does seem to be excluded (*CC*, pp. 25–6), but the French clerico-nationalist forerunners of Fascism

---

[4] I have discussed Walzer's substantive treatment of his 'social critics' more extensively elsewhere. See 'Complaining', a review of the *Company of Critics*, in *The London Review of Books*, vol. 11 no. 2 (23 Nov. 1989), 12. Some of the points made below were first aired here, though they have been reworked for the rather different purposes of the present chapter.

deplored by Julien Benda in *La Trahison des clercs* and indeed Fascism itself seem to satisfy Walzer's criteria well enough.

Social criticism, according to Walzer, is best conducted in the '"national-popular" mode.' 'The ideal critic in this mode is loyal to men and women in trouble—oppressed, exploited, impoverished, forgotten—but he sees these people and their troubles and the possible solution to their troubles within the framework of national history and culture' (*CC*, pp. 233–4). The trouble is that Maurras and Mussolini would have agreed enthusiastically with all that. Where they parted company with Walzer's good guys was in having a different theory about the way in which the lot of the oppressed, exploited, impoverished, and forgotten could be improved.

The general tendency of Walzer's writing is, however, to denigrate theory, crying up 'moral sensitivity' as an alternative. Deploying one of the false dichotomies that constitute a characteristic mode of argument, he asks rhetorically: 'Who can doubt that [the] language [of twentieth century politics] is better employed by a person of moral sensitivity without a theory than by a morally obtuse person with the grandest possible theory?' (*CC*, p. 229). But a grand theory is not necessarily a good theory, and a bad theory may actually guarantee moral obtuseness: the three critics whom Walzer seems to find most congenial—Silone, Orwell, and Camus—rejected the orthodox Communist line for precisely this reason. The relevant question is surely whether a person with any given degree of moral sensitivity is better off with a good theory than no theory at all.

The question can be pressed harder. All criticism—as opposed to lamentation—presupposes that it is possible for things to be better than they are now as a result of human action (*CC*, pp. 17–18). I think that Walzer skews his analysis by taking as his paradigmatic social critic the prophet Amos. (He is the major figure in the last third of *ISC*, and reappears at key points in *CC*.) For the burden of Amos' complaint is that the Jews (and in particular the rich) are failing to live up to the precepts of the Covenant—failing, for example, to return to their owners each night clothes given in pledge (*ISC*, pp. 81–2). Charles Dickens was a critic of this kind: avarice was, for him too, the root of evil. As George Orwell observed, Dickens's solution was that businessmen should model themselves on (post-spirit) Scrooge and the Cheeryble brothers. This is no doubt to be counted as social criticism of a sort, but typical social critics of the left in this century (including those in Walzer's list) have rejected as naïve the formula of social reform constituted by individual reform. A critic of institutions, as distinct from a critic of conduct, must surely have a social theory in order to explain why the reforms that he proposes will deal with the complaints that he articulates.

Thus, for example, Orwell had a theory (at any rate from, say, the late 1930s to the mid-1940s) to the effect that a capitalist economy was hopelessly inefficient in comparison with a socialist economy, and that the abolition of private education would have beneficial effects on the class system. This theory may have been a good one or a bad one but it was, I suggest, the belief that he knew of a better way that made Orwell a critic rather than a mere grouser.

II

So far I have presented Walzer's company of critics, and given an account of Walzer's conception of social criticism. I now want to discuss in some detail Walzer's defence of social criticism, so understood, against other modes of criticism. The essence of social criticism, on Walzer's conception, is interpretation. The social critic 'gives expression to his people's deepest sense of how they ought to live' (*CC*, p. 232). This forms a basis for criticism because there is always a gap between aspirations and reality: 'This is what we value and want, he says, and don't yet have. This is how we mean to live and don't yet live' (*CC*, p. 230). It follows from this that the content of social criticism must vary from society to society. 'Whenever it points to particular images and expresses particular aspirations, criticism is a pluralizing activity.' Thus, 'the critic . . . insists that there are . . . other, equally legitimate, hopes and aspirations' (*CC*, p. 232). This line of thought will be recognized by readers of the earlier *Spheres of Justice* as a generalization of Walzer's claim there that 'the questions posed by the theory of distributive justice admit of a range of answers, and there is room within the range for cultural diversity and political choice', so that 'principles of justice are . . . the inevitable product of historical and cultural particularism'.[5]

Walzer believes that social criticism as interpretation 'is not philosophically respectable' (*ISC*, p. 39), and I suppose that the quest for philosophical respectability might be said to have motivated the production of the two books under review here. How is this respectability to be achieved? By showing that the interpretative method yields better results than does the Platonic alternative that

[5] Walzer, *Spheres of Justice*, 5–6.

Walzer takes to be more respectable within mainstream Anglo-American philosophy. 'Some critics seek only the acquaintance of other critics; they find their peers only outside the cave, in the blaze of Truth. Others find peers and sometimes even comrades inside, in the shadow of contingent and uncertain truths. My own commitment to the cave leads me to prefer the second group. But that preference determines nothing. What is at issue is the cogency and force, the verisimilitude and nuance of the criticism that results from these different choices' (*CC*, pp. ix–x).

As a way of settling the issue as Walzer poses it, this proposal invites the objection that his criteria are either open to rival interpretations by the partisans of the two schools or simply load the dice. Thus the troglodytes are bound to come out ahead on nuance, but the virtue of nuance is presumably going to be a point at issue between the two sides. Verisimilitude will go by default to the interpretative school if it means fidelity to existing beliefs. But of course anyone who holds that 'moral principles are necessarily external to the world of experience, waiting *out there* to be discovered by detached and dispassionate philosophers' (*CC*, p. ix) will say that verisimilitude should be construed as correspondence to that external standard. Again, what counts as cogency and force will presumably be systematically different in the two cases. The Platonists would say that the most cogent and forceful kind of criticism will be that which derives most accurately from a transcendent moral reality, whether or not it achieves popular appeal. Social critics, by contrast, 'hope to be effective; it is the natural form of their ambition' (*CC*, p. 233); and effectiveness is at the minimum a matter of being read and touching hearts, and at the maximum one of changing behaviour (*CC*, p. 235).

I do not want to dwell on these difficulties because I think the whole issue is misleadingly posed by Walzer as a choice between Platonism and social criticism. As I see it, apperception of a transcultural and transhistorical Form of the Good stands at one end of a continuum and Walzer's radical particularism stands at the other end. There are many alternatives to both Platonism and particularism. One possibility, which has been explored by many people, including R. M. Hare and T. M. Scanlon, is that, while there is no transcendent moral reality waiting for us to get in touch with it, there is an inherent connection between morality and impartiality. This will lead us beyond particularism without committing us to Platonism.

The same false dichotomy infects Walzer's discussion of the social position of the critic. Sociologically, the metaphor of the cave can be cashed out to give a division between insiders and outsiders. On one side we have the social critics—represented at best by figures such as Silone, Camus, and Orwell—who draw upon the inherited stock of moral ideas within their own societies in order to make their criticisms. On the other side we have a figure who 'breaks loose from his local and familial world . . ., detaches himself from all emotional ties, steps back so as to see the world with absolute clarity, studies what he sees (scientifically, in accordance with the most advanced views), discovers universal values as if for the first time, finds these values embodied in the oppressed class', and so on (pp. 225–6). In the second chapter of *ISC*, the 'conventional view' of the critic makes him 'an outsider, a "total stranger," a man from Mars. . . . He stands outside, in some privileged place, where he has access to "advanced" or universal principles; and he applies these principles with an impersonal (intellectual) rigor' (p. 38). Walzer attributes this 'conventional view' especially to Sartre.

The first chapter of *ISC*, however, complicates the picture by suggesting that there are *two* alternatives to interpretation as a method of social criticism. One is discovery, the other invention. The paradigm of discovery is religious revelation, but it has secular versions, which include utilitarianism (*ISC*, pp. 7–8). The 'best known and most elegant' version of invention is 'that of John Rawls' (*ISC*, p. 11). This creates something of a puzzle. For it is hard to see that the Sartrean picture of *l'homme revolté* even begins to fit Bentham and the Mills, or for that matter Smart and Hare. Nor, as far as I am aware, has Rawls ever undergone the trauma of radical personal detachment that should have been required to propel him out of the orbit of social criticism.

The best way of salvaging something is to withdraw any suggestion that the Sartrean model represents the only alternative to social criticism and fall back on the more general idea that the alternative to social criticism is 'universal principles' applied with 'impartial (intellectual) rigor'. But this still embodies a false choice. Why should we suppose that the only alternative is particularistic principles applied slackly and with partiality?

Walzer prays in aid his favourite social critics, especially Silone, Orwell, and Camus, but I do not think that they support his case. They were 'connected' but they were not, or at any rate did not aspire to be, partial. A lot of what Walzer says seems to me to gain unwarranted plausibility from the running together of two ways in which somebody may identify with a group. In one sense, identification is a sense of belonging to a group, caring about what happens to it, and wishing to play a part in its collective life. This kind of identification is a part of being human. It is hard to conceive of life without it, and impossible to imagine that life could be lived well in its absence. The other sense of identification is far less benign. Identification is here a form of collective selfishness. It means refusing to judge the interests of one's group by the same standards as the interests of others—favouring one's own group simply because it is one's own group.

It is by no means apparent that identification even in the first sense is necessary for good criticism. Walzer may be right in saying that criticism of a society is more likely to be taken to heart by its members if it comes from someone who manifestly identifies with the society. But efficacy among the members of the society being criticized is not the only criterion of good criticism. It may be that the members of a society are systematically blinded by their belief system to grave defects in their practices and that an outsider is better placed to illuminate the darkness. The *antebellum* South, for example, was capable of generating criticisms of certain practices within slavery—gratuitous cruelty, breaking up of families, sexual exploitation—but scarcely anyone was able to rise to the level of condemning slavery root and branch. That had to come from outside.

Walzer could, and presumably would, say that criticism is pointless unless it is efficacious. I have two responses. First, most truths are pointless in that sense and none the worse for that. It redounds to the honour of the human race that there should be people going around saying that slavery is an absolute evil, even if this cuts no ice with the beneficiaries. My second response is that efficacy need not be defined so narrowly as to include only persuading the members of the group in question to mend their ways. Criticism may convince those outside the society to support or undertake action to change things—ranging from letter-writing campaigns organized by Amnesty International all the way up to military intervention.

Of course, if Walzer really believes that the only valid form of criticism is interpretative—that it must involve showing the members of a society that they are falling short of their own ideals—he would have to say that all such outside pressure is illegitimate. But the rest of us who are not relativists of that stripe should be careful not to accept a conclusion that covertly rests on that premiss.

For the sake of argument, however, let us concede that all criticism must stem from the first sort of identification. That does nothing whatever to advance the claims of the second sort of identification. Caring about a society and seeing one's own future as bound up with its fate does not mean wishing its good at the expense of injustice to others. It is quite compatible with insisting that its interests should be weighed in the same scales as everybody else's. The social critics that Walzer approves of (and my list would not be very different from his) undeniably identified with their societies in the first sense but did they do so in the second sense? Nothing in Walzer's account of them appears to me to show that they did. It would be absurd to declare categorically that they never showed partiality to their own societies. It is such a common failing that it is unlikely they managed to avoid it altogether. But what I do believe is that they would have recognized it as a failing and would not have been pleased with themselves if they had become aware of having succumbed to it.

III

Walzer appears to me deeply ambivalent about the room for manœuvre open to the social critic. The problem comes to a head when two people produce rival interpretations of the same cultural inheritance. In *ISC*, Walzer says that the issue between the prophet Amos and the priest Amaziah was over 'the core values of the Israelite tradition'—righteousness versus formal observance (p. 88). Although there is no mechanism guaranteeing 'definitive closure', Walzer says that 'we can recognize good and bad arguments, strong and weak interpretations' (ibid.). But these are arguments about who has the most authentic interpretation: '[Amaziah's] silence is a kind of admission that Amos has provided a convincing account of Israelite religion—also perhaps that he has found . . . advocates in the hearts of the people' (pp. 88–9). This implies that if Amaziah had come up with a really compelling argument to the effect that Israelite religion was more centrally concerned with ritual than righteousness, Amos would have been obliged to concede defeat. Now it may be that, given the source of Amos' claims—the Covenant between God and Abraham—this would have been unavoidable. But the implication is, once again, that Amos makes a bad paradigm social critic. For most social critics would surely retort that the issue is not who can claim *most* of the tradition but who can claim the *best* of it. They will say that the morally worthy parts of the tradition should be kept and built on while the rest should be dropped.

In *CC*, Walzer seems much more willing than he was in *ISC* to concede the creativity of social criticism. Indeed, he can hardly do otherwise if he is to count Breyten Breytenbach, a sympathizer with the African National Congress, as a social critic of his fellow Afrikaners. According to Walzer, Breytenbach manages to find a toehold in the Afrikaner belief system by appealing to their African identity and their love of the land (*CC*, pp. 210–24). But he can scarcely claim to be articulating their 'core values', nor has he been very successful in finding 'advocates in the hearts of the people'.

It is easy to see, however, why Walzer steered clear of acknowledging this kind of eclecticism the first time around. For it leaves his conception of social criticism in tatters. If once we allow a social critic to say that, although he is not offering the most authentic reconstruction of the whole cultural tradition, he is picking out the bits worth preserving, we cannot avoid asking: how does the critic decide which are the good bits, and how does he defend his decision to other members of his society? To do these things seems to call for discursive resources that Walzer has no room for.

We can press the point harder. Whatever may have been true of the self-consciously exclusive tribe addressed by Amos, no modern society has *a* tradition waiting to be expounded by a social critic. We are heirs of many traditions, religious and secular, which cannot without gross self-deception be presented as forming a harmonious whole. Any critic must therefore pick and choose among the available materials, simply because there is no way of reconciling them.

Once we admit that eclecticism is possible and indeed unavoidable, we have no difficulty in showing that utilitarianism and the Rawlsian theory of justice, so far from having to rest on discovery and invention respectively, flow quite naturally from selection among familiar beliefs. Thus, utilitarianism has, I suggest, at least two sources. One is the idea, with roots in Stoicism and the monotheistic religions, that everyone's life is equally valuable. Utilitarianism develops this idea by suggesting that the fairest way of treating everyone equally is to count everyone for one in an aggregative calculus. The other source is the virtue of benevolence, universally recognized and perhaps especially prized in the eighteenth century, judging by its frequent presence in the list of the virtues of the deceased on epitaphs of that period. Building on the virtue of benevolence, utilitarianism invites us to commit ourselves to the good of the social whole. If utilitarianism were as outlandish as Walzer implies, it would be incomprehensible that it became the working political morality of a whole society, that of Victorian England.

As far as Rawls is concerned, the essential point to be made is that it is highly misleading to dub Rawls's theory one of morality as invention, where this is contrasted with morality as interpretation. Walzer imagines that the function of the original position in Rawls's theory is to launch a system of morality *de novo*. But the construction has never been intended to be self-subsistent in this way. Rawls starts from a number of basic ideas that he believes his readers will share. (One is the importance of religious liberty; another is the indefensibility of deriving social advantages from morally arbitrary features such as natural ability or a privileged background.) He then seeks to create a choice situation that will incorporate these ideas in its construction (by denying the parties information about their religious affiliations or morally arbitrary personal characteristics) while embodying an idea so basic that he scarcely bothers to mention it, that of fundamental human equality. (This is done by putting everyone in the original position on the same footing.) Whether or not Rawls succeeds in the ambitious task that he sets himself, the point that matters here is that he is just as deeply committed to interpretation, understood in a catholic spirit, as is Walzer.[6]

The upshot is that we arrive once again at the conclusion that the package constructed by Walzer to contain interpretation and particularism comes unravelled. Interpretation can be (and I would say should be) made to lead in an impartial direction. If Rawls is correct, we shall find, when we examine our moral commitments, that they drive us towards impartiality. We simply cannot justify to ourselves or to others putting our family, religion, or ethnic group in a specially favoured position. If we pull back from our partial interests, we do so not as an arbitrary act of will, but because we recognize, on the strength of some very commonplace moral ideas, that we cannot otherwise be true to our deepest beliefs.

The same misunderstanding lies at the root of another sally that Walzer makes against Rawls. Walzer suggests (*ISC*, pp. 14–15) that

---

[6] I should mention that after a few pages spent elaborating the idea of morality as invention, Walzer suddenly concedes that there is a 'more plausible' account of Rawls's intentions (*ISC*, p. 16) in terms of 'reflective equilibrium'. However, he now substitutes another misconception of the original position, this time suggesting that 'values (like liberty and equality) that we all share' (*ISC*, p. 16) are to be assigned to people in the original position. The point, however, is not that the people in the original position have these values but that the whole construction embodies them and gets its entire *raison d'être* from doing so. In any case, the concession to Rawls made here seems completely *ad hoc*. There is no sign that Walzer recognizes its subversive implications. For within a couple of pages he is back with the assumption that the morality to be interpreted is particularistic rather than universalistic: 'the whole thing, taken as a whole, lends itself less to abstract modeling than to thick description' (*ISC*, p. 20), and so on.

the problem posed by Rawls is like that of designing a hotel on the assumption that you might have to live in any of the rooms. Naturally, you would design them to be all the same, but that doesn't mean you would want to live in the hotel once it was built. This is a good joke but a poor analogy. A better one would be designing a city. A lot of different people have plans for it: there are a variety of Protestant plans, several Jewish plans, at least one Catholic plan, several more from the 'secular humanists', as well as lobbies representing blacks and whites, English speakers and Spanish speakers, fit and disabled, young and old, men and women, and so on. The problem is to come up with a master plan that everybody accepts as fair. If agreement can be reached (and there is no guarantee of this) it is not likely to be on identical houses, or on there being only one place of religious worship (or none). Rather the agreement will presumably attempt to accommodate as many of the diverse demands as possible on terms that are seen to be fair to all. Walzer's error is, as before, to regard the specification of the original position as a gratuitous exercise in abstraction rather than a response to the actual situation in which Rawls's readers find themselves: one of apparently irreducible disagreements about religion, abortion, homosexuality, and so on.

I remarked near the beginning that there might be some significance in the absence from Walzer's company of critics of any Americans who have written in the last seventy years. What Walzer is looking for are writers on the left who can be presented (with some massaging) as partial and particularistic. But in the United States more than anywhere else, the left (relatively, of course, to the American political spectrum) finds succour in documents such as the Declaration of Independence and the Bill of Rights and the traditions of thought associated with them. There are, of course, other traditions, represented, for example, by the people who defended slavery and Jim Crow, banned the teaching of evolution in Missouri, and kept *The Grapes of Wrath* out of school libraries in California—all in the name of 'community standards'. But they are, obviously, not quite what Walzer has in mind.

There is, of course, Walzer himself: everything in the two books suggests that Walzer takes for granted his place in the Honourable Company of Social Critics. But is he really alone? Let me put forward the name of John Rawls as a candidate. I believe it can be shown that all the major substantive positions taken in Walzer's *Spheres of Justice* with respect to contemporary America are either a part of Rawls's theory of justice or (as with health care, which Rawls does not deal with) compatible with it. Rawls's theory entails, for example, that civil rights, education, desirable occupations, political office, and income should all be distributed according to different criteria, and his discussion of the institutional changes required to keep the spheres apart (especially politics and money) is much better worked out than Walzer's. If *Spheres of Justice* constitutes social criticism, then so does *A Theory of Justice*. The travesty of Rawls's theory that Walzer presents both in *Spheres of Justice* and *ISC* suggests that he has not managed to make much sense of it. If he did so, he might have to recognize that Rawls is the missing figure in his company of critics.

It is true, of course, that Rawls is an academic rather than a journalist, novelist, or essayist—but then so is Walzer. As far as I can see, the only other thing wrong with Rawls from Walzer's point of view is that he has (to adapt the words of Auden) committed a political philosophy. But, to repeat, Rawls's occupation of the intellectual high ground is not a gratuitous exercise in abstraction but an attempt to come to terms in a systematic way with the real dilemmas of a culturally pluralistic society. His theory has implications about the injustice of American society as currently constituted that are actually more radical than those reached by Walzer in *Spheres of Justice*, because he maintains, unlike Walzer, that the distribution of income is a matter of justice. The important difference between them is not so much substantial as methodological.

Walzer saddles himself with the highly unpromising task of trying to show that the major American institutions can be given a coherent justification only in ways that entail large changes in them—a strategy that is vulnerable to any plausible rationale for the internal consistency of the existing arrangements. Rawls digs deeper and seeks to unearth widely shared post-Enlightenment ideas on which the American polity (among others) is founded, and to show that these have subversive implications for almost all existing forms of inequality. In judging between these approaches, let us set on one side the matter of truth (something about which Walzer frequently expresses unease) and focus on his preferred criterion of efficacy. The Rawlsian approach of identifying principles of broad scope and universal aspiration and using them to attack entrenched inequalities has to its credit the success—partial but still significant—of the anti-racist and anti-sexist movements within the past thirty years. What comparably liberating achievements can Walzer claim for his approach?

2

HOW NOT TO DEFEND LIBERAL INSTITUTIONS

My object in this chapter is to ask how liberal institutions, liberal laws, and liberal policies can be justified. In particular, I want to ask what arguments are available to persuade people who are not liberals—people who do not have a liberal outlook on life—that they ought nevertheless to subscribe to liberal institutions. I shall examine four such arguments—three traditional and one recent—and conclude that they are either limited in scope or dependent on dubious factual premises. The implication to be drawn is the rather depressing one that the only people who can be relied on to defend liberal institutions are liberals.

Let me explain briefly, before I go any further, what I mean by liberal institutions. I believe that there are three features that defined liberal states as they emerged in the seventeenth and eighteenth centuries. These were: religious toleration, freedom of the press, and the abolition of servile civil status. Modern liberal institutions may be seen as extensions of each of these elements in the historic core. Thus, the principle of religious toleration has been generalized to the 'harm principle': the principle that people should be free to act as they wish provided they do not harm others. Freedom of the press has been generalized to cover freedom of expression of all kinds. And the principle that there should be no servile civil status has been generalized to a concept of equal citizenship rights due to everyone without regard to social class, race, or gender. There are, of course, many disputes about the formulation of these generalizations of the venerable liberal institutions. But nothing I have to say will turn on the precise way in which such disputes are resolved.

The other expression that I have used is 'a liberal outlook', and I want now to explain what I mean by that. Again, I suggest that we should approach the question historically. Liberalism is *par excellence* the doctrine of the Enlightenment, and by liberal ideas I intend to refer to the attitudes characteristic of the Enlightenment. There is no definitive list, but I shall again suggest three ideas that it would be hard to exclude. First is the belief that inequalities are a social artefact, and therefore have to be justified on a basis that starts from a premiss of the fundamental equality of all human beings. Second is the belief that every doctrine should be open to critical scrutiny and that no view should be held unless it has in fact withstood critical scrutiny. And third is the belief that no religious dogma can reasonably be held with certainty.

It so happens that I agree with these ideas, but it is no part of my purpose here to defend them. (In any case John Stuart Mill seems to me to have done a good enough job already.) What I am concerned with is, rather, the logical relations between these liberal ideas and support for liberal institutions. First, I shall seek to show (what is not very difficult) that the possession of liberal ideas is a sufficient condition for supporting liberal institutions. Then I shall address the central problem of this chapter: how far the possession of liberal ideas is a necessary condition of support for liberal institutions.

II FROM LIBERAL IDEAS TO LIBERAL INSTITUTIONS

If liberal attitudes had been defined in terms of support for liberal institutions, it would be a logical necessity that people with liberal attitudes support liberal institutions. As it is, however, the two have been defined independently. There is, nevertheless, a strong connection between them in that, given some reasonable assumptions about the way in which the world works, liberal attitudes should give rise to support for liberal institutions. Let us take in turn the key features of liberal institutions outlined at the beginning of the chapter, and see how each may be derived from elements on the list of liberal attitudes just presented.

We begin, then, with religious toleration. If all claims to religious truth (including dogmatic atheism) deserve a sceptical reception, it is surely a plausible implication that no religious faith should ever be put in a position that enables it to coerce people into adhering to it or be granted a monopoly of schooling. What about the modern extension of religious toleration to the idea of a 'private sphere' within which people should be free from state-imposed constraints? The connection with liberal attitudes is less immediately apparent here, but it can still be traced. For if religious beliefs are too doubtful to provide a solid basis for the persecution of deviant religions, they are by the same token too doubtful to underpin the suppression of behaviour which constitutes no threat to the public but is condemned as sinful by the tenets of some religion.

This would be conclusive if everybody who claimed that an act of a certain kind that was immoral though harmless to the community was explicit in grounding the claim upon the authority of some religion. However, we find people in contemporary societies who are prepared to say that, for example, homosexual acts between consenting adults are wrong, even though they are not willing to invoke any tenet of religion to back up their claim. What are we to make of this? I think that here (though only here) Alasdair MacIntyre's diagnosis of the modern predicament is valid.[1] That is to say, the moral condemnation of acts that are not harmful to others makes sense only against a background of religious belief. Take that away and words like 'wrong' and 'immoral' in such contexts become literally unintelligible. It is clear that the things subject to this kind of free-floating condemnation are precisely the same as those condemned on religious grounds. The phenomenon is one of a sort of religious hangover. From a liberal point of view, we may surely conclude that, if religiously based condemnation of harmless acts is inadequate to ground their legal suppression, then condemnation of harmless acts that does not rest on any intelligible basis at all is even less adequate.

Freedom of the press, and, by extension, freedom of expression in general would seem to follow pretty straightforwardly from the premium that the liberal outlook places on critical thinking. For although it could hardly be said that the absence of prohibitions is a sufficient condition for a society of free thinkers, we may at the same time say that it is hard to see how critical attitudes could be fostered by the suppression of ideas. Finally, the opposition to servile civil status, and by extension to other legal inequalities such as the legal disabilities of women, can be plausibly seen as the working out of the implications of the premiss of fundamental equality.

A point which is worth drawing attention to here, since it will be of crucial importance later in the chapter, is that support for liberal institutions by no means exhausts the policy implications of the liberal outlook. (This confirms their logical independence, as I have defined them.) Even in what I described as their modern extended form, these liberal institutions are quite limited in their scope, in that they are

[1] 'What I have suggested to be the case by and large about our own culture [is] that in moral argument the apparent assertion of principles functions as a mask for expressions of personal preference.' (Alasdair MacIntyre, *After Virtue* (Notre Dame, Ind.: University of Notre Dame Press, 1981), 18.)

concerned exclusively with civil rights. But the liberal vision of the good life points towards a more active role for the state. As the 'new liberals' pointed out,[2] the spirit of critical thinking and the practice of autonomous decision-making favoured by the liberal outlook can be fostered by positive state action. Formal rights embodied in liberal institutions have material conditions for their enjoyment. What is especially relevant here is that the kind of critical enquiring spirit valued by liberals will be aided by such things as subsidizing the dissemination of the results of social scientific research that challenges existing prejudices and stereotypes, and by underwriting the costs of publishing books and the costs of producing plays that present new ways of looking at things. Above all, an educational system designed to foster a liberal outlook will be one that encourages independent thinking and in particular works to undercut religious dogmatism by promoting the active questioning of all religious beliefs.

III LIBERALISM FOR NON-LIBERALS: TRADITIONAL ARGUMENTS

I shall take it that a liberal outlook has been established to be a sufficient condition of support for liberal institutions. The question now to be raised is how far it is a necessary condition. To answer this question we must ask whether there are valid arguments that can be addressed to non-liberals to show them that they too have good reason to support liberal institutions. Let us begin by looking at three arguments that have been put forward in the past. These are: the argument from *social peace*, the argument from *prudence*, and the argument from *inefficacy*.

The argument from social peace runs as follows. Suppose we have a society which is roughly equally divided between the followers of two sects, denominations or religions, each of which is officially committed to using state power to compel universal adherence to its tenets. Then it can be said (and frequently was in the seventeenth and eighteenth centuries) that the only chance of achieving social peace is for both sides to abandon their demands and instead settle for a general policy of religious tolerance. This argument is, obviously, perfectly sound as far as it goes. But it must be observed that its force presupposes that those addressed by it attribute a high value to social peace and are thus at any rate to that extent already secularized.

---

[2] See Michael Freeden, *The New Liberalism* (Oxford: Clarendon Press, 1978).

The argument from prudence avoids this problem by suggesting that under some conditions a concern for the ability to practise one's own religion should lead to agreement on a policy of toleration. Thus, suppose again that rival religious groups are evenly balanced within a society. Then it can be said to each group: if you fight, you may win and be able (at whatever cost) to impose your beliefs on all the members of the society. But it is equally possible that if you fight you may lose and have an alien set of beliefs imposed on you. In this situation, religious toleration presents itself as a maximin strategy for both sides, not giving either the outcome that it wants most but guaranteeing it against the outcome that it wants least.

This argument has the advantage over the first of making religious claims self-limiting. But it has in common with the first the feature that its cogency depends upon there actually being a balance of forces within the society. It thus brings no comfort to unpopular minorities, especially powerless ones. Since it is of the essence of liberal laws and policies that they should protect minorities, it is clear that these arguments cannot be said to provide general support for them.

The argument from inefficacy breaks out of these limitations. Rather, it seeks to show that persecution is pointless because it fails to achieve the ends of the persecutors. The argument, which was like the others commonly made in the seventeenth and eighteenth centuries, ran along the following lines: what matters is religious belief, not religious practice; but belief cannot be coerced. Therefore religious persecution is pointless, because it cannot achieve its justifying end.[3]

The argument depends on the following assumptions, all of which are questionable: (1) the sole purpose of coercion is the salvation of the person coerced; (2) salvation is a matter of inner belief rather than outward observance; and (3) coercion cannot produce alterations in inner belief. The first premiss is the most vulnerable. The persecutor may be less concerned with converting existing heretics than with preventing them from gaining new adherents from the ranks of the currently orthodox, and for this purpose it may well be sufficient to prohibit all outward manifestations of the heretical belief. Even more importantly, the persecutor may well consider that, in the great scheme of things, saving the souls of the present generation of adults is of trivial significance compared with what is at stake in saving the

---

[3] See Preston King, *Toleration* (London: Allen and Unwin, 1976), esp. p. 101. The most familiar version of this argument among Anglophones is John Locke's *Letter Concerning Toleration* (in J. W. Gough, ed., *The Second Treatise of Civil Government* (Oxford: Blackwell, 1946), 123–65), but what should be emphasized, and is made clear by King, is how widespread within Europe arguments of this kind were.

souls of their descendants. And here the historical record is extremely clear. Most of the contemporary adherents of Islam are the descendants of people who originally adopted it at the point of a sword, but the quality of their faith today is no less for that. The same goes for many Protestant and Catholic areas in Europe. The effectiveness of coercion in producing genuine belief over the course of a few generations is beyond question.

I pass more briefly over assumptions (2) and (3), simply observing in connection with (2) that, whatever may be the case with Christianity, some other religions appear to attach primary importance to the carrying out of prescribed rituals rather than to the state of mind of the person carrying them out. And as far as (3) is concerned, it is by no means evident that beliefs cannot be changed by coercion. If outward conformity is obtained by coercion, the machinery of cognitive dissonance reduction comes into play to create a pressure towards bringing belief into line with performance.

When we shift from beliefs to actions, this third argument becomes even weaker. Suppose we accepted that coercion is inefficacious in inducing belief. It is a good deal less implausible to think that it must be inefficacious in suppressing what is deemed to be wrong behaviour. If you believe that, say, homosexual acts are wrong, prohibiting them by law will, it seems reasonable to suggest, at any rate reduce their incidence.

A version of (3) could be maintained independently of any facts about human psychology by stipulating that God does not assign any value to religious beliefs acquired under duress. This would rule out coercion justified entirely by its beneficial effects on those concerned. But it would not rule out coercion motivated by the other ends mentioned above. And in any case it has to be observed that the relevant view of the Deity is one that is far from universal among religious believers. Moreover, this variant is no more successful in relation to actions than is the argument from inefficacy. For even those who take the view that true beliefs brought about under duress are of no value may well think that right acts brought about by duress, while no doubt less valuable than right acts chosen freely, are still not without value. Those who believe some kind of act to be wrong will normally think it better if such acts do not occur, even if the motive for refraining from them is fear of punishment.

Let me make it clear that I have no wish to disparage the significance of these three arguments. They were unquestionably crucial in the development of liberal states. The beginnings of liberal institutions antedate the prevalence of liberal attitudes, and it was precisely pragmatic arguments of the kind outlined here that led to support for such practices as religious toleration. Nevertheless, such pragmatic arguments are valid only under quite restrictive conditions and even then limited in the range of activities they cover.

It is true that we move away from pragmatism with the variant of the third argument that ascribes value only to freely chosen beliefs and actions. But this is in itself a viewpoint characteristic of liberal individualism and is by no means standard among religious believers. What we are looking for, it should be recalled, is an argument that can be addressed to non-liberals to induce them to support liberal institutions while retaining intact their non-liberal attitudes. This requirement is not met by showing that converting people with non-liberal religious ideas to liberal religious ideas would result in their supporting liberal institutions. The pragmatic arguments do meet the requirement, but with severe limits. We are still, therefore, left seeking an argument of general applicability that is (a) addressed to non-liberals and (b) not designed to operate by changing their basic non-liberal outlook.

IV LIBERALISM FOR NON-LIBERALS: NEUTRALITY

Can the problem tackled unsuccessfully by the traditional arguments still nevertheless be solved? In recent years several political philosophers have taken up the challenge, and proposed a principle that is claimed to generate support for liberal institutions without invoking liberal premises. This is the principle of neutrality: the principle that states should, as a matter of justice, be neutral between different ideas of the good. What is meant by this is that in their laws and public policies states should avoid doing anything to favour one idea of the good over others. 'Idea of the good' is here something of a term of art, including such things as religious beliefs, moral convictions or judgements of value such as the superiority of poetry to pushpin.

The names most prominently associated with the principle of neutrality are those of Bruce Ackerman, Ronald Dworkin, and John Rawls.[4] It is hardly surprising that the first two are professors of law who cut their teeth on the decisions of the Warren court, while the

---

[4] Bruce A. Ackerman, *Social Justice in the Liberal State* (New Haven, Conn.: Yale University Press, 1980); Ronald Dworkin, 'Liberalism', in Stuart Hampshire, ed., *Public and Private Morality* (Cambridge: Cambridge University Press, 1978), 113–43, reprinted in Ronald Dworkin, *A Matter of Principle* (Cambridge, Mass.: Harvard University Press, 1985), 181–204; and John Rawls, *A Theory of Justice* (Cambridge, Mass.: Harvard University Press, 1971).

closeness of Rawls's thought to American constitutional jurisprudence has often been noticed. For the best way of looking at the principle of neutrality is to see it as a generalization of the line of postwar Supreme Court cases that interpreted with increasing stringency the constitutional requirement that Congress shall make no law establishing a religion.

What is the rationale of the principle of neutrality? It might be defended on pragmatic grounds similar to those canvassed in the previous section. But even if such an argument were successful as far as it went, it would go no further than the pragmatic arguments in favour of liberal institutions themselves. What we are seeking is an ethical justification of the principle of neutrality. Does one exist?

There is indeed an argument, and it is one that claims to derive neutrality from a consideration of the demands of distributive justice. The argument runs as follows. We imagine a society as made up of a set of individuals each of whom has an ordered set of wants, derived from biological needs, conceptions of the good, and so on. The society at the same time disposes of various resources, a resource being defined as something whose deployment is a means to the satisfaction of wants. These resources include money (a means to the satisfaction of whatever wants lend themselves to satisfaction through the market), legal rights, such as the right of free expression and the right to worship the god of one's choice (as President Eisenhower once felicitously put it), and opportunities, such as the opportunity to enter Harvard Law School. We then pose the problem of justice as that of allocating these resources among the claimants. And the answer we give is that a prima-facie just distribution is an equal one. Our three theorists have somewhat different answers to the question of what justifies a departure from equality. We need not follow them into these ramifications, however. For there is one point on which they all agree, and that is the negative point that what *cannot* count as a good reason for allocating a smaller share of resources to one person than he would otherwise be entitled to is that he would use these resources to pursue unworthy ends. This is the principle of neutrality, the principle that public policy should not be based on an evaluation of people's conceptions of the good. If we go on to assert 'the priority of the right over the good', so that considerations of justice trump all others, we can conclude that the principle of neutrality should be the organizing principle of every society.

Now it is no part of my object to deny (though others have done so) that the principle of neutrality can be operationalized. Nor do I wish to deny that when the principle of neutrality is operationalized it leads to the endorsement of liberal policy prescriptions. If we follow up Rawls's hint that we are looking for the maximum equal liberty, it is hard to see how we could do other than support equal rights of worship and of expression, with no restrictions on what people can do in practising their religion or expressing themselves provided they do not harm others — 'harm' being interpreted pretty robustly here so as to exclude shocked sensibilities from its scope. Equal citizenship rights also follow straightforwardly from neutrality, at any rate when it is combined with the egalitarian premiss common to Ackerman, Dworkin, and Rawls.

So far so good. Have we then succeeded in deriving liberal policy prescriptions without relying on liberal attitudes? What might lead us to think so is, plainly, that we have called upon something called a principle of neutrality. If the principle of neutrality were itself neutral between different belief systems and conceptions of the good, we would be home and dry. But that is not so. The principle of neutrality does indeed put them all on the same footing, but to accept that this is how things ought to be organized it is necessary to have an outlook that is, in broad terms, liberal.

The simplest way of illustrating this point is to take Ronald Dworkin's idea that what he calls 'external preferences' should not be counted in the calculus of wants operated to determine public policies. What this means can be explained as follows. Suppose I have certain wants derived from my sexual orientation. These are unproblematic, and should go into the calculus. But suppose I also have a preference that you should be frustrated in satisfying wants derived from your sexual orientation, because it conflicts with my theory of the good. This is an 'external' preference and should not be counted because there is no reason why my preference for your not being able to pursue your conception of the good should lead to your having a less than equal opportunity to pursue it. This would be to impose an unfair burden on you. The case just given is referred to as 'the present argument' in the following quotation:

It is often said that [the] liberal thesis [that the government has no right to enforce popular morality by law] is inconsistent with utilitarianism, because if the preferences of the majority that homosexuality should be repressed, for example, are sufficiently strong, utilitarianism must give way to their wishes. But the preference against homosexuality is an external preference and the present argument provides a general reason why utilitarians should not count external preferences of any form. If utilitarianism is suitably reconstituted so as to count only personal preferences, then the liberal thesis is a consequence, not an enemy of that theory.[5]

To see what is wrong with this let us ask the following simple question: under what conditions could Dworkin's proposed formulation have any application? It would have none in a society of utilitarians, because in such a society the problem of what Dworkin calls 'moralistic preferences' could not arise in the first place. For there could be no 'popular morality' that held things to be wrong for any reason other than that they were contrary to the maximization of utility, since, by definition, everyone would apply the utilitarian principle in determining what was wrong.

Now consider a society whose common morality was based upon some set of beliefs antithetical to utilitarianism, for example a society in which people took their morality from the priests or mullahs. Obviously the members of such a society would have no time for utilitarian criteria in any shape or form. So once again Dworkin's reformulated utilitarianism would hold no interest for them.

The only use I can see for Dworkin's proposal is that it might be construed as advice to the utilitarians in a society many of whose members were not utilitarians. On this interpretation, it would tell them how to factor in the preferences of these non-utilitarians when applying the utilitarian calculus in order to decide what they thought public policy should be. And if in such a society the utilitarians controlled the government, public policy would then be founded upon Dworkin's version of utilitarianism. However, although Dworkin's proposal would have application in such a context, a problem still remains. For the moral beliefs of the non-utilitarians would then be treated in a way that they would regard as a travesty. It could therefore scarcely be put forward as a way of dealing in a generally acceptable fashion with differing 'conceptions of the good'.

What I mean by saying that the non-utilitarians could not accept Dworkin's proposal is that to do so they would have to abandon their own conception of the status of their moral convictions. They could never agree that these convictions should be discounted as 'external preferences' because they would regard 'preference' as a wholly inappropriate category in which to put them.

Once concede that it is merely a matter of whose preference gets satisfied and it is indeed hard to deny that someone who wants to have

[5] Ronald Dworkin, 'Reverse Discrimination', in *Taking Rights Seriously* (Cambridge, Mass.: Harvard University Press, 1977), 223–9, quotation from p. 236.

his 'external preferences' to count is being greedy. But of course someone who really believes that homosexual acts are sinful and wicked will disclaim any notion that they should be prohibited to please him. Rather, he will say that if it is a matter of pleasing anyone it is a matter of pleasing God. But really, he will add, pleasing is not what it's all about. Homosexual acts are wrong and that is why the law should prohibit them.

It is not essential to the argument from neutrality that one should follow Dworkin's crass suggestion that moral convictions ought to be treated as mere 'preferences' and then rejected as a basis for public policy on the ground that they are an inappropriate kind of preference. John Rawls has proposed an alternative approach that leaves moral convictions to be regarded as falling into the category of beliefs rather than that of preferences, but suggests that they should be held in a special way that precludes their being translated into public policy.

According to Rawls, we should seek in a contemporary pluralistic society to base public policy on uncontroversial beliefs. All conceptions of the good (in which Rawls includes religious doctrines) are, Rawls says, inherently controversial. Therefore neutrality between different conceptions of the good must be the watchword of such a society.[6] On this view, people with illiberal beliefs—about the wickedness of homosexuality, for example—can continue to hold them without challenge. But they must hold these beliefs in a special way: as private opinions that they do not seek to impose on anybody else through the machinery of the state.

There is no doubt that some people do in fact adopt the position recommended by Rawls. John F. Kennedy, to give a prominent example, undertook when running for the Presidency not to allow himself in exercising the office to be influenced by the teachings of the Roman Catholic Church on public issues. But the point to be made about this phenomenon is essentially the same as that already made in the context of Dworkin's idea that people should not ask to have their 'external preferences' put into the calculus of public policy. This point is simply that any understanding of the Church's teachings that treats them as matters of personal opinion is profoundly at odds with the claims that the Church itself makes for its teachings. Exactly the same can be said of those who derive their notions of right and wrong

---

[6] 'Briefly, the idea is that in a constitutional democracy public conceptions of justice should be, so far as possible, independent of controversial philosophical and religious doctrines.' John Rawls, 'Justice as Fairness: Political not Metaphysical', *Philosophy & Public Affairs*, 14 (1985), 223–51, quotation from p. 223.

directly from an authoritative book such as the Bible rather than from an authoritative organization such as the Roman Catholic Church. Either way, for someone to be prepared to say 'Homosexuality is wrong but that's just my private opinion', he or she must already have swallowed a large dose of liberalism.

What such a person is saying is that wrongful acts fall into two categories. There are those which are wrong because they injure others. These are legitimate objects of prohibition, though the principle of *de minimis non curat lex* may imply that in some cases they should not actually be prohibited. Then there are those which are wrong because they are condemned by some authoritative religious book or body. Some of these acts will also be wrong because they injure people (e.g. murder). Others, however, will be wrong only in the second way, and these are not legitimate objects of prohibition. Of course, even if one believed that a wrongful but harmless kind of act could legitimately be prohibited, one might still be against actually prohibiting it for practical reasons.[7] But on the view we are now discussing prohibition is ruled out in principle, so that the practical issues do not even come into play.

We should observe that this second sense of 'wrong', which has no potential implications for law or public policy, is a very weak one. Operationally, saying that something is wrong in the second (and not also in the first) sense would seem to commit one to little more than refraining from the act oneself. This is plainly to withdraw what are usually the major implications of saying something is wrong. When I said that the position presupposes that the person holding it has already swallowed a large dose of liberalism, what I had in mind was this: that it is hard to see how anyone could hold it except on the basis of a sceptical attitude towards the religious teachings which provided the basis for the belief in the wrongness of certain non-harmful acts.

If I am right about this, we have to abandon as illusory the hope that people might be left undisturbed in their dogmatic slumbers while somehow being cajoled into accepting liberal policy prescriptions. Dogmatism must give way to scepticism before the appropriately

---

[7] Since, *ex hypothesi*, these would be 'victimless crimes' their enforcement would be a greater threat to liberty than other forms of law enforcement, since it would require collecting information about consensual transactions. Corruption of the police and opportunities for organized crime tend to arise from the prohibition of harmless acts. And, to the extent that members of the society do not see anything wrong in harmless acts, the law is liable to fall into disrepute. Another point often made is that the pursuit of victimless crimes diverts police effort from more important crimes. But this in effect presupposes that preventing harm is what matters, so it is essentially a variant on the view considered in the text.

attenuated concept of wrongness can become attractive. I would, indeed, speculate (though the truth of this speculation is inessential to my overall argument) that the position advocated by Rawls, and many other liberals, finds few adherents. From a psychological point of view I suspect that it is radically unstable, and tends to function as a half-way house between the thought that homosexual acts (say) are wrong in the old-fashioned sense and the thought that they are not wrong at all. Thus if we take the proportion of the population that, according to British or American survey evidence, would like to see homosexual acts prohibited, and make a guess about the proportion that thinks there is nothing wrong with homosexuality, it looks as if people who believe it is wrong but should not be prohibited must be very thin on the ground. To put it bluntly, I wonder how many of the philosophers who espouse the Dworkinian or Rawlsian position personally believe that there are kinds of act that are wrong in spite of not being harmful. My guess is that the doctrine is usually offered for general consumption by people who have no use for it themselves.

V SHOULD LIBERALS EMBRACE NEUTRALITY?

The conclusion at which I arrive is, then, that a liberal outlook is not only a sufficient condition for supporting liberal institutions but is also (except in circumstances where the arguments discussed in section III apply) a necessary condition. Or, more precisely, this is the conclusion that must be held until we find some better argument than that from justice for the principle of neutrality—and I find it hard to believe that any such argument is waiting to be discovered.

What I have suggested is that there is no way in which non-liberals can be sold the principle of neutrality without first injecting a large dose of liberalism into their outlook. But I now want to add that, unattractive as the principle of neutrality must be to non-liberals, it is not necessarily very attractive even to liberals. For although a liberal outlook does support liberal institutions, it goes beyond them, as I suggested in section II. And the destination to which it goes is not neutrality.

This point can be brought home by examining the reasons give by Ackerman for espousing the principle of neutrality. One is that 'you might think that you can only learn anything true about the good when you are free to experiment in life without some authoritative teacher intervening whenever he thinks you're going wrong. And if you think this, Neutrality seems made to order.' Another is that 'you may adopt a conception of the good that gives a central place to autonomous deliberation and deny that it is possible to *force* someone to be good. On this view, the intrusion of non-Neutral argument into power talk will seem self-defeating at best—since it threatens to divert people from the true means of cultivating a truly good life.[8] The ideas that Ackerman outlines here clearly correspond to my description of liberal attitudes. But the confidence with which he asserts that they naturally lead to support for neutrality seems misplaced. In fact, Ackerman's arguments would seem to underwrite support for liberal policy prescriptions but not for the principle of neutrality. For the liberal conception of the good—which is what Ackerman is in effect building on—can be promoted by the state in the kinds of way mentioned in section II. If we want to prevent intervention by authoritative teachers, we shall do better to insist that parents should not be allowed to send their children to schools that teach some inherently dubious doctrine as unquestionable truth than to allow them to do so on the ground that we have (for purposes of public policy) no idea whether such indoctrination is a good thing or not. Similarly, autonomy is not likely to be fostered by a society which treats the ideal of human good that gives a heavy weight to autonomy as just one among many and no better than any others. The bogey of forcing people to be good can be laid to rest once we bear in mind that enforcing the criminal law is only a tiny part (albeit an important one) of what a modern state does, and that much of its activity is facilitative rather than repressive.

I think that there is nevertheless a line of argument that can be addressed to liberals. As we have seen, the problem with neutrality is that it asks people with moral convictions to treat them as external preferences or matters of personal opinion. This goes as much for those with liberal beliefs as for those with non-liberal ones. It can, however, be suggested that liberals suffer substantially less than non-liberals from the truncation exercised on their beliefs by the operation of the principle of neutrality. For although liberals believe, of course, that it is better if people are more rather than less capable of making up their own minds and steering their own course through life, it is only in really extreme cases that they have a sense that departure from their standards is actually wrong, as against simply being unfortunate. A liberal will tend to regard the denial of autonomy as actually wrong only in cases where it is so gross that it can reasonably be regarded (at

---

[8] Ackerman, *Social Justice*, p. 11 (italics in original).

any rate from the liberal point of view) as constituting harm. Non-liberals, by contrast, characteristically do think that a variety of practices that would be protected by the principle of neutrality are wrong, typically on the basis of some religious authority. If we take the view that being prevented from prohibiting what you believe to be wrong is a more severe restriction than being prevented from promoting what you believe to be good, we can conclude that the principle of neutrality bears more harshly on non-liberals than on liberals.

Another way of approaching the same conclusion is to observe that neutrality underwrites the liberal policy prescriptions outlined in section I, and that these are congruent with liberal attitudes. Non-liberals, however, will tend to find that the liberal policy prescriptions, at any rate as extended from the classical core to include the notion of a 'protected sphere', run counter to the policies that they would favour. Thus, we once again arrive at the point that neutrality suits liberals better than it suits non-liberals.

It has to be said that nothing immediately follows from this. But it does lend some support for the idea that liberals could afford to be generous and pull back from the implementation of the full liberal programme, adopting instead the principle of neutrality. In doing so they would perhaps be lending some credence to the jibe that a liberal is someone who is not prepared to take his own side in an argument. But it could be suggested that this kind of forbearance—in effect applying liberal scepticism to liberal beliefs—redounds to their credit.

It has to be observed, however, that this line of reasoning does nothing to advance the cause of neutrality as a general solution for conflicts among rival conceptions of the good. It would be nice if the liberal could say 'There you are. We adopt neutrality when in power. So you should reciprocate by adopting it when *you* are in power.' But this is liable not to cut much ice with a non-liberal. Nor, I suggest, is there any good reason why it should.

It is a familiar idea that to be consistent a society committed to liberal policy prescriptions should tolerate Nazi or Communist propaganda. But this has no implication that a Nazi or Communist regime should allow liberal propaganda. Liberalism is true to itself by opening the public sphere to Nazis and Communists. But Nazism and Communism (at any rate as understood in the Soviet Union until now) would be false to themselves by failing to control the flow of information so as to ensure that only 'correct' ideas are disseminated.

This provides an analogy (though I emphasize that it is no more than that) for the point to be made about neutrality. If we apply liberal scepticism to liberal beliefs we get neutrality. But there is no similar pressure from considerations of internal consistency to get a dogmatist to apply liberal scepticism to his beliefs. A dogmatist is consistent all the way down by holding his beliefs dogmatically.

I have presented an argument that can be addressed to people with a liberal outlook to press them towards neutrality. I have, however, been careful not to endorse the argument myself. I shall conclude this essay by offering two reasons for doubting that liberals should embrace neutrality.

The first reason for questioning the argument is that it relies on the implicit assumption that liberal beliefs are on all fours with dogmatic beliefs. But we must ask if this kind of self-depreciating stance is warranted. A dogmatist, for the purposes of this discussion, is not simply someone who adheres to a dogma, but someone who adheres to it dogmatically. This means that he wishes the young to be brought up in it without any opportunity to question it, and wishes to shield it from public debate. Inasmuch as his dogma condemns certain types of action, he considers it legitimate to use the state to attempt to suppress them, even if they would be immune under liberal policy prescriptions.

A liberal, by contrast, has no objection to anyone holding a dogma, so long as it is not held dogmatically — that is to say, so long as it has to take its chances in competition with other ideas. Again, liberals want to open up more opportunities for people to express themselves rather than prevent them from doing things that pose no harm to the public. It seems reasonable to suggest on the basis of these contrasts that departures from neutrality in a liberal direction have a different status from departures in a non-liberal direction. It is not simply a matter of saying 'This kind of thing is all right when I do it but not when you do it' because the 'kind of thing' involved is actually different in its nature.

The second reason for doubting that liberals should abandon liberalism for neutrality is that the defence of liberal institutions requires those with a liberal outlook to go on the offensive and promote liberalism actively. If I am right in this essay, there is little chance of selling neutrality to non-liberals, which means that non-liberals will continue to hold views about the proper role of state action that run counter to liberal policy prescriptions. Even if he has no wish to promote liberal attitudes as an end in itself, anyone attached to the liberal institutions sketched in section I is going to have to recognize that their prospects of survival depend on there being in the population a large proportion of people with a liberal outlook.

The optimistic hope of the Enlightenment was that the cessation of persecution and censorship would over time lead to the triumph of liberal attitudes. We know now that things do not work like that. These purely negative conditions leave the outcome to the play of social forces that are not necessarily favourable to liberal values. The rise of fascism within societies with liberal institutions showed the vulnerability of those institutions in the most dramatic way possible. Currently the retreat from liberalism is far less dramatic but the evidence is there for all to see. The churches that have made the biggest concessions to liberalism are losing ground while those that strain credulity the most gain the most adherents. (The international success of the Mormons is the most remarkable exemplification of this rule.) The popular press in Britain (and wherever else Rupert Murdoch has penetrated) reinforces and makes respectable the more atavistic impulses of its readers. The idea is gaining ground that schools should teach what parents want taught. And so on.

Under these conditions, I do not think that liberals can afford the luxury of unilateral disarmament. Very likely we are headed for a new Dark Age, and nothing philosophers of a liberal persuasion can do will prevent it. But given the choice between trying to persuade non-liberals to accept the principle of neutrality and trying to discredit their beliefs, I think that the second is clearly the better strategy.

3

AND WHO IS MY NEIGHBOUR?[1]

I remember, . . . about 1646 (or 1647) that Mr. John Maynard (now Sir John, and serjeant) came into Middle Temple hall, from Westminster-hall, weary with business, and hungry, when we had newly dined. He sate-downe by Mr. Bennet Hoskyns (the only son of Sergeant Hoskyns, the Poet) since Baronet, and some others; who having made an end of their Commons, fell unto various Discourse, and what was the meaning of the Text (Rom. v. 7.) 'For a just man one would dare to die; but for a good man one would willingly die.' They askt Mr. Maynard what was the difference between a just man and a good man. He was beginning to eate, and cryed:—Hoh, you have eaten your dinners, and now have leisure to discourse; I have not. He had eate but a Bitt or two when he reply'd:—I'le tell you the difference presently: serjeant Rolle is a just man, and Mathew Hale is a good man; and so fell to make an end of his dinner. And there could not be a better interpretation of this Text. For serjeant Rolle was just, but by nature penurious; and his wife made him worse: Mathew Hale was not only just, but wonderfully Charitable and open handed, and did not sound a trumpet neither, as the Hypocrites doe.

J. Aubrey, *Brief Lives*

It is often said that the most important division in moral philosophy is between the view that what makes actions right or wrong is their consequences and the view that some kinds of actions are right or wrong intrinsically, and should be done or not done regardless of the consequences in any particular instance. The strongest objection to the first doctrine is that an adherent of it might be manipulated into doing something extremely evil by the threat on somebody else's part that he will otherwise do something with even more horrible consequences. The strongest objection to the second doctrine is that there seems to be something almost crazy in saying that, once an act has been

[1] This chapter departs from the original form of publication a good deal further than do any of the others in this volume. It is based on a revision of the original (1979) review essay which was carried out in 1983 with the objects of making the order of exposition more natural and also making the discussion relatively independent of the terms set by a rather crass book. At that time the discussion of the relevant literature was carried up to 1983.

determined to fall under a certain description, no consideration of consequences can be relevant in assessing the moral quality of that act.

I believe that both objections are well taken and that any satisfactory view of the matter must accommodate both of them. In this chapter I shall argue for a position that does this. It denies that any act can be immune to moral censure simply in virtue of its falling under some description. But at the same time it allows what an unqualified consequentialist doctrine cannot allow, namely that it makes a difference in the moral quality of an act whether its foreseeably bad consequences follow directly from it or whether they arise from the act's occasioning the predictably wrong act of another.

The doctrine that some kinds of acts are intrinsically right or wrong, irrespective of their consequences, must of course be filled out by specifying what it is about actions that makes them right or wrong. One view that has achieved some considerable currency is this: what makes an act wrong is that it injures somebody and what makes an act right (which in this context means 'permissible' rather than 'required') is that the actor had a right to do it, or, in different words, that the act fell within his sphere of absolute discretion. I shall criticize both halves of this theory.

An even more fundamental question in moral philosophy is whether morality rests on convention or whether some things would be wrong in a society whatever its institutions and whatever the beliefs of its members. I shall not be so bold as to tackle this great question head on but I shall nevertheless try to throw some light on it. I shall, as before, suggest that the strongest arguments on both sides are correct. It is true that much adverse judgement of other cultures is mere prejudice. The stock example of missionaries objecting to the scanty clothing of their 'natives' is entirely to the point here. But it is also true that genocide is wrong whatever the social context in which it occurs. I shall seek to put forward a view that gives full weight to the moral relevance of convention without collapsing into total relativism.

The essay will be cast in the form of a critique of a book published in 1978, Charles Fried's *Right and Wrong*.[2] I shall at times wander pretty far from Fried's text, but the book still provides the framework for my discussion. Although it must be conceded that Fried is hardly the subtlest of thinkers, there are some advantages in having the view to be discussed presented in a fairly stark form. If Fried is willing to draw conclusions from which others who share his outlook might shrink,

[2] Page references in the text of this chapter are to Charles Fried, *Right and Wrong* (Cambridge, Mass.: Harvard University Press, 1978).

that is surely to his credit. Truth, as Bacon said, arises more readily from error than from confusion.

I shall set out my criticisms under two heads: that Fried is mistaken in reducing morality to a matter of rights and wrongs (sections I and II); and that the notion of saving one's soul does not survive translation into secular terms (section III). I shall take up the question of convention in the course of the discussion in section II. I shall conclude (section IV) by returning to the question with which I opened this chapter and ask where the intervening discussion leaves the doctrine of consequentialism.

I WRONGS

The title of Fried's book is *Right and Wrong*; and, not being a man inhibited by excessive modesty, he claims to be able to tell us what is right and what is wrong. However, the two major parts into which the book is divided are called 'Wrongs' and 'Rights'.[3] The shift from right and wrong to rights and wrongs is momentous. Wrongs are things we do to particular people: we wrong them when we do certain things to them. To assume, as Fried does, that we can talk about wrong by talking about wrongs is to commit ourselves to a substantive moral doctrine of a peculiar kind. Other things being equal (at least), it is wrong to wrong people. But cannot there be wrong without anyone being wronged?

Consider these examples. First, let us suppose that a woman could conceive a child now, while she is taking a drug that will cause her child to be gravely deformed at birth; or she could postpone conception for a few months and have a normal child. If the woman goes ahead and conceives the defective child, we can say that the child she bears is much worse off than the child she might have borne later. But we cannot say that the woman has harmed the child that is born, because that child would not have otherwise existed. The child therefore has not been wronged, unless we say that bringing it into existence at all was wronging it (a case of wrongful birth). Let us stipulate, however, that the child is not so miserable as to regret having been born. It still seems reasonable to say that the woman did wrong by conceiving the defective child, and to say this without

---

[3] There is also a third part of the book (pp. 165–94) which consists of only one chapter. This is entitled 'Roles' and discusses the implications of the theory for professional ethics. Although I regard the chapter as highly obnoxious I shall not take it up here since the rest of the book is self-contained without it.

taking into consideration the effects of the birth on other people who would have existed anyway. We can maintain that the woman did wrong, however, only if we accept that it is possible to do wrong without wronging anybody.[4]

What is in effect a generalization of the same example is the following. Suppose those currently alive deplete resources and create pollution with the result that subsequent generations suffer great hardship. Provided this course of action results in different people being born, compared with what would have happened if a more responsible course had been followed, nobody is wronged. For the would-be complainants would not otherwise have come into existence.[5] Yet it seems absurd to suggest that the members of the current generation are not open to moral criticism for their conduct.

If the only points at which the equation of wrong with wronging came unstuck were those involving alternative populations, we might feel secure in saying that under normal circumstances doing wrong and wronging can be identified. For problems involving possible people are very hard to make sense of anyway. (For a review of the difficulties, see chapter 18 below.) But I believe that the same slippage between wrongdoing and wronging also occurs in cases where the population affected is given. It is still possible to do wrong in relation to people without wronging anybody.

Imagine, then, that a hospital has a limited supply of a scarce drug. The doctor in charge could either use the drug in one massive shot to save the life of one person (less will be of no use to him) or divide it into five equal doses which will save the lives of five people. Would he do wrong to give all of the drug to the one person rather than to divide it among the five?[6] Or, imagine that several people are stranded on one rock, and that one person is stranded on another rock. Assuming that there is not enough time to rescue the people on both rocks before the tide rises and drowns them, does someone with a boat do wrong by rescuing only the lone person? The reason for saying that the doctor or the man with the boat does not do wrong would be that nobody is wronged. Nobody has any cause for complaint, the argument goes, so long as the drug or the boat was used and not wasted.

---

[4] This example was introduced by Derek Parfit. The best exposition of his views is to be found in his *Reasons and Persons* (Oxford: Clarendon Press, 1984), 351–79.

[5] This is seriously maintained by Thomas Schwartz 'Obligations to Posterity', in R. I. Sikora and Brian Barry (eds.), *Obligations to Future Generations* (Philadelphia: Temple University Press, 1978), thus illustrating the point that one person's proof is another's *reductio ad absurdum*.

[6] The example was introduced by Philippa Foot, 'Abortion and Double Effect', *Oxford Review*, 5 (1967), 5–15, at 9.

As Miss Anscombe put it: 'Why, just because he was one of the five who could have been saved [by the drug], is he wronged in not being saved, if someone is supplied with it who needed it? What is *his* claim, except the claim that what was needed go to him rather than be wasted? But it was not wasted. So he was not wronged. So who was wronged? And if no one was wronged, what injury did I do?' Similarly, the man with the boat 'doesn't act badly if he uses his resources to save X, or X, Y and Z, *for no bad reason*, and is not affected by the consideration that he could save a larger number of people. For, once more, who can say he is wronged? And if no one is wronged, how does the rescuer commit any wrong?'[7]

We can be grateful to Miss Anscombe for making it so clear that the argument rests on the assumption that if no one is wronged nobody can have done wrong. But why should we accept that assumption? Why should we not say that it would be wrong to save fewer lives rather than more? It seems to me spurious to argue that the drug or the boat were not wasted: they were wasted in the sense that they were not used to the best advantage. Suppose the doctor treated one of the five patients with an adequate dose and poured the remaining four-fifths of it down the sink. If giving all the drug to one patient would have been all right, is there anything wrong with that? If so, why? In both cases one person is saved where five might have been. Or suppose that the man with the boat goes to the rock with lots of people and takes off just one person picked at random. He is surely wasting life-saving space in the boat as much as if he went to the rock on which just one person is stranded and rescued that person. The question 'Who is wronged?' is irrelevant. We need not show that anyone is wronged before we can say that it would have been better to use the life-saving resource to save more lives.

Someone who agrees that saving fewer is wrong might try to salvage the equation of wrongdoing and wronging by suggesting that the greater number who might have been saved but were not can legitimately be said to have been wronged. I am inclined to think that this claim would appeal only to someone who was for some reason already committed to the principle that wrongdoing requires a wronged party. It is, of course, true that the greater number suffer grievously as a result of the wrong choice made by the possessor of the medicine or the boat. But all that can be claimed of each of the losers is that it would have been efficient (in life-saving terms) to have saved the group of which he or she was a member. The same person, by

    [7] G. E. M. Anscombe, 'Who is Wronged?', *Oxford Review*, 5 (1967), 16–17, at 17.

happening to go to the rock with the smaller number of people, would have lost the claim to be saved. But it seems to me that it is one thing to say that a calculus of life-saving shows that so-and-so was a member of the group that should have been saved and another to say that so-and-so was wronged by the failure to follow the results of applying that calculus. To anticipate the discussion in the next section for a moment, let us pose the question in terms of rights: did each member of the larger group have a right to be saved? If we want to say that wrongdoing is the violation of somebody's rights, we may be driven by the wish to conclude that it is wrong not to save the larger number into saying that each of them has a right to be saved. I cannot see any knockdown argument to show that this is a mistake but I would again ask if one would ever feel drawn to say that the larger number had a right to be saved while the smaller number did not except in order to arrive at the conclusion that it was wrong not to rescue the larger number.

What, after all, is going on here? There is no way of saying who has the right to be saved until the calculation has been carried out to determine which course of action will be most efficacious in saving lives. The only thing that distinguishes those with the right to be saved from those with no right to be saved is that the former emerge from the calculation as those whom it is more efficient to save. This state of affairs does not seem to me to be very perspicuously rendered by talking about some people having a right to be saved and others not. Such talk makes it sound as if the members of the larger group have a right to be saved and therefore ought to be saved, whereas it is actually the other way round: they ought to be saved and, once we have determined that, we could if we choose say (but without adding any new point) that they have a right to be saved.

In the course of his discussion, Fried refers to an article later than Miss Anscombe's which, he says (p. 219), develops the argument with 'great power and subtlety'. Although I should myself be inclined to substitute 'perversity' for 'subtlety', I do think that the central point that the article makes is important and must be faced in any analysis of the notion of a duty to rescue. The author, John Taurek, puts forward the following case.[8] Suppose that we have once again the situation in which the available amount of some drug could save one person in a single dose or some larger number of people divided into smaller doses. And now suppose further that the person who would require

[8] John Taurek, 'Should the Numbers Count?', *Philosophy & Public Affairs*, 6 (1977), 293–316.

the whole amount to be saved owned it. Would we say that he was morally condemnable if he used it on himself? If we would not, then, Taurek argues, this must show that there is no duty to maximize the number of lives saved. So we can generalize the case and say that if some third party owned the drug, we could not consistently say that he was wrong to give it to the one rather than the five.

This argument clearly depends, if it is to be valid, on our acceptance of the proposition that, if A cannot be blamed for doing something to save his own life at the expense of several other people's lives, then nobody else can be criticized for choosing to save A's life at the expense of those other people. But this move seems to me to be without foundation. It is true that in 'common sense morality' we make allowances for people in extreme situations. We do not condemn people for failing to be heroes, and to hand over the drug that would save your life so that the lives of five others could be saved would surely be heroic. But that certainly does not mean it would not be better if the five lives were saved instead of the one.[9] Since it would not be heroic for a third party who owned the drug to give it to the five rather than the one, he *can* be criticized for not doing so.

How, then, should we deal with the case of the man with the boat, to take account of what is valid in Taurek's argument without drawing his invalid conclusions? The answer I wish to give is that, instead of asking simply 'Was what he did right or wrong?' we shall ask more fine-grained questions, and according to the answers respond in a variety of ways. Thus, in some circumstances we would treat him as a moral leper if he failed to rescue the people—he happened to be passing the rock anyway, the sea was calm, and he could have taken them off at almost no inconvenience or risk to himself. In others, we might award him a medal for heroism—the sea was stormy and he was putting his own life at risk by going out to rescue the people. In between is a continuous gradation: the further the rock, the severer the storm, the less seaworthy the boat, the less robust the man's health, for example, the better his deed in rescuing the people.

If the man would be risking his life, many other questions become relevant. How did these people come to be stranded? Did they go on to the rocks knowing and accepting the risk? If they did not know, should they have known? Or did they know of the risk but thought they had covered it by arranging to be taken off by a boat which has

---

[9] Cf. Derek Parfit, 'Innumerate Ethics', *Philosophy & Public Affairs*, 7 (1978), 285–301, and Gregory S. Kavka, 'The Numbers Should Count', *Philosophical Studies*, 36 (1979), 285–94.

failed to appear? And what about the man? What dependants has he? Given their particular circumstances and the prevailing social system, how will they fare if he dies in the rescue attempt? And so on. That these questions are relevant shows that we cannot simply postulate a duty to do as much good as possible, counting in one's own welfare as one unit among many. But they also show the inadequacy of the idea that it would be wrong to save nobody but beyond moral criticism to save one rather than many.

After saying everything that can be said about the situation, we may ask whether, taking everything into account, rescuing should be regarded as praiseworthy and not rescuing as acceptable conduct in the circumstances, or whether not rescuing should be regarded as blame-worthy and rescuing as no more than could be reasonably expected of any decent person in the circumstances. But people will probably not all draw the line in exactly the same place: some people set higher standards (for themselves and for others) than do the rest of us. And it does not have to be a *line* at all. After the morally relevant facts have all been established, we may feel disinclined either to say that, in that situation, rescuing was praiseworthy or not rescuing blameworthy. (This is not, of course, to deny that rescuing would always be better than not rescuing.)

What about 'wrong'? We can certainly say that what the man with the boat did was wrong, if it falls so far below the minimum standards of conduct required by the social norms of our community as to lead to universal disapprobation; or we can say more loosely that what he did was wrong if we believe that the social norms should be such as would lead to his severe condemnation. The only thing we cannot do is pretend that we are trying to duplicate the actions of a sort of secular equivalent of the Recording Angel.[10]

II RIGHTS

The strong drive underlying Fried's *Right and Wrong* is the wish to come up with a fixed and finite list of things that people can be morally required to do such that if they do not infringe these rules they can count as 'morally good'. The opening sentence runs: 'This book is about how a moral man lives his life' (p. 1), and the connection between sticking to the rules and being 'morally good' comes out later in, for example, this passage from near the end of the book:

[10] Cf. Joel Feinberg, 'On Being "Morally Speaking a Murderer"', in *Doing and Deserving: Essays on the Theory of Responsibility* (Princeton, NJ: Princeton University Press, 1970), 38–54.

We must recognize a discontinuity: Between the merely just man and the chiseler comes the dividing line of right and wrong, while the whole distance between the saint and the merely just man occurs within the range of the morally good, and thus the categories of condemnation and compulsion are wholly inappropriate within that range. At most, what are in order are judgments of regret, but even those are questionable. The scale of judgement is marked, if at all, in degrees of praise only (pp. 175–6).

This Pharasaical conception of moral goodness as the satisfaction of certain rule-based minimal requirements can be questioned on two grounds. First, we can point out that it has had a long run for its money and if it has fallen into disrepute this was for good reasons, based on extensive experience with it. Victorian novels and biographies are thickly populated with self-righteous prigs who never did anything wrong in Fried's sense but still managed to make life hell for everyone around them. (One might recall the description of Dr Temple, the mid-Victorian headmaster of Rugby School, as 'a beast: but a just beast'.)

The second point that can be made goes to the root of the whole conception. Is a legal or theological model appropriate to what purports to be a secular account of the content of morality? In law and in any rule-based religious system, there is no room for better or worse, only for right and wrong, or, more precisely, permitted, required, and prohibited. Any act is either legal or illegal. There are no degrees of legality. Similarly, an act can be more or less sinful only in the sense that it constitutes a more or less grave sin. The borderline of any given category of sin is an area of increasing doubt about its application, not a continuum of decreasing sinfulness.[11]

The question that must be raised is whether it makes sense to construe morality on the legal model, as Fried does, in the absence of a divine lawgiver. Miss Anscombe observes that 'it is not possible to have [a *law* conception of ethics] unless you believe in God as a lawgiver: like Jews, Stoics and Christians'.[12] I think she is right. Since Fried does not call on supernatural authority to underwrite his theory, we must say that his 'wrong' is, to adapt Hobbes, the ghost of sin sitting upon the grave thereof.

We can see both the inadequacy and the arbitrariness of this law conception of morality by examining Fried's doctrine of rights. The

---

[11] See G. E. M. Anscombe, 'Modern Moral Philosophy', *Philosophy*, 33 (1958), 1–19; reprinted in Judith J. Thomson and Gerald Dworkin (eds.), *Ethics* (New York: Harper & Row, 1968), 186–210, at 201. (All page references in this chapter are to the reprint.)
[12] Ibid. 192.

drive to establish minimal standards the meeting of which absolves anyone from criticism emerges very clearly in the definition of a right that is offered by Fried:

I want to do something. It is not wrong, but it has (bad) unfortunate concomitants. Do I have to weight these, and forbear if the balance is unfavorable? Usually yes, *unless I have a right to do whatever it is I am doing*. If I have a right to marry whom I want (who wants to marry me), then this just means I do not have to consider how our happiness compares to the unhappiness our marriage will cause my rivals or hers, our parents, the neighbors (pp. 83–4, italics in original).

Fried claims to give us 'an account of moral choice and substantive moral values that is rich, complex and true to the facts' (p. 2). This claim is palpably false. Whatever plausibility Fried's claim may have is gained entirely from the false dilemma he constantly poses that, if one rejects his theory, there is no alternative to accepting universalistic consequentialism—that is to say, the theory that we have a duty to maximize total human wellbeing.

In fact, however, any account fully sensitive to the complexities would regard almost all the substance of morality as falling outside either the sphere of rights or wrongs (understood as Fried proposes to understand them) or the sphere of universal consequences. Counting everyone's interests equally is something legislators and administrators often should do. For a private individual to adopt it, counting himself as one, is (depending on the context) heroic, selfish, meddlesome, or crazy. But, equally, there are very few kinds of case where consequences can be totally discounted in arriving at a moral judgement. Rape and physical injury would be among the few examples to the contrary: nobody would be criticized for refusing to submit in such instances however a utilitarian balance of advantage might come out. Marriage, Fried's own example, surely is not such a case.

If a right is what Fried says it is, there is no right to marry whom you please. (Of course there is, and ought to be, a legal right. But there are many reasons why people should have legal rights, and none of them depends on the existence of moral rights in Fried's sense.) If I have a right to marry whom I please, let us recall, 'I do not have to consider how our happiness compares' to that of others affected. It would be one thing to say that, having considered everything, I would rarely be blameable for preferring my interest to that of third parties. But that is a far cry from saying it is totally irrelevant to any judgement of the moral quality of my act how others would be affected. In this context, it is interesting that P. H. Nowell-Smith, in his book *Ethics*, gives just two illustrations of 'moral obligation', of which the second is: 'I am not free to marry the girl of my choice, because I know that it would break my mother's heart and I am obliged by filial duty.'[13] If the case of marriage fails to convince, take divorce. There is and ought to be a legal right to divorce, but surely the decision to seek a divorce is open to evaluation on the basis of its impact on the interests of all those affected?

If a right were what Fried says it is, there would be no rights to act. For there is no class of actions (such as decisions about whom to marry) with the property that any choice made is beyond moral criticism. The only rights would be rights not to be wronged. We could speak of a right not to be assaulted or raped. This would be a way of saying that assault and rape are always subject to condemnation, whatever the circumstances. But there are no actions of a kind that are never liable to criticism.

We should observe that none of this entails that there are not rights to act in a sense other than a legal one. But it does mean that such rights cannot be construed on the lines proposed by Fried. Thus, we recognize moral rights as well as legal rights. These arise out of the positive morality of a society in a way parallel to that in which legal rights arise from the positive law of a society. We are here concerned with the sphere within which morality (*mores*) can properly be assimilated to the legal model. Thus, just as contracts give rise to legal rights, so promises give rise to moral rights. If you have promised me something, then, whether or not the promise is legally binding, I have a right to demand fulfilment, even if it would be burdensome to you to carry out your promise and of trivial advantage to me to have you do so.

But there is a disanalogy between moral and legal rights, and I suspect it is failure to take account of it that leads Fried into error. If I have a legal right to do something, I never do wrong legally by exercising it, however inopportunely. Substituting 'moral' for 'legal' in both places turns a correct statement into an incorrect one. It is not true that if I have a moral right to do something I never do wrong by exercising it, however inopportunely. The analogy between moral and legal rights, is, rather, that the exercise of either a moral or legal right is always open to moral appraisal and, potentially, to moral condemnation. As Justice Frankfurter put it, 'much that is legally

    [13] P. H. Nowell-Smith, *Ethics* (Harmondsworth: Pelican, 1954), 210.

permitted is repugnant to the civilized mind'.[14] The same may be said of moral rights.

Thus, suppose that I have a moral right (based, say, on an earlier agreement that is not legally binding) to play the piano for an hour every evening in the apartment above yours. That means you cannot require me to refrain; but if I do not enjoy it much and you hate it, I would certainly be a better person if I chose not to exercise my moral right to play. Thus, we often say both that somebody is 'within his rights' in doing something and wrong to do it.[15] That is a kind of complexity that Fried cannot accommodate in his theory of rights.

Just as we found Fried's ideas about wrongs more sharply presented by other writers, Anscombe and Taurek, so here we can fruitfully shift our discussion to Judith Jarvis Thomson's well-known argument against rights of recipience, in her article 'A Defense of Abortion'.[16] This is particularly handy for the continuation of the discussion begun in section I in that it bears on the duty to rescue.

Thomson supposes that you have been kidnapped by a society of music-lovers and that a famous violinist has been plugged into your kidneys for nine months of recuperation. If you unplug him he will die. The question she asks about your accepting this and not unplugging the violinist is posed as follows: 'Is it morally incumbent on you to accede to this situation? No doubt it would be very nice if you did, a great kindness. But do you *have* to accede to it?'[17] Before we know where we are, this is turned into the question whether the violinist has a 'right to life' that trumps your right to determine the use your own kidneys are put to. The answer is 'no', and that is equally true, according to Mrs Thomson, if he only needs to be plugged into your circulation for an hour.[18]

In a second example, we are to suppose that your life would be saved by the cool touch of Henry Fonda's hand upon your fevered brow.[19] Does he have to supply it? If we look closely at what she says about the case, it again becomes clear that she sees the question as one about what you have a right to receive from Henry Fonda. If we feel any temptation to say you have a right to have him cross the room to soothe your fevered brow, how far exactly does he have to come

---

[14] Gerald Grant, 'The Character of Education and the Education of Character', *Daedelus*, 110 (1981), 135–49 at 141.
[15] See Jeremy Waldron, 'A Right to Do Wrong', *Ethics*, 92 (1981), 21–39.
[16] J. J. Thomson, 'A Defense of Abortion', *Philosophy & Public Affairs*, 1 (1971), 47–66; reprinted in R. M. Dworkin (ed.), *The Philosophy of Law* (Oxford: Oxford University Press, 1977), 112–28. (Page references to reprint.)
[17] Ibid. 113.   [18] Ibid. 123.   [19] Ibid. 118.

before the right ceases to exist? Across the street, across town, halfway
round the world? Any particular cut-off point seems absurd. 'So I
have a right to it when it's easy for him to provide it, though no right
when it's hard? It's a rather shocking idea that anyone's rights should
fade away and disappear as it gets harder and harder to accord them to
him.'[20] We are thus driven to conclude that you either have an
unconditional right to a touch of his cool hand on your fevered brow
or you do not, and in that case it seems evident that you have no such
right. But why cannot we simply say (as I suggested we should in the
case of the man with the boat) that the further he has to come the less
badly we think of him if he does not? And cannot we condemn him for
not crossing the room, *just because* it would be so easy? This would be
like the man with the boat passing right by the rock and refusing to
rescue the people from drowning even though he could do so in
perfect safety and at very little personal inconvenience. Why need we
seek to say more?

I am perfectly well aware that lurking in the background of all this
talk about 'rights' by Mrs Thomson is a policy question about positive
law: should the law enforce a 'right to life'? But why should we
suppose that in order to answer a question about what the law should
be we must first find out about the existence or non-existence of some
other, spooky, kind of right? In the end, it turns out, even Mrs
Thomson concedes that what she calls 'Minimally Decent Samaritan
laws' could be defended.[21] But does that not mean that saving a life by
crossing a room (a less fanciful analogy would be going a few yards
out of your way to pull a drowning child out of a puddle) could be
made (or, indeed, morally just *is*) something you 'have to' do? If so, it
must be that the person you 'have to' save does not have a 'right' to be
saved (in the 'natural right' sense) because we should then get back
into the position of having to say that the right comes and goes
according to whether or not there happens to be somebody around
who could save him while being no more than Minimally Decent. But
if we can argue about the pros and cons of enforcing (either by legal
sanctions or social pressure) Minimally Decent Samaritanism,
without ever mentioning natural rights, why cannot we do the same
for Good Samaritanism? I shall argue below that we can.

Fried, like Mrs Thomson, poses the question: what right do others
have to demand services from us, over and above not deliberately
being harmed? And he comes up with the answer: precious little. The

---

[20] Ibid. 123.   [21] Ibid. 125.

'negative right' not to contribute to the good of others if we choose not to has the effect of ruling out just about any enforced beneficence. Most of Fried's discussion of enforced beneficence is carried out as if the kind of 'enforcement' in question was solely legal enforcement. Thus, in his discussion of blood and kidney donors, he writes as if there were only two alternatives: *either* people have a right (of bodily integrity) to do what they like with their blood and tissues (including giving them, selling them, or keeping them) *or* it would be permissible for a squad of medical policemen to drag you off, clamp you to a table, and extract your blood or organs without your consent (p. 140).

Fried then applies his conclusion (that forced donation is out) to the question of whether people must develop and employ their talents to benefit the community. Fried construes talents on the model of blood and kidneys: you can use your talents to benefit yourself or to benefit others. (In the latter case you can either sell them or give them away.) You can choose not to develop your talents, or, if you have developed your talents, you can let them deteriorate or simply not use them. Thus, a tax on people's earning potential would be bad because it would penalize those who choose to be lazy; an income tax is bad (though less bad) because it penalizes those who choose to be hard-working (pp. 143–7).

Towards the end of the book, Fried suddenly extends all this earlier discussion of legal enforcement to exclude moral criticism of refusal to help other individuals or serve the community.

It would violate the rights of individuals, to *enforce* notions of fairness or efficiency in respect to the deployment of what I have called a man's discretionary resources. But should we not at least recognize a *moral* duty to use these resources for the good of all mankind—fairly and efficiently? Yet if a man may not be compelled but may be blamed (and should blame himself) if he does not use his liberty to maximize the good of all mankind, then we have accomplished very little by affirming that negative rights establish the core of moral personality. For if total claims upon us, while not enforceable, are nevertheless morally valid, then moral personality is established on a foundation which makes it morally immune only from coercion but not from condemnation. But surely we would want moral personality to have a more secure foundation. It is not enough that a man cannot be forced to act like a utilitarian maximizer; it should also be the case that he cannot be morally condemned if he does not act that way (p. 172, italics in original).

I hope that by this point it is not necessary to emphasize that the choice posed here between being free from any possibility of moral criticism for not doing something for others and being morally required to act as a 'utilitarian maximizer' is a wholly bogus one. What I do want to argue is that Fried's case against 'positive rights' is given a quite unwarranted plausibility by his first presenting it as if it were a question of legal enforcement and then calling on the conclusion of that discussion later to rule out moral criticism. A society may well establish a legal right of its members not to have their blood taken without their consent or not to contribute their talents to the common good if they choose not to. But there are many reasons why something should not be made subject to legal enforcement. The case against may be quite strong without in the least implying that there is a 'right' in Fried's sense not to do it, that is to say that the decision not to contribute must be beyond moral criticism. We can therefore agree that it should not be legally required to give blood or contribute to the common good, without agreeing that people should not feel bad (or be made to feel bad) about failing to do so. Why it should be an assault on somebody's integrity to feel that the decent thing to do would be to give blood is completely beyond me.

I cannot create a full-blown alternative here but let me sketch what one might look like. I suggest, then, that the value of fairness calls for doing good to others in so far as there exist widely practised social norms that one should do that kind of good. People can quite properly be criticized for failing to live up to such norms. The basic idea is that a whole variety of alternative norms would be consistent with the requirements of justice. Which norms exist in a society is a matter of culture and tradition. One can criticize these norms even if the existing norms fall within the range of justice. A utilitarian may say they should be more stringent; a libertarian that they are too stringent, for example. As a theory about the basis for appraising such norms, 'actual rule utilitarianism'—that norms should be judged by the consequences of observing them—was inadequate but not a bad first shot. What sank it was the idea that, in order to be consistently utilitarian, one must try to show that each instance of obeying the rule would help maximize total utility. On the view I am proposing, however, the moral basis for obeying the existing rule is that it is unfair to be a 'free rider', taking advantage of the contributions of others and not contributing yourself.[22]

This general idea is familiar enough where the source of the norm is a legal enactment. Thus, within broad limits the level of taxation is

---

[22] H. L. A. Hart, 'Are There Any Natural Rights?', *Philosophical Review*, 64 (1955), 175–91. Reprinted in F. A. Olafson (ed.), *Society, Law and Morality* (Englewood Cliffs, NJ: Prentice-Hall, 1961), 173–86.

neither just nor unjust, but if others with your income are paying their assessed share it is unfair of you not to. It is neither just nor unjust to ban open fires in the middle of a city to cut down air pollution, but if others comply it is unfair of you not to. Note that it is the behaviour creating the benefits that creates the obligation of fairness, not the law itself. Thus, if nobody else takes any notice of the city ordinance requiring owners of dogs to clean up after them, it is not unfair if you do not either.

The positive morality of a community can be the source of benefit-creating behaviour just as can its positive law, and the same analysis can be applied. Let us call the degree to which people expect and are expected to help one another individually and contribute to the common good the *level of public morality* of a society. This level will be different in different societies. It is, for example, relatively high in small, ethnically and socially homogeneous countries such as New Zealand, lower in Britain, and lower still in the USA.

The argument I am making is that the different levels of public morality in different societies are conventional (in at any rate one sense of the term) but that they provide the basis for judgements of fair and unfair behaviour, and for criticizing those who fall too far short of the standard. What would be an unfair refusal to help others in New Zealand would be perfectly fair among the Ik of Uganda, of whom Colin Turnbull wrote in the Acknowledgements of his book about them: 'It is difficult to know how to thank the Ik; perhaps it should be for having treated me as one of themselves, which is about as badly as anyone can be treated.'[23] (Note, again, that one can treat people *badly*, even among the Ik; one simply cannot treat them *unfairly*.)

Fried's theory entails that it would be wrong, because it is an attack on inalienable negative rights, for a society to have a high level of public morality. I suggest, on the contrary, that to erect to the status of natural law the alienation of contemporary American society is provincialism, and to put forward as binding on all mankind the latest intellectual fashion in Cambridge, Mass., is parochialism.

It is also, I believe, limited imagination rather than superior insight into the 'nature of things' that leads Fried to regard the idea that being a kidney-donor might be a matter of morality as so utterly absurd that it can be used as the cornerstone of a whole theory of negative rights. There are, I think, three features of being a kidney-donor that make it relatively unsuitable to be the subject of a social norm, as against, for

[23] Colin M. Turnbull, *The Mountain People* (New York: Simon and Schuster, 1972), 13.

example, being a blood-donor.[24] First, giving up a kidney involves a serious operation and some increased risk of eventual renal failure (though the prospect of this would be much less grim if one could be sure of a ready supply of donors in case one's remaining kidney were to fail). Second, rather a small proportion of the population would be donors, even if all who could benefit from a transplant got one, raising the question 'Why me?' (Similarly, conscription runs into increasing trouble the *smaller* the proportion of those eligible who are drafted.)[25] And, third, the question 'Why me?' is less persuasively answered by saying 'Because our tissue-typing shows that you are the person in the whole country who is most compatible with somebody who needs a transplant' than is the answer 'Because you're there' when you are the only person on the beach and somebody is drowning just offshore.

For all these reasons, it may well be that kidney-donation by live donors never becomes a social norm anywhere. Even in conscript armies, the Western tradition has been that dangerous missions requiring small numbers should be filled by volunteers, and giving a kidney seems most aptly assimilated to that kind of exceptionally meritorious offering of oneself for the good of others. (A closer equivalent to blood-donation would be giving permission for one's organs to be used for transplants after death, and it seems to me quite possible that this will some day be the norm in countries with a high level of public morality.)

The upshot is that the donation of kidneys, so far from being a case from which we can confidently move to others, is in a number of ways quite distinctive. Anybody who has clear intuitions that even the mildest form of social pressure towards being a kidney-donor would be unjust should beware of being stampeded into the kind of reckless generalization from that case engaged in by Fried and Nozick.

And what if it *did* become a norm, to (say) the weak extent that being a blood-donor in Britain (particularly in the case of those with a rare blood group) might be thought of as a norm? Would that really be such a terrible assault on individual integrity? Or would it be one of the highest expressions of human fellowship?

[24] See Richard M. Titmuss, *The Gift Relationship: From Human Blood to Social Policy* (London: George Allen and Unwin, 1970), 215, 225, 242–3.
[25] See for a discussion of conscription chapter 14 of this book.

III FROM SOUL-SAVING TO FACE-SAVING

In the introduction to *Right and Wrong,* Fried writes as follows:

Individualism is often seen as a selfish doctrine allowing individuals to ignore the interests of others. Right and wrong, however, emphasize not the individual's selfish concerns but his moral integrity, and in this we come closer to the historic heart of individualism. If deontology, the theory of right and wrong, is solicitous of the individual, it is primarily solicitous of his claim to preserve his moral integrity, to refrain from being the agent of wrong, even if such fastidiousness means forgoing the opportunity to promote great good or to prevent great harm. In this respect the primacy of right and wrong is a doctrine that shows its traditional religious origins in contrast to the secular, melioristic foundations of those theories which hold that it is consequences alone which count. . . . Religious views . . . expect the secular future to share the imperfections and suffering of the present and the past. With such expectations it follows that the focus must be on personal moral perfection. Thus Christianity rejects consequentialism on the (consequentialist) ground that man is unlikely to gain the whole world (or its betterment) even if he were prepared to lose his soul. And of course one need believe neither in original sin nor in any theology at all to share this sense of our situation (p. 2).

I believe that the 'of course' in the last sentence here is too easy. If we substitute 'moral perfection' for 'a state of grace' and replace 'saving your soul' with 'protecting your moral integrity', it is in my view a serious question whether we are left with a credible (or creditable) doctrine.

To illustrate, let me turn to Fried's chapter on the absolute wrongness of lying, whatever the human consequences of telling the truth. In the course of his discussion, Fried cites Augustine's *De mendacio.*

Having argued that God destroys all who tell lies, he [Augustine] asks: If this truth be granted, who of those who assent will be shaken by such argument as are given by those who say: 'What if a man should flee to you, who by your lie can be saved from death?' . . . In very truth, some are indignant and angry if someone is unwilling to lose his soul by telling a lie so that another may grow a little older in the flesh (p. 70).

Granted the premisses, this seems fair enough. If life on earth is the blink of an eyelid compared to eternity, which is going to be spent in bliss or torment depending on how you conduct yourself here, and if telling a lie will shift you from being saved to being damned (or even has any finite probability of doing so), you would surely be quixotic to lie in order to add a few years to somebody else's life on earth (which is also the blink of an eyelid). If that is really how things are, Augustine is quite right. But suppose that none of it is true: there is no God, this is the only life we have, and violent death is one of the greatest evils we know. Is anything left of the argument? Fried says that he can offer 'secular versions' of Augustine's arguments, and the one corresponding to that quoted above is as follows:

The frequent references to lying as defilement might fairly be given the following interpretation: if lying is (absolutely) wrong, then to treat lying as something which is simply bad, undesirable, but to be traded off to procure other goods, to avoid worse harms, is to pursue good ends by impermissible means. To use a Kantian formulation, the violation of the categorical imperative is inestimably worse than any harm one may fend off by such a violation, since the categorical imperative and our obligation under it are what found our moral nature. Any violation for a mere contingent good trades what gives us moral status at all for something which has moral status only insofar as it is attributable to a moral being. This, then, is the Kantian version of the notion of gaining the whole world but losing one's soul (pp. 70–1).

I have to say that I find the secular translation a step from the sublime to the ridiculous. We are, after all, talking about a case where, by telling a lie, you can save a man's life. If I were the man who was fleeing death, I should not think much of the moral nature or moral status of somebody who was agonizing about whether to pollute his precious 'integrity' to save my life. 'Moral status' is a very poor substitute for 'soul'. It seems to me that the moral theory being put forward by Fried needs the original article. 'Moral status' simply will not carry the weight. If we take God and the soul out of the picture, the emphasis on 'integrity' becomes a form of narcissism. The question Fried would have us keep in the forefront of our minds is always 'How do I come out of this looking?' There certainly are people like this, but the idea that we should be expected to admire them seems to me bizarre.

The reasoning which this moral dandy is supposed to offer to the refugee runs as follows:

We are responsible for the wrongs we do ourselves and not for those which by our wrong we fail to prevent others from committing. This argument is necessary . . . to maintain the distinction between the wrong and the bad. The category of the wrong speaks in the first or second person, but not in the third person: it tells me what I must not do, and I violate it just by doing the forbidden thing. But though the norm is universal in its application, a violation by another person is not a wrong except in relation to that other person. In relation to me it is bad, so that my lying to prevent a wrong by another is a case of my doing wrong in order to prevent something which *from my point of view* is a bad. To be sure, what the other will do *is* wrong, but it is *his* wrong (p. 71, italics in original).

Thus, the fact that by revealing your whereabouts, I give the pursuer the opportunity to work his nefarious will is neither here nor there. That he will kill you is the foreseeable but unintended consequence of my act; and anyway, it is his wrong, not mine. If this is Kant, I prefer to spell it with a *c*.

To keep the record straight, I should add that Fried finally extricates himself from the conclusion that it is wrong to lie in this case by adducing a complicated argument extending over seven pages to the effect that the pursuer has no right to the truth so he is not wronged by being lied to. (See pp. 72–8.) However, the point is not whether or not it is possible with enough of a struggle to get out the obviously right answer. The point is that, as Fried admits, 'a struggle is necessary in the context of my argument' (p. 72). Bernard Williams has correctly argued that the object of setting up hard cases for utilitarians is not to see if the right answer can be arrived at by utilitarian calculation with enough effort, but to point out that the effort is needed.[26] The same argument can, I suggest, be deployed against Fried here. Any theory that requires seven pages of fancy footwork to establish that it is all right to lie to a would-be murderer in order to save his prospective victim's life has something seriously wrong with it.

The last long quotation raises two questions, one about double effect, the other about responsibility. In my view, the first is fairly straightforward, the second far more complicated than Fried, with his sweeping metaphysical assumptions, admits. Fried raises the issues in the following example: a man seeking to free a prisoner (1) blows up the prison wall with the predictable consequence that a guard will be killed by falling masonry or (2) shoots the guard so as to obtain the keys. (See p. 23.) Fried apparently wants to say that there is a difference in the moral quality of the two acts: in the first case the death of the guard is a foreseen but unwanted by-product of blowing up the wall, whereas in the second case the guard's death is deliberately brought about as a means to the escape. But in my view, not only is the man who brings about the guard's death equally responsible in both cases, but he is equally culpable. That the death of the guard is in the first case a by-product and in the second case a means is irrelevant, and

[26] Bernard Williams, 'A Critique of Utilitarianism', in J. J. C. Smart and Bernard Williams, *Utilitarianism: For and Against* (Cambridge: Cambridge University Press, 1973), 99, 117.

if the doctrine of double effect implies the contrary (as Fried apparently holds) that is sufficient basis for dismissing it.

As another example, take the much discussed case of bombing in wartime. Suppose that it is known that (given the inaccuracy and dispersion inherent in aerial bombing) the only way to have a reasonable chance of hitting an important military installation is to drop a number of bombs that can be foreseen to kill thousands of civilians. Can the man who plans the raid say: 'I am not responsible for the civilian deaths—they are the foreseen but unintended by-product of the raid on the military target'?

I think not. Fried cites with approval 'the international law of war' as condemning 'intentional infliction of civilian casualties, while permitting the causing of such casualties as a side-effect, even a certain one, of military action against military targets' (p. 21). But surely the *responsibility* for the outcome is just the same whatever the intention of the actor. It is monstrous if (as seems to follow from Fried's views) a man can disclaim responsibility for almost anything that happens as a result of what he does just so long as he picks his intentions carefully enough.

Holding the military planner responsible for all the consequences—both the destroyed military installation and the dead civilians—does not preclude our condemning him if he aims at the civilians while acquitting him of a war crime if he aims at the military installation and hits the civilians as a by-product. But he must *answer* for all the consequences. He must, to be excused, show that the military target was really important, that there was no way of hitting it at reasonable cost to his own side that would have killed fewer civilians, and so on. Relieving him of responsibility for the foreseen but unintended consequences of ordering the bombing raid would mean that he did not have to justify it in terms of the balance between (military) gains and (civilian) losses.

Consider any situation in which it is claimed (1) that we properly hold somebody fully responsible for an act of his under some description (e.g. aiming at a military target, organizing a peaceful civil rights march) but (2) that we should acquit him (wholly or partly) of responsibility for (some of) the consequences of the act (e.g. killing innocent people, creating the occasion for a race riot). I suggest that, whenever the claim is plausible, we will find it to be a case where we hold somebody else (partly or wholly) responsible for those consequences. The simplest way in which somebody other than the actor is held responsible is where there is a *novus actus interveniens* between the actor and the foreseeable consequence of his act. The more subtle way is where, although the act produces its natural consequences without any other act coming between, we hold someone responsible for the circumstances in which that act has those consequences.

Thus, Alan Donagan has argued that, in a war that is legitimately being fought, 'the deaths of noncombatants who are killed in direct attacks on military installations are to be deemed accidental, on the ground that it is the enemy's fault that noncombatants are there'.[27] This seems to me implausible, if such things as munitions factories, railway marshalling yards, and so on, are military targets, given the radius within which bombs aimed at them are bound to fall. But the point that the responsibility may shift to those who create the circumstance seems reasonable. If the enemy puts civilian hostages on military trains[28] or straps innocent persons to the front of its tanks 'so that the tanks cannot be hit without hitting them'[29] it is responsible for their deaths. But notice that responsibility here is assigned by saying something like, 'You can't expect people fighting a war to call it off because the other side fixes things so as to make it impossible to fight without killing innocent people.' Some judgement about what it is reasonable to expect cannot be escaped here.

Suppose, to modify the example of the tanks, that I am tired of people driving too close behind me so I grab a child who is playing in the street and lash it to the back of my car before setting off. If you drive behind me at a distance that does not leave you with ample room to avoid running into my car (even if it would be considered enough normally), then I would say that, in the event of a collision, you are partly responsible for the resulting injuries to the child. Why? Because in this case 'business as usual' is *not* reasonable.

In the case of the *novus actus interveniens*, Fried regards the solution as simple: an act always breaks the chain of responsibility. So the last actor before the consequence is always responsible for the consequence—subject, of course, to the proviso about responsibility for the circumstances being what they are in the first place. Thus, 'we must not do wrong even in order to prevent more, greater wrongs by others. If those others do wrong it is their wrong, for which they are responsible' (p. 2). Once again, I find Fried's theory too simplistic.

Fried is haunted by the nightmare of our being saddled with

---

[27] Alan Donagan, *The Theory of Morality* (Chicago: University of Chicago Press, 1977), 87.
[28] See Michael Walzer, *Just and Unjust Wars: A Moral Argument with Historical Illustrations* (New York: Basic Books, 1977), 174, for an example from the Franco-Prussian War of 1870.
[29] Robert Nozick, *Anarchy, State, and Utopia* (New York: Basic Books, 1974), 35.

excessive personal responsibility for the state of the world. Thus, in his opening paragraph he writes:

My central concern is to discern structure and limits in the demands morality makes upon us. . . . We are constrained but not smothered by morality once we acknowledge that there are limits to our responsibility for the world's good and ill, that we are responsible for some things but not everything (p. 1).

Within limits, the concern to restrict our liability for consequences is quite appropriate. It would, indeed, be intolerable if people could always get us to do things by suffering if we didn't do them.[30] It would be even worse if we could always be manipulated by people threatening bad consequences unless we did what they demanded. But Fried's desperate struggles to escape suffocation take him much too far. In slashing away at the clammy tentacles of consequentialism he also cuts off a large chunk of live morality.

The legal model again misleads here. In the law, people are in general held solely responsible for their own actions. But moral judgements can be far more finely nuanced. We can allow for all kinds of relations between the actions of different people that would, and should, never get into a court of law. As Hart and Honoré put the point:

The use of the legal sanctions of imprisonment, or forced monetary compensation against individuals, has such formidable repercussions on the general life of society that the fact that individuals have a type of connexion with harm which is adequate for moral censure or claims for compensation is only *one* of the factors which the law must consider, in defining the kinds of connexion between actions and harm for which it will hold individuals legally responsible.[31]

A good example of the point at issue here is provided by advice-giving. Except in special cases such as professional advisers or counsellors of crime people are not legally responsible for the advice they give others, even if following it has disastrous consequences. The responsibility falls squarely on the person who decides whether or not to take the advice. Morally, however, if someone does something bad on our advice, especially if the advice pertained to a matter of

---

[30] One might recall Scobie, in *The Heart of the Matter*: 'He had always been prepared to accept the responsibility for his actions, and he had always been aware too, from the time he made his terrible vow that [Louise] should be happy, how far *this* action might carry him.' Philip Stratford (ed.), *The Portable Graham Greene* (New York: Viking Press, 1973), 92–367, at 154.

[31] H. L. A. Hart and A. M. Honoré, *Causation and the Law* (Oxford: Clarendon Press, 1959), 62.

fundamental choice rather than the means to an end the person definitely was going to pursue anyway, we share the responsibility.[32] Other examples are provocation and temptation. From a moral point of view we tend to hold people rather widely responsible for provoking and tempting others—far more widely than in law.

More generally, it seems to me that we cannot absolve ourselves totally from responsibility for the foreseeable actions that others do as a result of our actions. Suppose that I have a contractual right to keep my employee late at work once a week. I know, however, that he tends to beat his wife when I keep him at work late, and that he rarely does so at other times. No doubt the beating is the employee's wrong, not mine. But if I know what the facts are and still keep the employee late, do I not have some moral responsibility too? Should I be able to excuse myself on the ground that the result, although foreseen, was not intended?

Again, suppose that Martin Luther King announces a civil rights march in some Southern town, and the local worthies prophesy violence. Or suppose that somebody proposes to deliver a speech on some controversial topic and zealots on the other side threaten to break it up. It seems to me important here to keep two things in focus, and not let either force out the other. One is that the racists and bigots are fully responsible for whatever bloodshed occurs. The other is that the organizers of the march or rally are also responsible for the bloodshed: not necessarily blameable but answerable.[33] Their answer may be a satisfactory one that relieves them of blame (and it need not be couched in terms of strictly utilitarian considerations). But they must be prepared to answer. Otherwise, if we simply say of the racists and bigots 'It's their wrong,' we cannot say that the organizers were wrong not to take every precaution to minimize violence, consistent with carrying out their object. Yet this is surely morally relevant. That the organizers did not intend that their actions should lead to violence but merely foresaw violence as a consequence is undeniably relevant but not the end of the story. What the law should be is another matter and there may be good reasons founded in the value of free speech and

---

[32] 'If people ever took advice', Virginia Woolf noted defensively in her diary, 'I should feel a little responsible for making up Ralph's mind [to marry Carrington]. I mean I am not sure that this marriage is not more risky than most.' Her biographer comments: 'Her doubts were well-founded. . . .' Although there is no question that Ralph Partridge did the marrying—it was his act—Virginia Woolf was surely right to feel qualms about her role. See Quentin Bell, *Virginia Woolf: A Biography* (New York: Harcourt Brace Jovanovich, 1974), 80, 81.

[33] For the suggestion that the root meaning of 'responsible' is 'answerable', see H. L. A. Hart, *Punishment and Responsibility: Essays in the Philosophy of Law* (London: Oxford University Press, 1968), 264–5.

assembly for saying that the responsibility for violence should be laid
solely at the door of those who commit it and that those who provide
the occasion for it should not be held legally responsible for failing to
minimize the risk, provided their contribution does not amount to
what the law will take cognizance of as provocation.[34]

Fried is concerned that too strong a sense of responsibility for the
world's sufferings will be bad for our moral health. (See pp. 34–5.) As
the old Chinese song put it:

> Don't escort the big chariot;
> You will only make yourself dusty.
> Don't think about the sorrows of the world;
> You will only make yourself wretched.[35]

I am inclined to believe that there is relatively little risk, in the
countries where Fried's book is most likely to be read, of that danger.
In arguing so strenuously for limited liability, Fried is simply telling us
what we would like to hear. Think of the kind of context in which
people characteristically say things like: 'My conscience is clear.' This
is generally a defensive statement made to deny responsiblity for the
consequences of one's acts: the ruin of a business competitor, the
suicide of a subordinate, and so on. Fried would say that, provided it
was not your intention to procure the competitor's ruin or deliberately
drive the subordinate to suicide, your conscience is quite properly
clear. I suggest that it is a lot less simple than that. We do not have to
choose between holding someone responsible for all the consequences
of his acts and limiting liability for consequences as stringently as Fried
does.

Obviously, if this is so, the right answer is going to be very
complicated. In developing it I predict that we shall get more help
from the novelists than from the lawyers. One particular way in
which the law is a poor model is that, where responsibility for an
outcome is divided, the total normally adds up to 100 per cent: if one
driver was 70 per cent responsible for the collision at an intersection
then the other one contributed 30 per cent to it. Fried, following this
logic, assumes that, if we are to hold one person 100 per cent
responsible for his actions we must absolve everybody else of
responsibility for them. But attributing moral responsibility is not a
fixed-sum game. Just as there can be overdetermination of events
there can be, so to speak, overresponsibility for outcomes.

---

[34] See Hart and Honoré, *Causation and the Law*, pp. 333–4 for a somewhat inconclusive
account of English law on this point.
[35] Arthur Waley, *The Book of Songs* (London: George Allen, 1937), No. 286.

Underlying all of Fried's book is, as he often repeats, a Kantian notion of human freedom according to which we do not merely have the freedom to choose what to do but also the freedom to choose what to choose: we are literally responsible for making ourselves.

I choose my life plan freely. . . . Though the system of wants I have constructed for myself is supremely important to me, it is after all I who have constructed it. . . . The . . . conception I offer holds a man responsible for his wants. . . . The respect we are entitled to as regards our wants . . . depends on the fact that as free beings we have freely chosen this conception of the good (pp. 124–6).

If Fried's theory is correct, society is due for a great leap backward. Marx and Freud—and everything they stand for—will go out of the window. There can be no room for the subversive notion that people are the products of their social environment or that their actions may have deep-rooted psychological causes. You can do anything if you try, and it is metaphysically guaranteed that you can always try. So out go any suggestions that there are causes of suicide, recidivism, alcoholism, baby-battering, inability to hold a job, failure to use contraception, and so on. Pleas of insanity or diminished responsibility will disappear from the legal system. Social workers and psychiatrists will be out of a job. Society will inscribe on its banner not, as Marx thought, 'From each according to his ability, to each according to his need' but:

> It matters not how strait the gate,
> How charged with punishment the scroll,
> I am the master of my fate:
> I am the captain of my soul.[36]

Fried might reply that this is to take him too literally. But if we once allow Fried's metaphysical absolute to be turned into an empirical claim about actual people, I do not see how we can avoid concluding that nobody fully has the ability and opportunity to shape his own life. And can we avoid concluding that the extent to which people are in fact able to shape their own lives varies greatly from country to country and within countries from class to class?

Fried at no point offers any defence of his conception of freedom. At one point he says that 'in moral philosophy we may often be forced to swallow some quite unchewed metaphysical morsels' (p. 20). But

---

[36] W. E. Henley in F. T. Palgrave (ed.), *The Golden Treasury* (London: Oxford University Press, 1929), No. 397, p. 476.

does that also apply to forcing these unchewed morsels on everybody? In a liberal society everyone has the privilege of believing what he likes—even that the earth is flat or that men are noumenal beings. But when it comes to questions of public policy, it matters a lot to everyone whether the premisses on which proposals are made are in fact true.

Let us grant that the freedom to shape our own lives and achieve our own ends is of central importance. As Fried puts it: 'Happiness is . . . the aim and outcome of individual *choice*, the success of the self in realizing its own values through its own choices and efficacy' (p. 34, italics in original). I maintain that it is nothing better than a cruel hoax to say that everyone has such freedom by virtue of being a noumenal self. Only a privileged minority of the human race have ever had the opportunity either to choose their own ends (to the extent that anyone can ever do so) or to be efficacious in pursuing self-chosen goals. To develop a core of identity, to be able to integrate short-term and long-term aims into a coherent 'life plan', and to acquire the skills necessary for having a reasonable opportunity to carry out that plan: none of these abilities just accrues to people as a concomitant of their metaphysical status. What chance has an unemployed high-school dropout in the ghetto or a Mississippi plantation worker to 'realize his own values' through his own 'choices and efficacy'?

It makes a big difference politically whether or not we swallow the unchewed metaphysical morsels that Fried offers us. If we say that freedom is something human beings are guaranteed metaphysically, we almost inevitably finish up with Fried's complacent kind of liberal conservatism. If, by contrast, we take freedom as empirically problematic, as something that has to be created, we find ourselves committed to a social and economic revolution to create the conditions in which alone freedom can thrive.

IV　THE REVOLT AGAINST CONSEQUENTIALISM

Although not much is left by this stage of Fried's *Right and Wrong*, it is still significant as a straw in the wind—the wind of anti-consequentialism that has been blowing with increasing force since the 1960s. In this concluding section, I shall put Fried's book in its context and ask how we should assess consequentialism.

Let us begin with the term 'consequentialism' itself. It was, I believe, introduced into Anglo-American philosophical discourse by Elizabeth Anscombe in 1958 to mean the doctrine that one should judge the morality of an action by its consequences.[37] The contrast is with an act's being judged by its nature. The judgement of an action would then turn on its being an action of a certain sort, where 'being of a certain sort' could not include 'having such-and-such consequences'. Candidates for the role of a 'sort of action' might be specific descriptions ('killing an innocent person' or 'betraying a friend') or more general characterizations such as the Kantian one of 'treating a person as a means only and not as an end in himself'.

In principle, a consequentialist could have any criterion for judging consequences as better or worse, however bizarre: he could say that good actions are those that have the effect of raising the level of the sea, increasing the amount of radiation at certain frequencies, and so on. But, in practice, the consequences are usually defined in terms of human interests. Thus, an egoistic consequentialist judges actions by the way they affect himself, a patriotic consequentialist by the way they affect his country, and a universal consequentialist by the way they affect all human beings. (A 'non-speciesist' universalist might judge actions by their consequences for all sentient beings. I shall not consider this extension of universalism in the present discussion.)

The most familiar version of consequentialism is utilitarianism, the doctrine that one act (or policy, institution, etc.) is better than another if it yields more aggregate happiness to human beings. We should note, however, to avoid confusion, that the term 'utilitarianism' is often extended to include the whole of what I am calling consequentialism. Thus, for example, G. E. Moore proposed an 'ideal utilitarianism' according to which value inheres in such things as the existence of beautiful objects and the creation of certain kinds of personal relationships, and acts are to be assessed in terms of their value-producing effects.[38] I have not followed this usage. I take utilitarianism (as I have defined it) as the prime example of consequentialism, because of its historical importance and its relatively definite specification.

What we have seen in recent years is, I believe, a shift from consequentialism, the doctrine that actions are right or wrong according to their consequences, to absolutism, the doctrine that actions are right or wrong according to their nature. In Anglo–American philosophy, the prevailing way of looking at morality used to be consequentialist, with some qualms about lying, breaking promises or killing innocent people in a good cause. It has now shifted towards

[37] See Anscombe, 'Modern Moral Philosophy', p. 8. Cf. Donagan, *Theory of Morality*, p. 190; Williams in Smart and Williams (ed.), *Utilitarianism: For and Against*, p. 84.
[38] G. E. Moore, *Principia Ethica* (Cambridge: Cambridge University Press, 1903).

absolutism, with residual doubts about catastrophic consequences. The conclusions may not have altered drastically but there has been a sea-change in the premisses. It may be asked whether it matters much what the premisses are if there is so much play in their application. The answer is, I think, that it does in the long run make a difference where you start. For this will determine what you take to be the easy problems. Thus, you can start from consequentialism and then build in some side-constraints on particularly repellent actions or you can start from absolutism and add some escape clause for situations where the consequences of following such a rule would be too horrendous. In principle, it is indeed possible to imagine that you could get to the same concrete judgements starting from either end. But in practice it tends to make a big difference which cases are taken as clear and central and which as difficult and exceptional. For what is at stake is no less than one's fundamental conception of what morality is all about, and it would be surprising if that did not have some implications for conduct. I do think that in fact the shift to absolutism has a quite clear tendency to reduce the scope of the diffuse obligations to others that are generated by universal consequentialism.

This kind of shift is nothing new: we can find a number of analogues. The most striking was perhaps the rapid repudiation of logical positivism after the Second World War which led A. J. Ayer to complain that he went from being a Young Turk to being old hat without an intervening period of solid respectability.[39] Putting it very schematically, we might think of a shift in starting-point as having four stages. In the first stage, a dominant paradigm (to use the inevitable Kuhnian terminology[40]) rides high. Scholars devote their research to developing the dominant paradigm, exploring its implications, and trying to clear up anomalies. There are some objectors, either left over from a previous paradigm or reacting on their own initiative against the dominant paradigm, but they are voices crying in the wilderness. In the next stage, the criticisms of the dominant paradigm build up but it still remains true that the paradigm holds the field. It is still, as it were, the thing to beat. The decisive stage is the third one in which a new paradigm is established and becomes the focus of attention. Taking the offensive is not always the way to conduct a war (as Marshall Foch demonstrated) but in the war

[39] A. J. Ayer, *A Part of My Life: The Memoirs of a Philosopher* (London: Oxford University Press, 1978), 294-5.

[40] Thomas S. Kuhn, *The Structure of Scientific Revolutions* (Chicago: Chicago University Press, 2nd edn., 1970).

between paradigms it is critical. As Imre Lakatos in particular emphasized, a paradigm becomes dominant when it generates a research programme that looks interesting and holds out hopes of being feasible.[41] As the new paradigm begins to take hold, those who continue to support the previously dominant one are relegated to the wilderness. The final stage is that in which the new paradigm is triumphantly established. History is now rewritten—history is, of course, always written by the victors—so that those who in some way anticipated the current paradigm (and especially the prophets who were previously crying in the wilderness) are presented as the major figures while the heroes of the earlier paradigm fall into obscurity.

I may, of course, be hopelessly wrong in my reading of the entrails. But it seems to me that the evidence for some fundamental shift is persuasive. Ten or twenty years ago, such work as was being published on substantive questions of morality was almost all located within the utilitarian paradigm. As I have emphasized, to say that work is located within a paradigm is to say only that the paradigm provides the focus of attention; the attention may be either positive or negative. In this respect, we can, I suggest, trace a change between the 1950s and the 1960s. Although the period of the mid-1950s hardly corresponds fully to my ideal typical first stage, it would not, I hope, be over-intepretation to sum up the prevailing mood as follows: utilitarianism, in some shape or form, has just *got* to be the right general answer, and the research programme is to apply enough technical ingenuity to crack the problems of application (thresholds, co-ordination, etc.) in order to get out the right specific answers. This was the period of mixed strategies, varieties of rule utilitarianism, and so on.[42] If we now turn to the books and articles of the mid-1960s we find very few people investing in attempts of this kind to make utilitarianism work. At any rate with hindsight, we can see that period as a classical pre-revolutionary one. The old regime still survives, but it is the subject of widespread yet diffuse disaffection and finds few

[41] Imre Lakatos, 'Falsification and the Methodology of Scientific Research Programmes' in Imre Lakatos and Alan Musgrave (eds.), *Criticism and the Growth of Knowledge* (Cambridge: Cambridge University Press, 1970), 91–197.

[42] The basic approach was well expressed by Samuel Gorovitz as follows: 'As a normative principle, the principle of utilitarianism has an enormous intuitive appeal. It calls on an agent to perform that action which will do more good for more people than any other, and it is hard to imagine how such an action could fail to be the right thing to do. Even though many objections to utilitarianism as a moral theory have been raised, this basic appeal remains for many people, who are more inclined to try to meet the objections than to abandon what is initially such a plausible moral theory.' Introduction to Samuel Gorovitz (ed.), *Utilitarianism, John Stuart Mill, with Critical Essays* (Indianapolis: Bobbs-Merrill, 1971), p. xiii. This is a useful selection of the kind of work I am referring to; it is noticeable that the bulk of the pieces are from the mid-1950s.

thoroughly convinced defenders. By 1973, we find Bernard Williams pronouncing sentence of death: 'The important issues that utilitarianism raises should be discussed in contexts more rewarding than that of utilitarianism itself. The day cannot be too far off in which we hear no more of it.'[43]

It is instructive to review the career of John Rawls in this context. His early 'Two Concepts of Rules' is presented as a variant of utilitarianism, closely related to Urmson's interpretation of Mill.[44] By the time of *A Theory of Justice*,[45] the theory is presented as an alternative to utilitarianism, but it is clear from the form of the argument that the object is taken to be weaning the reader away from his putatively utilitarian loyalties. At the same time, the line of analysis developed, especially in the second half of the book, makes the theory really incommensurable with utilitarianism. The question is not (as it might first appear) between average and maximin utility but between basically incompatible visions of man and society. Subsequent developments in Rawls's thinking carry this process further. Meanwhile, the rewriting of history is taking place with respect to *A Theory of Justice*: I would hazard the guess that most people now read it in a more Kantian light than when it first appeared, both because of Rawls's own subsequent glosses on it and the concomitant changes in the mental climate that I am trying to depict here. Thus, although *A Theory of Justice* did not shift the paradigm when it appeared, it can be mobilized to form an important part of the intellectual ammunition of the neo-Kantians.

In order for the critics of the old paradigm to go from the defensive to the offensive, it is necessary to have a critical mass of work that exemplifies the new approach and provides handholds for those less adept to scramble up after the virtuosi. Or, to put it more mundanely, you cannot have articles until you have books. You can, of course, have a lot of articles peppering the old paradigm; but to obtain the reassuring sense of cumulative development characteristic of 'normal science' there must be a solid body of literature forming a common reference point.

Right and Wrong may be seen as a contribution to the building up of that critical mass. To appreciate it in this context, one must also

---

[43] Williams in Smart and Williams (eds.), *Utilitarianism: For and Against*, p. 150.

[44] John Rawls, 'Two Concepts of Rules', *The Philosophical Review*, 64 (1955), 3–32; J. O. Urmson, 'The Interpretation of the Moral Philosophy of J. S. Mill', *The Philosophical Quarterly*, 3 (1953), 33–9. Both reprinted in Gorovitz (ed.), *Utilitarianism* on pp. 175–94 and 168–74 respectively.

[45] John Rawls, *A Theory of Justice* (Cambridge, Mass.: Harvard University Press, 1971).

consider two books that were published at about the same time: Alan Donagan's *The Theory of Morality* and Michael Walzer's *Just and Unjust Wars*. The three books are different but complementary. Donagan's is the most ambitious work. In a relatively brief compass, *The Theory of Morality* undertakes to expound the substance of what Donagan calls the Hebrew-Christian moral tradition and also to ground it in a Kantian meta-theory of morality. The book is sharp, spare, and clear. Walzer's book, in contrast, is diffuse and theoretically unrigorous. (It may even be ultimately incoherent.) But its bulk provides one essential ingredient: it gets onto the table a mass of problems in one large and important area of morality that can be referred to and worked over by others. Fried's book is different again. The talent that is most on display in *Right and Wrong* is a talent for synthesizing the work of other recent writers with his own earlier work.[46] But if it is potential influence that we are concerned with, we should never underestimate the importance of a work of synthesis.

The books by Fried, Walzer, and Donagan are not primarily critiques of consequentialism. They are devoted to the working out of a non-consequentialist ethic, and their criticisms of consequentialism are incidental to that purpose. More important, if we are looking for a body of work that will form a common reference point, is that all three ground their non-consequentialist systems in traditional Hebrew and Christian religious morality. Its major interpreters such as Aquinas and Maimonides are referred to as authorities. If the essence of a paradigm shift is a shift in focus, these books certainly provide it. All three, for example, devote careful and detailed attention to the doctrine of double effect, and I quoted from all three in my discussion of the doctrine in section III. As it happens, they come out in different places: Fried embraces it with uncritical enthusiasm, Walzer accepts it with substantial qualifications, while Donagan in the end rejects it. But, to repeat, the important thing is what is regarded as an important question, not what is said about it. So the point here is that we find three highly respected academics taking seriously a doctrine that most people had thought of as a quaint survival from the Middle Ages, like the custom of venerating the relics of saints. At the same time, fine discriminations between different varieties of utilitarian theory that would until recently have been treated as raising serious issues tend to be dismissed summarily. The function of the term 'consequentialism' is indeed to make this change of focus seem natural.

---

[46] There is a valuable reference section at the end of the book (pp. 197–219), which is not keyed to specific points in the text but provides a kind of running bibliographic commentary on the sources (many of them also at Harvard) drawn upon.

As with all the best historical stages, each of the ones I have outlined develops within the womb of the preceding one, and we can already begin to discern roughly how the anti-consequentialist history of morality is going to look. First there was Hebrew and Christian traditional morality and its scholarly expositors. Then there came the dark age of utilitarianism during which the traditional doctrines took refuge in Roman Catholic moral theology. Miss Anscombe's 'Modern Moral Philosophy' may well be the only piece of academic moral philosophy to be rescued out of the period 1870–1970. The 1970s, beginning with *A Theory of Justice*, will then presumably count as the beginning of a new era.[47]

Fried's role in all this is primarily as a sort of intellectual broker. He brings together two anti-consequentialist lines of thought: the Hebrew-Christian tradition of 'Thou shalt not' and the 'libertarian' doctrine of natural rights which has recently enjoyed such a curious revival in American academic philosophy. He then adds some 'integrity' from Bernard Williams: in conjunction with the first, integrity means keeping your hands clean, while, in the second, it means doing your own thing. The result is a potent brew with something for (almost) all tastes. It is quite a feat to accommodate within a single theory the God of the Pentateuch, Robert Nozick, Pontius Pilate, and Henry David Thoreau. (A quotation from Thoreau's 'On Civil Disobedience' leads off the book.) Of the mainstream moralists recognized in Britain and North America only Jesus and John Stuart Mill are left out in the cold.[48]

I must now confess that I have been using the term 'consequentialism' with less precision than I might have done. However, I can immediately add that I have in this been reflecting a similar lack of precision that runs through the literature. I began this section by ascribing the word 'consequentialism' to Elizabeth Anscombe, and defined it as the doctrine that all actions are to be judged by their consequences. However, Miss Anscombe did not actually define the term in the article I referred to, and the form of words I used is capable of being interpreted in (at least) two ways. According to one interpret-

---

[47] The reference notes in Fried's book may be read as a first sketch of this revisionist history.

[48] As Miss Anscombe says, 'Christianity derived its ethical notions from the Torah.' 'Modern Moral Philosophy', p. 191. That traditional Christianity has more in common with the Torah than with the Gospels was a commonplace of classical utilitarianism: we find it in both Bentham and John Stuart Mill. The same incompatibility was noted by Maimonides, who wrote that 'Jesus the Nazarene, may his bones be ground to dust . . ., interpreted the Torah and its precepts in such a fashion as to lead to their total annulment, to the abolition of all its commandments and to the violation of its prohibitions.' 'Epistle to Yemen', in Isadore Twersky (ed.), *A Maimonides Reader* (New York: Behrman House, 1972), 441.

ation, consequentialism may be defined as a negative doctrine: it denies that it is possible to specify a list of act-descriptions in terms of their 'nature' such that it would never under any circumstances —whatever the consequences—be right to do an act of a kind that was on the list. This appears to be what Miss Anscombe had in mind by 'consequentialism'. Her point was to contrast it with what she called the 'Hebrew-Christian ethic', according to which 'you are not to be tempted by fear or hope of consequences'. As she says: 'the prohibition of certain things simply in virtue of their description as such-and-such identifiable kinds of action, regardless of further consequences is . . . a noteworthy feature of [this ethic].' But 'it is pretty well taken for obvious among [modern academic philosophers] that a prohibition such as that on murder does not operate in face of some consequences.'[49]

Ironically, Fried, for all his expressed admiration for Miss Anscombe, is himself a consequentialist in her terms. For he says that 'we can imagine extreme cases where killing an innocent person may save a whole nation. In such cases it seems fanatical to maintain the absoluteness of the judgement, to do right even if the heavens will in fact fall' (p. 10). Interestingly enough, Miss Anscombe mentioned exactly this case in her dismissal of any claim that the 'Oxford Objectivists' (of whom the best known is Sir David Ross) could be exempted from the charge of consequentialism. 'Oxford Objectivists of course distinguish between "consequences" and "intrinsic values" and so produce a misleading appearance of not being "consequentialists". But they do not hold—and Ross explicitly denies—the gravity of, e.g., procuring the condemnation of the innocent, is such that it cannot be outweighed by, e.g., national interest.'[50]

Fried is himself a consequentialist, then, in what I shall call the weak sense of the term. In this sense, to recapitulate, consequentialism is the doctrine that it is possible for any prohibition based on the 'nature' of an act to be overridden if the consequences of adhering to the prohibition are sufficiently horrendous. What, then, we are bound to ask, is the object of Fried's crusade? In what sense of 'consequentialism' can he be counted as an anti-consequentialist?

The alternative conception of consequentialism, which I shall call the strong conception, is the doctrine that each person has a duty to act

---

[49] All quotations from Anscombe, 'Modern Moral Philosophy', 198. Alan Donagan, who follows Miss Anscombe by claiming to expound 'the Hebrew-Christian ethic', also understands consequentialism in this way, as the denial of absolute prohibitions.

[50] Anscombe, 'Modern Moral Philosophy', p. 196 n. 4.

at all times so as to maximize the total amount of good. Fried's identification of the enemy with 'utilitarian maximizing' clearly shows that the consequentialism with which he contrasts his own theory is to be understood in this way.[51]

It is curious to note that this strong consequentialist doctrine has exactly the same formal characteristics as Fried's own theory, for it too divides all acts into the required, the prohibited, and the permissible, with no room for the better or worse. Consequentialism is a particularly implausible way of assigning content to the trichotomy because it narrows the range of moral indifference to cases where two or more acts would have equally good consequences. One way of looking at Fried's theory is to say that he takes over the framework and simply expands the area of the morally permitted with his doctrine of negative rights.

There is no question that strong consequentialism is defective. By demanding that everyone's interests count equally in the computation (including the agent's) and then making it a duty that the agent act to maximize net benefit, it makes acts that would be heroic into routine duties. It also, in its hedonist form, entails that 'a man who, *ceteris paribus*, chooses the inferior of two musical comedies for an evening's entertainment has done a moral wrong, and this is preposterous'.[52] Notice, however, that there is nothing at all preposterous in saying that, if the alternative theatres were equally conveniently located and equally comfortable (etc.) and if nobody else was affected one way or the other by the choice, it would certainly have been *better* if this man had gone to the more enjoyable show. In fact, it is hard to see how anyone could deny it.

The decline in popularity of utilitarianism as a moral theory in recent years can, I think, be to some extent explained by the way in which utilitarianism has come to be understood as a variety of strong consequentialism. We may observe that strong consequentialism goes back to William Godwin, who, in *Political Justice*, quite explicitly maintained the duty of each person to maximize the aggregate happiness.[53] It then seems to have become dormant until G. E. Moore maintained in *Principia Ethica* that 'the assertion "I am morally bound to perform this action" is identical with the assertion "this action will

---

[51] Similarly, Bernard Williams's attack on 'utilitarianism' makes sense only as an attack on consequentialism in this strict sense.

[52] Urmson, 'The Interpretation of the Moral Philosophy of J. S. Mill', p. 170 in Gorovitz (ed.), *Utilitarianism*.

[53] William Godwin, *An Inquiry Into Political Justice*, abridged and edited by K. Codell Carter (Oxford: Clarendon Press, 1971).

produce the greatest possible amount of good in the Universe"'.[54] To find out what one must do it was necessary to determine what constituted 'the good', and one answer could be that given by utilitarianism.

The resulting conception of utilitarianism, as a strong consequentialist doctrine, would not fit Bentham or J. S. Mill, neither of whom asserted a duty to maximize aggregate happiness. Bentham seems to have thought of the problem of practical morality as one of setting up institutions that would result in people who are pursuing their own interest acting at the same time in ways that conduce to the general interest. The market, as understood by Adam Smith and Bentham, is, of course, the paradigm institution here, but all of Bentham's pieces of social invention—for choosing governments, for getting officials to behave honestly, and so on—can be seen as attempts to pull off the same trick of creating conditions in which a 'hidden hand' will guide individuals motivated by self-interest in the direction indicated by the greatest happiness principle. This does not mean that he did not believe in non-self-interested behaviour. He acknowledged its existence but, like Hobbes and Hume, he thought benevolence was too weak a force to rely on for achieving anything important in society. As he wrote: 'All that the most public-spirited, which is as much as to say the most virtuous of men can do, is to do what depends upon himself towards bringing the public interest, that is, his own personal share in the public interest, to a state as nearly approaching to coincidence, and on as few occasions amounting to a state of repugnance, as possible with his private interest.'[55]

Mill was (perhaps deliberately) ambiguous and trying to decide what he 'really meant' in *Utilitarianism* is probably unfruitful. But chapter V does explicitly say that 'duty' can be understood only within the context of a system of social norms. The criterion of a good state of the world and the ultimate test of the system of rules constituting a society's positive morality is general happiness. It is clear, however, that this is not equivalent to defining the duty of each individual as being the maximization of happiness.[56]

A version of utilitarianism that would avoid the disadvantages of strict consequentialism and would, I believe, articulate the common ideas of Bentham and Mill might run something like this:

[54] *Principia Ethica*, Ch. V, sec. 89. See also G. E. Moore, *Ethics* (London: Oxford University Press, 1912), 140.

[55] Quoted in David Baumgardt, *Bentham and the Ethics of Today with Bentham Manuscripts Hitherto Unpublished* (Princeton: Princeton University Press, 1952), 423.

[56] J. S. Mill, *Utilitarianism* in Gorovitz (ed.), *Utilitarianism*, pp. 13–57.

Utilitarianism is a theory about what constitutes good states of the world. It is no part of utilitarianism so understood to try to answer the question how far individuals can be 'required' to sacrifice themselves for the greater good of others, if this is taken to be a question asked in abstraction from any legal system or set of social norms, for we acknowledge no supernatural source of 'requirements'. All we can say is that a society is likely to be a better society the more its members have a self-sacrificing disposition. For, given the tendencies to self-interest in human beings, it is hardly likely that people will be so self-sacrificing as to reduce the amount of good in the world by acting in accord with an excessively self-sacrificing disposition. We can add the advice that moral rules and institutions are better the better the state of the world they give rise to, given whatever general level of self-sacrifice can be predicted to occur in the society; and, to the extent that the moral rules and institutions themselves affect the general level of self-sacrifice, institutions that elicit more self-sacrifice are better than those that elicit less, other things being equal.

I believe that a general framework like this can, indeed, be put to good use even if we drop the classical utilitarian postulate that the criterion for testing institutions is their contribution to aggregate happiness. I should like to claim as much for the sketch of an alternative to Fried's theory that was put forward in section II. The criteria for judging moral norms that were there employed included fairness as well as utility, but the overall approach was, I think, the one just outlined.

Let me conclude by comparing the strong and the weak forms of consequentialism. Weak consequentialism holds that there is no class of cases, definable in advance, such that the consequences are never relevant to the question of what is the right thing to do. Strong consequentialism holds that there is at all times a duty to act so as to maximize the amount of good—to maximize aggregate happiness if one is a utilitarian, to maximize something else if not. Strong consequentialism entails weak consequentialism and the denial of weak consequentialism entails the denial of strong consequentialism. But it is logically possible to accept weak consequentialism and reject strong consequentialism. In fact, Fried does this and so do I.

If we agree about both types of consequentialism, how can we disagree about so much else? The answer is, of course, that our being able to do so illustrates how weak is weak consequentialism and how strong is strong consequentialism. To accept weak consequentialism requires only that, for any proposed absolute prohibition, one can think of *some* hypothetical set of circumstances in which it should be departed from. To deny strong consequentialism requires only that one should be able to find one hypothetical case in which an act admitted to have the best consequences is not considered to be a duty. It should be plain that a vast range of positions on real issues are compatible with the acceptance of weak consequentialism and the denial of strong consequentialism.

I can illustrate this by referring to Bernard Williams's much-discussed example of Jim, who, while on a botanical expedition, 'finds himself in the central square of a small South American town' where a 'captain' is about to shoot twenty Indians, following 'recent acts of protest against the government'. The captain, Pedro, offers Jim the privilege of shooting one Indian, upon which he will let the others go. If Jim refuses, the twenty Indians will be killed as planned.[57] What should Jim do? A number of commentators have protested at the artificiality of the dilemma as presented: how, for example, does Jim know that Pedro will shoot all the Indians if he does not shoot one; or release the rest of them if he does? However, I think that the case will do with no more than probabilities attached to the alternatives. For the point of the example is that both strong consequentialists and deniers of weak consequentialism have no need to find the problem difficult. If Jim is a strict consequentialist, the fact that it is he who is to shoot an Indian has no moral significance (though if he has squeamish feelings about killing that should go into the calculation as a psychological datum). His only qualms should be over the probabilities. But if the evidence for Pedro's intentions is clear (for example, he has already shot one batch of twenty when Jim arrives) and Jim sees after he has shot one that the rest are released, he can feel that he has done a good job in saving nineteen Indians, and that is all there is to be said. Equally, if Jim does not accept weak consequentialism, he need feel no responsibility for the deaths of the Indians, since he can say of Pedro (in Fried's words) 'It's *his* wrong'. If we find both of these reactions too simple, we must, it seems to me, accept weak consequentialism and reject strong consequentialism.

My complaint against Fried is that he treats the rejection of strict consequentialism as if it licensed him to move to a position in which consequences play a role only in very occasional and extreme cases. His only example of something that would compensate for doing wrong is 'saving a whole nation'. Fried's argument, such as it is, proceeds much of the time as if it were only necessary to mention the implications of 'utilitarian maximization' to derive his own conclusions. I have suggested here that there are many reasons for rejecting his conclusions while agreeing with the rejection of strong consequentialism.

[57] Williams in Smart and Williams (ed.), *Utilitarianism: For and Against*, p. 98.

4

LADY CHATTERLEY'S LOVER AND DOCTOR FISCHER'S BOMB PARTY

Liberalism, Pareto Optimality, and the Problem of Objectionable Preferences

In the ten years since Amartya Sen announced 'the impossibility of a Paretian liberal', the alleged 'liberal paradox' has come in for a good deal of critical discussion.[1] I shall argue in the first section, 'Lady Chatterley's Lover', that, on a sensible understanding of 'liberalism' and of the significance of something's being 'socially preferred' (in the sense of being picked out by a social welfare function), there is no incompatibility between liberalism and Pareto optimality. In the second section, which is called 'Doctor Fischer's Bomb Party', I ask on what grounds we might nevertheless disapprove of deals that the parties have a right to make. This is, in my view, the serious question of substantive morality that is left after we have cleared away the problems that are internal to social choice theory. In the third section, 'What's Wrong with Social Choice?', I broaden the discussion to argue that the so-called liberal paradox illustrates the general weakness of social choice theory as a mode of political philosophizing. The basic conception of a 'social welfare function' constructed out of 'preferences' is, I suggest, fundamentally misguided. The fourth and final section, 'Paradox Lost', attempts to make clear exactly what my dissolution of the liberal paradox amounts to. (This part of the chapter has not previously been published.)

I LADY CHATTERLEY'S LOVER

The basic idea of the impossibility result is simple enough. Suppose that we take three conditions that we should like a social welfare function to satisfy: unrestricted domain (U), Pareto optimality (P),

[1] A. K. Sen, 'The Impossibility of a Paretian Liberal', *Journal of Political Economy*, 78 (1970), 152–7; and *Collective Choice and Social Welfare* (San Francisco, Calif.: Holden-Day, 1970), 78–88. An extensive review is provided by A. K. Sen, 'Liberty, Unanimity and Rights', *Economica*, 43 (1976), 217–45. The two articles are reprinted in Amartya Sen, *Choice, Welfare and Measurement* (Cambridge, Mass.: MIT Press, 1962), 285–90 and 291–326.

and liberalism (*L*). Then the theorem is that these three requirements, *U*, *P*, and *L*, are incompatible. 'Unrestricted domain' means that we do not place any restrictions on the range of individual preferences entering into the social welfare function. Pareto optimality is the requirement that if everybody prefers one state of affairs to a second then the first state of affairs is 'socially preferred'—that is to say, ranked higher on the social welfare function. (The question of what exactly is the significance of a social welfare function is one that I shall duck here, not because I want to slight its importance but because I want to take it up at length later.) What the liberal condition means here is that each individual should be 'socially decisive' over some pairs of alternative social outcomes. Candidates for the role of such pairs would be the two states of the world that are identical in every respect except that in one I sleep on my belly and in the other I sleep on my back, or that in one my kitchen walls are painted pink while in the other they are painted crimson. In other words, if I prefer to lie on my belly rather than on my back, the social welfare function should produce the conclusion that, of two states of the world differing only in respect of which way up I lie, the state of the world in which I lie on my belly is socially preferred.

We had better at this point, for the sake of brevity, resort to *p*s and *q*s. *L* specifies that for each *i* there is a pair of alternatives *p* and *q* such that if *i* prefers *p* to *q*, the social welfare function ranks *p* above *q* (and conversely if *i* prefers *q* to *p*); and *P* specifies that, if everyone prefers *p* to *q*, the social welfare function ranks *p* above *q*. The thesis of the 'impossibility of a Paretian liberal' states that conditions *L* and *P* are inconsistent, given *U*. The proof is very simple and, as far as it goes, incontestable. It runs as follows. Let *i* be decisive over the pair $\langle p, q \rangle$ and *j* be decisive over the pair $\langle r, s \rangle$. If *i* prefers *p* to *q* and *j* prefers *r* to *s*, then, by condition *L*, *p* is socially preferred to *q* and *r* is socially preferred to *s*. But if *i* and *j* both also prefer *q* to *r* and *s* to *p*, then, by condition *P*, *q* is socially preferred to *r* and *s* is socially preferred to *p*. So *p* is preferred to *q*, *q* to *r*, *r* to *s*, and *s* to *p*. This is, obviously, a violation of 'acyclicity', which is normally taken as an absolutely minimal demand to make of a social welfare function.

The entire literature tends to revolve around an example which Sen introduced in 1970 involving the reading of D. H. Lawrence's novel *Lady Chatterley's Lover*. (This of course dates the original treatment fairly precisely, for today stronger meat might be required to make the case plausible.) The example runs as follows. Mr *A* (the prude) has the following preference order with regard to this supposedly lubricious book: $\bar{a}\bar{b}$ (nobody read it); $a\bar{b}$ (he read it rather than contemplate the lewd Mr B wallowing in that filth); $\bar{a}b$ (Mr B read it); then ab (both read it). Mr B has the following preference order: ab (it would do Mr A good to read it and he would enjoy reading it himself); $a\bar{b}$ (if only one is to read it, let Mr A widen his literary horizons); $\bar{a}b$ (read it himself); $\bar{a}\bar{b}$ (waste of a good book).

It may help to set this out in tabular form. The preferences, then, are in the following order:

A (the prude)	*B (the lewd)*
$\bar{a}\bar{b}$	ab
$a\bar{b}$	$a\bar{b}$
$\bar{a}b$	$\bar{a}b$
ab	$\bar{a}\bar{b}$

As may immediately be seen, ab is Pareto-superior to $\bar{a}b$. That is to say, both A and B prefer it. Yet the liberal principle, according to Sen, demands that the lewd Mr B should read the book and the prudish Mr A should not, since each should decide on his own reading matter. Since I want to maintain that there is no such liberal (or libertarian) principle entailing this conclusion, it would be as well to quote Sen's words:

> On libertarian grounds, it is better that the lewd reads the book rather than nobody, since what the lewd reads is his own business and the lewd does want to read the book; hence [$\bar{a}b$] is socially better than [$\bar{a}\bar{b}$]. On libertarian grounds again, it is better that nobody reads the book rather than the prude, since whether the prude should read a book or not is his own business, and he does not wish to read the book; hence [$\bar{a}\bar{b}$] is better than [$a\bar{b}$].[2]

Thus, we get the 'preference cycle' that constitutes the 'liberal paradox'.

What drives this result is, of course, the fact that both A and B have what Sen calls 'nosy' preferences: A, the prude, is more concerned to prevent B, the lewd, from reading what he regards as a pornographic book than he is to avoid reading it himself (either to save B's soul or because he can't bear to think of him enjoying it); and B is more interested (whether maliciously or in a missionary spirit) in inflicting *Lady Chatterley* on A than he is in reading it himself.[3] But is it true that

[2] A. K. Sen, 'Personal Utilities and Public Judgments: or What's Wrong with Welfare Economics', *Economic Journal*, 89 (1979), 537–58, at 550. Cf. Sen, 'Liberty, Unanimity and Rights', p. 218.

[3] Note that it is not merely that A and B have 'nosy preferences', in the sense of caring about each other's reading habits, but that they have *strong* nosy preferences. That is, the 'paradox'

such nosy preferences subvert liberalism? It seems to me that this is not so. Sen claims, as we have seen, that the liberal principle says that it is 'socially better' that the lewd read *Lady Chatterley* and the prude not, but I simply deny there is any such liberal principle. Hence Sen's claim that he has shown 'the incompatibility of the Pareto principle . . . with some relatively mild requirements of personal liberty, for consistent social decisions, given unrestricted domain'[4] simply falls to the ground. For liberal principles do not say in a context like the *Lady Chatterley* case who should read what; rather, liberalism is a doctrine about who should have a right to decide who reads what. Sen, citing Mill and Hayek, suggests that 'considerations of liberty require specification of . . . e.g. whether a particular choice is self-regarding or not . . . , or as falling within a person's "protected sphere"'.[5] Quite so, but let us take note of the purpose for which this information is required. It is brought in at the stage at which we argue about the allocation of rights: we say that when it comes to (say) what they read, people should have power to take their own decisions because this is 'self-regarding' or should be within the 'protected sphere'. But we do not then judge the *use made* of these rights in terms of any principle of liberty: the notion that any principle of liberty that would be endorsed by Mill or Hayek is violated by the prude choosing to read *Lady Chatterley* and the lewd not doing so (provided, of course, that they are freely exercising their rights, as in the case stated) is pure fantasy.

Liberalism cannot be connected up to Sen's statement of an alleged liberal principle because it is not a doctrine about what constitutes a 'socially better' state of affairs, where a state is defined by things like 'A reads *Lady Chatterley* and B doesn't'. Rather it is a doctrine about who has what rights to control what. When the liberal principle says that there should be a protected sphere,[6] what that means is that there are some things (e.g. which way up to lie in bed, what colour to paint one's kitchen, or how to spend one's money) about which an individual should be able to decide what to do, without any coercive

---

would not arise if each had a preference concerning the other's behaviour but, when it came to the crunch, cared more about his own. This would yield the following orderings:

A	B
$\bar{a}b$	ab
$\bar{a}\bar{b}$	$\bar{a}b$
ab	$a\bar{b}$
$a\bar{b}$	$\bar{a}\bar{b}$

Since both prefer $\bar{a}b$ to $a\bar{b}$, conditions L and P both endorse the same outcome here.

[4] Sen, 'Personal Utilities and Public Judgments', p. 549.
[5] Ibid.   [6] Sen, 'Liberty, Unanimity and Rights', p. 218.

interference by or on behalf of society. Indeed, further than that, the force of society will be put behind the claim of each individual to do what he likes in such a protected sphere without being subject to coercion by anybody else.

We can express this idea perspicuously by making use of the conceptual apparatus developed by James Coleman.[7] In this schema, actors can control certain events, either individually or jointly. They also have interests in events—not necessarily the same ones as those over which they have control. In the case of a binary choice, an actor's interest in getting the alternative that he prefers may be understood as the difference between the utility that he expects to derive from the favoured alternative and the utility that he expects to derive from the less favoured one. Clearly, as Coleman says, a utility-maximizing actor will seek to 'do two things: first, gain control over those events that interest him, and secondly, exercise that control in such a direction that the outcome he favors occurs'.[8]

And, once we have a structure of rights to control events and of interests in those events:

the principal activities of actors in attempting to realize their interests consist of actions through which they gain effective control of events they are interested in, through giving up effective control over events they are not [or less—B.B.] interested in. In economic activities, this consists of an explicit exchange of control; in other areas of life, including political activities, it consists of less explicit exchange of control often based on informal agreements.[9]

Let us apply these notions to the *Lady Chatterley* case. The initial distribution of control over events provided by a liberal scheme for assigning rights is as follows:

A (the prude)   controls $\begin{cases} A \text{ read } Lady\ Chatterley \\ A \text{ not read } Lady\ Chatterley \end{cases}$

B (the lewd)   controls $\begin{cases} B \text{ read } Lady\ Chatterley \\ B \text{ not read } Lady\ Chatterley \end{cases}$

If each makes his choice independently, A will choose not to read *Lady Chatterley* and B will choose to do so. However, if we look at the structure of interests, we see that, because both actors have nosy preferences, the structure of rights is out of alignment with the

[7] J. S. Coleman, *The Mathematics of Collective Action* (London: Heinemann Educational, 1973), Ch. 3.   [8] Ibid. 73.   [9] Ibid. 75.

structure of control. Each is more interested in what the other does than in what he does himself.

Ranking of interests by A	Ranking of interests by B
1. B not read *Lady Chatterley*	1. A read *Lady Chatterley*
2. A not read *Lady Chatterley*	2. B read *Lady Chatterley*

It is this structure that makes it mutually advantageous to the two parties to exchange control over the event in which they are less interested for control over the event in which they are more interested. *A* surrenders his right not to read *Lady Chatterley* in return for the more valued control over the reading matter of *B*, and *B* in return surrenders his right to read *Lady Chatterley* in return for the ability, which is more important to him, to have *A* read it.

It is essential to notice that the initial assignment of rights plays a crucial role in bringing about this post-trade outcome in which the prude finishes up reading *Lady Chatterley* and the lewd finishes up not reading it.[10] Suppose, for example, that the rights were not distributed so as to give each actor control over his own reading-matter, but instead that the prude could determine both what he himself read and also what the lewd read (a lewd minor, perhaps). Then, the outcome that would be brought about by an own-utility-maximizing prude (one, for example, not constrained by considerations of fairness in deciding how to exercise his rights) would be one in which neither reads *Lady Chatterley*.

It should be borne in mind that Pareto optimality is in itself indifferent to distributive considerations. Thus, for example, the outcome in which neither reads *Lady Chatterley's Lover* would be Pareto-optimal, since there is no alternative to it that both parties would prefer. This is the outcome we might expect if the initial assignment of rights allowed the prude to decide on both what he himself reads and what the lewd reads. For clearly, since the lewd has no rights over his reading-matter, he has no bargaining counter to offer in order to gain control over events controlled by the prude and move the outcome in a direction he favours. To put it another way, since the prude has all the power, the Pareto-optimal outcome is simply the one that puts *him* as high up his preference rankings as he

[10] Of course, if symmetry were maintained but the initial assignment of rights gave each control over the other's reading-matter, there would be no transfer of control (given the nosy preferences that we are postulating) because the structure of control and the structure of interest would then be congruent. However, if each were more interested in what he read than in what the other read, they would transfer control so that the prude did not read *Lady Chatterley* and the lewd did.

can get, and to hell with the preferences of the lewd. An exception would arise if the lewd were lucky enough to have his preferences enter into the prude's utility function—but presumably the prude, being a meddlesome prude, does not give weight to others' lewd preferences in arriving at his own preference ordering of outcomes.

The essential point about Pareto optimality, then, is that it simply calls for all mutually advantageous deals to be made, but to pick one Pareto-optimal outcome out of the infinite number of Pareto-optimal outcomes we have to have an initial assignment of rights. The liberal principle is a criterion for the assignment of these rights which tells us who should start with the power to control what events. If we knew the assignment of rights and what Coleman calls the structure of interests, we could, given his own theory, in principle work out the unique Pareto-optimal outcome corresponding to that assignment of rights. In the absence of such a strong theory as Coleman's, the assumption that mutually advantageous exchanges of control over events would be made until no opportunities remained would not generate a unique outcome. There might, in other words, be alternative Pareto-optimal outcomes compatible with a given initial assignment of rights. (We might recall that in the theory of economic bargaining—over an exchange of apples for oranges, say—it requires a very strong theory to pick out a unique point on the contract curve.)

It is important to be clear that there is all the difference in the world between having a right to decide something, where the contents of the decision may be made contingent on the offers other people make in order to influence that decision, and not having a right at all. Only by eliding that distinction can Sen achieve the effect of making us think that there is nothing between totally isolated decisionmaking in personal matters and a situation in which all preferences, including nosy ones, are thrown into a common pot and some sort of utilitarian calculus applied to them to arrive at politically enforced decisions about what people must or must not do (in effect, a set-up in which there are no rights at all).

Thus, in considering how one might come to drop the condition of liberalism, Sen offers this possible argument for doing so: 'The idea that certain things are a person's "personal" affair is insupportable. If the color of Mr. *A*'s walls disturbs Mr. *B*, then it is Mr. *B*'s business as well. If it makes Mr. *A* unhappy that Mr. *B* should lie on his belly while asleep, or that he should read *Lady Chatterly's* [*sic*] *Lover* while awake, then Mr. *A* is a relevant party to the choice.' He then goes on to say: 'This is, undoubtedly, a possible point of view, and the popularity of rules such as a ban on smoking marijuana, or suppression of homosexual practices or pornography, reflect, at least partly, such a point of view. Public policy is often aimed at imposing on individuals the will of others even in matters that may directly concern only those individuals.'[11] But, he says, to deny the weak liberal condition (which after all requires only that there be *some* alternative over which each person is decisive) is to 'deny even the most limited expressions of individual freedom. And also to deny privacy, since the choice between x and y may be that between being forced to confess on one's personal affairs (x) and not being so forced (y).'[12]

I hope it will be clear by now that this confuses two quite different ideas: that people should never fail to act on their personal preferences in what 'directly concerns' them, and that people should not be *required* to violate their personal preferences in what 'directly concerns' them. The second is, indeed, an authentically liberal idea. But the first is not, as Sen suggests, an essential part of every reasonable conception of liberalism. It might even be said to be antithetical to a conception of liberalism that emphasizes the freedom of individuals to make their own choices with as few constraints as possible. For surely we are more free to choose if we can trade a decision over something we have a right to control in return for control over a decision that we value more, which some other person has a right to take, than we are if some agent of the social welfare function restrains us from doing so. The simple answer, then, is that there is no inconsistency in principle between liberalism and Pareto optimality. Liberalism is, indeed, a principle that picks out a protected sphere, but one that is protected against unwanted interference, not against use in trading with others.

To sum up, if a social welfare function tells us what constitutes a better state of the world, there can be no conflict between any social welfare function, whatever its content, and the principle that there should be a protected sphere within which people shall be legally free to do what they choose. For the two have different subject–matters: one is about what is 'socially better', the other about what people shall be able to do without legal coercion.

The only way in which we can create a conflict between a social welfare function and a genuinely liberal principle of this kind is by supposing that what is socially better should be enforced. But then no elaborate argument is needed to establish incompatibility, since that idea is *itself* in conflict with the liberal principle. Thus, again, nothing

[11] Sen, *Collective Choice and Social Welfare*, p. 82.   [12] Ibid. 83.

turns on the particular content of the social welfare function. If the choice between x and y is within A's protected sphere, this entails that A should neither be forced to do x nor be forced to do y.

To ask (on this interpretation of what it implies to say something is socially better) how we should determine, in accordance with liberalism, whether x or y is socially better is a question obviously doomed to produce an absurd answer, so it is hardly surprising that it is possible to show that any particular answer is absurd. To say 'A's own preference shall determine whether x or y is socially better' is not a 'liberal' answer, because it still presupposes (on this interpretation of what it means to say that something is socially better) that either x or y should be enforced—yet this is exactly what the notion of a protected sphere is designed to deny.

II   DOCTOR FISCHER'S BOMB PARTY

So far in this chapter I have sounded, most of the time, like a born-again disciple of Milton Friedman, with the slogan 'Free to Choose' inscribed on my banner. It is now time to dispel that impression. As I said at the outset, I do not find Sen's *Lady Chatterley* example very compelling. But I do share the intuition that seems to lie behind Sen's anti-Paretianism: that some Paretian deals raise problems. However, Sen has misdiagnosed the issue by talking about a 'liberal paradox'. And he has, subsequent to 1970, compounded the error by saying that he prefers 'libertarian' to 'liberal'.[13] For, in the contemporary jargon, a libertarian is precisely somebody who believes that no limits should be set on the drive towards Pareto optimality. The state should not, for example, step in between a willing seller of labour (willing, that is, compared to the alternatives) and a willing buyer by prescribing minimum wage rates. Nor should it prevent people from entering into onerous contracts (e.g. at usurious rates of interest) if they regard that as advantageous to themselves. Thus, it is clear that libertarianism, so conceived, is in no sense incompatible with Pareto optimality. Rather, Pareto optimality is a natural part of the kind of social philosophy (in effect an ideology constructed out of outdated introductory economics textbooks) known as libertarianism.

This ideology assumes, in effect, that if people are to have a right in general to do what they choose in some area (e.g. buy or sell labour, lend or borrow money), it is better for there to be no legal restrictions

[13] Sen, 'Liberty, Unanimity and Rights', p. 218.

on the exercise of the right. But there are in some cases good reasons for setting limits to the range of transactions that should be permitted. Minimum wage laws and usury laws can operate so as to strengthen the position of the weak, providing by legal enactment the equivalent of an agreement that the weaker parties would have found it advantageous to conclude among themselves, if the problem of collective action did not arise. On somewhat similar lines, legal systems characteristically do not allow the consent of the victim to count as a defence to a charge of inflicting bodily harm or death. The rationale is, plausibly, that the position of potential victims would be weakened if they could validly consent. The prohibition of contracts of servitude and of debt peonage can be justified in the same way. These limitations do, of course, prevent the achievement of Pareto optimality, if we take a regime of unrestricted rights as our baseline and look at potential transactions one by one. But it is also inconsistent with libertarianism, as I have defined it.

It is, then, quite reasonable to assign rights in society so as to take account of the strategic relations of the parties. In the cases I gave, one side actually has an interest in being prevented from entering into certain kinds of legally effective agreements, thus illustrating, *contra* Friedman, that it is not always advantageous to be 'free to choose'. Although in general people can do better for themselves (i.e. achieve more preferred outcomes) by being legally free to deploy their rights in any way they wish, there are some cases where they can achieve a more preferred outcome if their rights are restricted so that they are prevented from giving up their rights or from exchanging them on particular terms.

At this point, however, we may begin to wonder whether the notion of Pareto optimality is well defined in such contexts. I said that limits on the exercise of a right prevent the achievement of Pareto optimality if we take as a baseline the absence of restrictions and if we consider the potential transactions one by one, independently of one another. But why should we? What we have here is a situation in which someone may be better off doing a certain deal than not doing it if he is permitted to do it, but would be better off still if he were not permitted to do it. Since *ex hypothesi* his position in the second rights regime is preferable to any open to him (either by dealing or not dealing) in the first rights regime, we cannot say that either of the regimes is Pareto-superior to the other. We have, rather, two regimes with different distributions among the actors, neither of which dominates the other. On this line of reasoning, we can say that both regimes have the possibility within them of attaining (different) Pareto-optimal outcomes.

Fortunately, conundrums of this kind do not have to be straightened out before I can present the problem to which this section of the chapter is devoted. Let us suppose that we have some system of rights established, and that it is of a conventional liberal nature. That is to say, although it restricts the exercise of rights along some of the lines just mentioned, it leaves open a wide range of discretionary behaviour. In addition to the resources for exchange offered by the market, then, we will suppose that people have many other opportunities to trade rights over things they control for things that other people control.

The question I want to raise is the following. When people operate within this established framework of rights, are there Pareto-optimal deals which they can properly be condemned for making? We are thus looking at cases where someone uses a right he unquestionably has (e.g. to read or not read *Lady Chatterley*) in order to try to influence, by making a contingent offer to act one way rather than another, the use another person makes of a right that *he* unquestionably has (e.g. to read or not read *Lady Chatterley*). Interestingly enough, Sen himself, in an article written three years after the survey article from which I was quoting before, broke away far enough from the social choice terminology to present the question in these terms, though without repudiating the implicit claim that what he said could be translated into the language of social welfare functions. He said there that a trade between the lewd and the prude:

raises a deeper question, viz., whether *having a right* based on the 'personal' nature of some decisions (in this case the right to read what one likes and shun what one does not wish to read) must invariably imply being free *to trade that right* for some other gain, irrespective of the nature of the gain (in this case the lewd's gain consists in getting pleasure from the prude's discomfiture, and the prude's gain in avoiding the discomfort of knowing that the lewd is reading a book that he—the prude—disapproves of). If the answer to this question is yes, then clearly the criticism of the Pareto principle would not apply to this case. I believe it is possible to question such an affirmative answer, but I resist the temptation to go further into this complex issue.[14]

It is precisely that complex issue that I wish to address here.

To begin with, let us get it quite clear that there is nothing wrong in general with attempts to manipulate one's use of rights to advance

----

[14] Sen, 'Personal Utilities and Public Judgments', p. 552, italics in original.

nosy preferences. Suppose that I have a purely disinterested nosy preference for your giving up smoking (it is not that the smoke bothers me, etc.) and you have likewise a preference for my losing weight based on a disinterested concern for my health rather than a desire to look at someone trimmer. It seems hard to see how any moralist could object to our making a deal in order to further our nosy ends. There is, surely, a version of the *Lady Chatterley* case that comes close to this, where the contingent offers are well intentioned in a somewhat parallel way. It is only by attributing nasty motives to the lewd (making the prude squirm) and reducing the prude's concern for the lewd to a self-centred one (avoiding his own discomfort at knowing the lewd is reading the book) that Sen is able to make us feel any qualms at all about the propriety of a trade. Even then, the case is one that I find hard to take seriously. There is no question that the lewd and the prude of Sen's depiction would be better people if they had different preferences but, given the preferences they have, I still feel reluctant to say that they should not act to further them. In fact, it seems to me that they deserve one another.

Let me take up instead the second novel that I have included in my title, Graham Greene's *Doctor Fischer of Geneva or the Bomb Party*.[15] The eponymous Dr Fischer is a very rich Swiss who, for reasons that we need not enter into here, wishes to have his contempt for the human race reinforced and justified. To this end he assembles a group of wealthy toadies (or Toads, as his daughter calls them) who endure all kinds of insults and humiliations at the hands of Dr Fischer in return for lavish gifts. Although they could, as Dr Fischer frequently emphasizes, quite well afford to buy the same things for themselves, they are too mean to spend their own money and greedy enough to put up with a lot of indignities in order to get them free. The climactic 'bomb party'[16] is unsuitable for our purposes because I suspect that, even under Swiss law, consent is no defence to a charge of bodily harm, and Dr Fischer, by offering his guests Christmas crackers which have either a large cheque or a small bomb in them, and inviting them to pull one each and take the consequences, is on shaky legal ground. And even if he is not legally guilty, we may still wish to hold the right to bodily integrity to be morally inalienable. Let us therefore take the earlier dinner party which the narrator (who is married to Dr Fischer's daughter) attends, since this raises no problems of violating

---

[15] Graham Greene, *Doctor Fischer of Geneva or the Bomb Party* (New York: Simon and Schuster, 1980). [16] Ibid. 65–6.

the rights of the guests. At this party, Dr Fischer dines on caviare, while his guests are offered nothing but cold porridge. As Dr Fischer points out, they are perfectly free not to eat it if they choose not to. As the narrator recounts it to his wife afterwards:

'Mrs. Montgomery [one of the Toads] said I should have been sent from the table as soon as I refused to eat the porridge. "Any of you could have done the same," your father said. "Then what would you have done with all the presents?" she asked. "Perhaps I would have doubled the stakes next time," he said.'
    'Stakes? What did he mean?'
    'I suppose he meant his bet on their greed against their humiliation.'[17]

I shall take it as uncontroversial that Dr Fischer would have been a better man if he had not had the desires that led him to give such dinner parties. But can we say that Dr Fischer ought, morally, not to have acted as he did? Can we say that it was not merely bad-producing conduct (like painting one's kitchen in clashing colours) but wrong?

I do myself feel strongly inclined to say this. If I try to determine what special features of the case make me want to say that it was wrong for Dr Fischer to act on his objectionable preferences, I seem to find two. The first is that this is a case of playing on a weakness of character—in this case greed—for one's own satisfaction. The other, somewhat related point is that Dr Fischer is deliberately corrupting the Toads, that is to say, making their characters worse in respect of the flaw of excessive greed. When Dr Fischer's invitation to the narrator to come to the dinner party arrives, his wife says: 'He wants you to join the Toads.' The following dialogue ensues: 'But I've nothing against the Toads. Are they really as bad as you say? . . .' 'They weren't always Toads, I suppose. He's corrupted all of them.'[18]

Dr Fischer played on human weakness. Another type of case is that where what is taken advantage of is economic weakness. Thus, where there are great disparities in economic circumstances between the parties, and in particular where one is in desperate need, the other (better-off) party may take advantage of the economically weaker one. Note that the resultant deal is certainly Pareto optimal in that the weaker party prefers the deal to the status quo ante. Our criticism is of the stronger party for offering those terms. The underlying idea is again that there are ways in which people should not treat others.

Examples of this second kind of case would be as follows:
    (*a*) Offers that express contempt, by emphasizing the worthlessness

---

[17] Ibid. 73–4.   [18] Ibid. 40–1.

of the person. An example would be paying people to dig holes and fill them up again. We might contrast this with the superficially similar case of a landlord paying men (as sometimes happened in earlier centuries) to carry out ornamental work on his estate purely in order to provide employment for them. In such a case, one may well object to the distribution of initial resources that puts the parties in the position where that is a Pareto-optimal deal but not, it seems to me, to the transaction itself.

(*b*) Offers that are intrinsically degrading—to do such things as eating excrement, blaspheming against one's religion, prostitution. (This is, of course, on the analysis that prostitution is taking advantage of poor alternative employment for women. Note, however, that this analysis can be used either to criticize prostitution or to criticize the economic position of women. In other words, if you cannot convince people that working in a match factory or a sewing room for the available pay is bad, you may still be able to convince them by pointing out that many girls prefer prostitution. This was, of course, Shaw's strategy in *Mrs Warren's Profession*.)

A third case of offers that ought not to be made is, I would suggest, those that are really coercive offers even though they are not caught within the usual (or legally enforceable) conception. In effect, these involve not appealing to psychological or economic weakness but to the recipient's better nature in an inappropriate way. Examples would be: 'If you don't marry me, I'll kill myself'; 'If you don't give me the job, it will blight my life'; 'Only by doing what I want can you save me from committing a mortal sin.' The point of these cases is that the person is not making a threat ruled out by the usual bans on coercion. Yet at the same time there is no doubt that the other person's decision is taken under duress. 'If you don't do it, I'll kill myself' may well be much more really coercive than 'If you don't do it, I'll punch you on the nose.'

To sum up, the question has been one of actions taken to encourage someone to do what you want him to, taken against a background where he is free to choose to accept or reject whatever offer you make. I have suggested that everything turns on that phrase 'free to choose': being free to choose is not simply equivalent to not being coerced, in the sense of threatened with the deprivation of a right. It has got to include the idea that not going along with the deal that is offered is an acceptable state of affairs. The second and third types of exception I gave are both ways in which this condition fails: in the third you are going to be made to feel bad if you do not accept (so it may be treated as an implicit sanction) and in the second you are not really free to reject it because the status quo is so unbearable that you have to take anything that promises to alleviate it. (A subset that gets closer to implicit coercion is where in the absence of a deal things get worse and worse, not because of the other's action but simply in the nature of the case—the obvious examples being where you are running out of money without a job, running out of water in the desert, etc.) The Dr Fischer case fits in more awkwardly, but we might say that weakness of will in the face of temptation is a lack of freedom to choose. In the absence of such conditions—so that the person to whom the offer is made is genuinely free to refuse it—is there any reason why, *given* the preferences, it is wrong to try to change the incentives facing somebody?

I do not think so. When it comes down to it, the only really objectionable cases do seem to be the three kinds of case I have picked out already. And the only plausible way of getting the *Lady Chatterley* case in is by imagining that the prude is presented with the offer as a challenge to his integrity. Suppose that the lewd says 'You always say that it matters a lot to you that people don't degrade themselves by reading filth. Here's a chance to stop me doing so, and the only cost to you is reading it yourself—and you're so incorruptible it won't matter to you.'

Examples of objectionable attempts to get compliance with nosy preferences generally rely on a background of inequality. For example, the efforts of the Victorian middle class to regulate the lives of their servants over and above what was defined in doing the job for which they were employed is no doubt revolting to any reasonable person. But is this not because their market position was such that they could impose these conditions as the norm? Suppose that a couple now wanted to employ a live-in nanny for their children and insisted on no visits from boyfriends. In the present market this would presumably require quite a hefty premium over the standard pay for the job. But then if somebody thinks it is worth the premium and takes the job on those conditions do we have any reason to think that that is a bad arrangement? Given a correct distribution of rights, then, my conclusion is that we can afford to be pretty tolerant of efforts to further nosy preferences, even unworthy ones.

III   WHAT'S WRONG WITH SOCIAL CHOICE?

This chapter has raised two questions. The first is whether there is some inherent conflict between the Pareto principle and some liberal principle of a kind that would be endorsed by J. S. Mill or F. A. von Hayek. The second is whether we have grounds for the moral condemnation of the use people sometimes make of the area of discretion granted them by a system of rights in offering to act in a certain way in return for some change in behaviour by another. This may be paraphrased as a question of whether Pareto-optimal moves can be undesirable. The answer to the first question is a clearcut 'no': there is no such contradiction. The answer to the second is a more hesitant 'yes': under some circumstances mutually preferred actions may be open to censure.

The key to the first question is that the Pareto principle and the liberal principle have different subject-matters, so they cannot conflict directly. The Pareto principle is a criterion for judging the goodness or badness of states of affairs, whereas the liberal principle à la Mill or Hayek is a criterion for assigning rights to individuals (and perhaps collectivities).

To spell this out a little more fully, here is a statement by Leontief of the Pareto principle, as quoted by Sen: "The social welfare is increased whenever at least one of the individual utilities on which it depends is raised while none is reduced."[19] And, in Sen's translation into his own lingo: 'For all pairs of states x, y, . . . if everyone has at least as much utility in x as in y, and someone has more utility in x than in y, then x is socially better than y.'[20] Note that this is a statement about what makes social welfare greater or makes one state of affairs socially better than another. It says nothing about what rights individuals should have or indeed what use they can, with propriety, make of those rights.

Now recall Mill's famous 'simple principle', which is, I suppose, a paradigmatic statement of the kind of liberal principle that is supposed to conflict with the Pareto principle:

The object of this Essay is to assert one very simple principle, as entitled to govern absolutely the dealings of society with the individual in the way of compulsion and control, whether the means used be physical force in the form of legal penalties, or the moral coercion of public opinion. That principle is, that the sole end for which mankind is warranted, individually or collectively, in interfering with the liberty of action of any of their number, is self-protection. That the only purpose for which power can be rightfully

---

[19] Sen, 'Personal Utilities and Public Judgments', p. 537.   [20] Ibid. 538.

exercised over any member of a civilized community, against his will, is to prevent harm to others. His own good, either physical or moral, is not a sufficient warrant. He cannot rightfully be compelled to do or forbear because it will be better for him to do so, because it will make him happier, because, in the opinions of others, to do so would be wise, or even right. These are good reasons for remonstrating with him, or reasoning with him, or persuading him, or entreating him, but not for compelling him, or visiting him with any evil in case he do otherwise.[21]

Not only does this not conflict with principles for the evaluation of states of affairs but it presupposes them. For Mill's whole point is that an individual's own good might be increased by his doing something where nobody else is adversely affected, and that this is nevertheless no ground for 'interfering' by means of legal or social sanctions. (Note, however, that 'remonstrance' is not a sanction.) It is thus historically bizarre to suppose that Mill would be fazed by any 'dilemma of a Paretian liberal', since he quite explicitly dissociated his 'simple principle' from any judgement of consequences. He accepts that an individual may, in exercising his rights, pass up a chance to make himself better off and nobody else worse off; but he denies that that is any reason for the rest of us to make him do it if he chooses not to.

There is no need for present purposes to take up the hoary question of whether, if the run is sufficiently long (e.g. measured in centuries), and the definition of utility sufficiently elastic (e.g. 'the permanent interests of man as a progressive being'), Mill's 'simple principle' is compatible with a very indirect sort of utilitarianism. The point that matters here is that a conflict between a liberal system of rights and the Pareto principle can arise only if (*a*) every single act is to be assessed according to the Pareto principle; and if (*b*) enforcement is considered to be an appropriate response to infractions of it. And it is made quite clear by Mill that this is exactly what he wants to deny; in fact the 'simple principle' might be said to consist of the denial.

It is, then, undeniable that if we propose a criterion for a good state of affairs like Pareto optimality, or, more full-bloodedly, maximizing aggregate utility, and if we also say that legislators and government officials should seek on a case-by-case basis to enforce the pursuit of this end, then farewell legal rights. And if we also assign a duty to everybody to co-ordinate social sanctions in order to maintain pressure towards the pursuit of the collective end, we have Mill's night-

[21] J. S. Mill, 'On Liberty', in J. M. Robson (ed.), *Essays on Politics and Society* (Toronto: University of Toronto Press, 1977), vol. i, pp. 213–310, at 223–4.

mare (how quaint it seems now!) of an excessive weight of public opinion on individual freedom. But what must be emphasized is that there is absolutely no inconsistency between holding that it would be a better state of the world if someone refrained from doing x (because doing it will be 'physically' or 'morally'—Mill's terms—deleterious to him, with no offsetting gains to others), and at the same time holding that he should not be legally or socially coerced into refraining from doing x.

It should be observed that I have been talking about the absence of enforcement (legal and, in Mill's extension, social) in certain areas as the essence of liberalism, and this seems to me historically correct. There is no inconsistency between liberalism and the view that, as a matter of individual morality, each person has a duty to maximize the amount of good in the universe. Thus, Godwin, in *Political Justice*, is archetypically liberal (even anticipating Mill's extension of the doctrine from law to public opinion) in looking forward to the end of all legal and social sanctions, while at the same time putting forward a fanatically rigorous doctrine of individual morality according to which every shilling in my pocket has its destined recipient, namely the person in all the world who will derive the most happiness from spending it.[22] This kind of strict consequentialist doctrine has few adherents as a theory and probably none in practice, but there is nothing anti-liberal about it. It can be combined, as it was in Godwin's case, with a strong endorsement of individual rights against coercion. Indeed, there is much to be said for Godwin's view that the relaxation of legal and social controls can be tolerated only when it occurs in a society within which stringent standards of individual morality are widespread. These standards need not be strictly consequentialist but they must acknowledge, in Justice Frankfurter's words, that 'much that is legally permitted is repugnant to the civilized mind'.[23]

To sum up, we can say that there are (at least) three things to be distinguished: what constitutes a good state of the world (this is what a social welfare function [SWF] should tell us); what rights individuals should be granted, that is to say in what areas of conduct they should be free from legal and (if we follow Mill) social coercion; and what, morally speaking, individuals have a duty to do. ('Duty' is of course just one out of the family of terms used in moral judgement, which are

[22] W. Godwin, *Enquiry Concerning Political Justice with Selections from Godwin's Other Writings*, abr. & ed. K. C. Carter (Oxford: Clarendon Press, 1971).

[23] Quoted by Gerald Grant, 'The Character of Education and the Education of Character', *Daedalus*, 110 (1981), 135–49, at 141.

not interchangeable. For the present strictly limited purpose, however, it can stand in for the rest.) How these three are related is a question, or set of questions, in moral and political philosophy. It is a substantive issue and is not to be settled by consulting the meanings of words. (Moore, for example, was simply wrong in regarding the proposition that one has a duty to maximize the amount of good in the universe as an analytic truth.) This is not the place to discuss the substantive issue. The point that has to be made here is that the *only* way in which a conflict arises between liberalism and Pareto optimality is if we adopt the meta-principle that not only do individuals have a moral duty to pursue the good (i.e. implement the SWF), but that 'mankind, individually or collectively' is warranted in *enforcing* the SWF, using legal or social sanctions. But, to repeat, there is nothing in the notion of an SWF that entails that what is 'socially better' must be (or may be) brought about by coercion.

Suppose that my 'personal' preference (i.e. consulting nobody but myself) is to have a crimson kitchen or to read *Lady Chatterley's Lover*. And now suppose that somebody with nosy preferences makes me an offer to change my mind, e.g. offers me $1,000 to switch to pink (thus appealing to my preference for more rather than less disposable income), or offers to read *Lady Chatterley* if I do not (thus appealing to *my* nosy preference in regard to his reading-matter). And suppose that the offer is, given my overall preference scheme, attractive: I was almost indifferent between crimson and pink anyway, and would actually have been happy to change for $10; I was only mildly keen on reading *Lady Chatterley* but attach great importance to the other's reading it. Then clearly Pareto optimality (which does here seem to be no more than an expression of elementary rationality) says that it is a better state of the world if I accept the offer: both parties gain and nobody else is affected either way. But nothing immediately follows from this about social intervention. Unless we adopt the additional principle that the SWF is to be enforced, I still have the right to paint my kitchen any colour I like or read whatever books I like. If I choose to act like a damn fool and turn down a deal that would move me up my preference ordering, the fact that I am also failing to move the outcome up a notch on the SWF does not mean that anybody can call a policeman and make me consummate the deal.

It is essential to distinguish between, on the one hand, an actual system—a constitution and a set of laws—that specifies who can control what events and, on the other hand, a criterion on the basis of which one might judge that a certain state of society is morally preferable to some alternative state of society. An SWF is a proposal for a criterion that will tell us what is a better state of society. Sen, by talking about 'social decision functions' and 'collective choice rules' as well as 'social welfare functions', makes it sound, to the unwary reader, as if the topic under discussion were actual constitutional rules. But it is not. It is still simply ideas people might have about what are better or worse states of affairs.

Now it is, of course, true that an interesting theoretical question arises if I support some decisionmaking rule, that is to say some actual system for the allocation of power, and disapprove of what comes out of it. For example, I may think that the majority has (via some representative system) a right to decide what is done about something and regard the majority decision as unjust. Or I may think that you quite properly have the right to the last word about the colour of your kitchen walls but also think that your decision is deplorable. Undeniably, I may say, you should have the right to decide on their colour. But why should that choice be beyond criticism on the basis of some reasonable criteria for good outcomes? Pareto optimality is by no means the only criterion for criticizing the choice of colour scheme. It might be said that, although you are quite within your rights in having any colours you choose in your kitchen, it would have been better if you had taken account of the sensibilities of others, or shown a less vulgar taste, or spent the money on something other than redecoration, or any of a thousand things. Liberalism says that nobody can make you paint your kitchen any colour you don't want it painted. It does not say that everybody else has to like it, or agree that your choice is the 'socially best' one.

The point is in fact a quite general one that applies either to (real) social decision procedures or to individual rights. In the first case it spawns the so-called 'paradox in the theory of democracy' (not to be confused with the 'paradox of voting') that Richard Wollheim claimed to have discovered.[24] In the second case it gives us the puzzle of how there can be a 'right to do wrong'—for a right only to do right would be no right at all.[25] However, we do not in practice find any great difficulty in voting one way and still accepting that, if we were in the minority, the actual decision should go with the majority. Similarly, we do not in practice (most of us, anyway) feel that there is really any contradiction in saying that somebody should have a right to do either

[24] R. Wollheim, 'A Paradox in the Theory of Democracy', in P. Laslett and W. G. Runciman (eds.), *Philosophy, Politics and Society*, 2nd ser. (Oxford: Basil Blackwell, 1962), 71–87.
[25] See J. Waldron, 'A Right to do Wrong', *Ethics*, 92 (1981), 21–39.

x or y but that what he or she really ought to do is x—even if y is the choice made by the right-holder. And in my view we are quite correct in this.[26]

It must be acknowledged that if one believes that each individual has a duty to maximize the good, and if the good (or SWF) includes Pareto optimality among its criteria, there will be a moral duty to pursue Pareto optimality wherever it leads. This would clearly entail that, if nobody else was affected, you would have a duty to get as high up your own preference rankings as possible. And it would mean that, since your all-things-considered highest preference on almost anything could always be changed by a big enough contingent offer, you could be manipulated into finding that almost anything might be your duty.

Of course, problems arise here about the meaning of 'preference'. If we say that the desire not to be manipulated is itself a wish that can enter into an all-things-considered preference, you may be able to say that you *prefer* not to accept a fantastic offer. But then preferences and actions become analytically indistinguishable. If we retain a more normal concept of preference (of the kind that Sen himself requires) so that we can say that something is preferable, on my scale of preferences, but I nevertheless choose not to do it, we will have to conclude that a duty to pursue Pareto optimality will be a moral constraint on what might reasonably be thought of as an area of individual discretion. The solution if we do not like this is to reject the premiss that gives the trouble: the idea that each person has at every moment a duty to pursue the good (including his or her own good where that of others does not enter into competition with it).

One possible way of accounting for Sen's invention of condition L—but I must insist that this is speculative—is that it is an attempt to incorporate a sphere of moral indifference into a strictly consequentialist moral system. There is some evidence for this interpretation in that he began a relatively recent article by saying that in it, 'without disputing the acceptability of consequentialism', he intended, among other things, to argue that Paretianism 'deserves rejection in its general form'.[27] And one way of interpreting the driving force behind condition L is that there ought to be not merely a protected sphere in the Mill/Hayek sense of one immune to legal or social coercion, but one in which what I do is *morally* my own business, in other words

---

[26] I have tried to make this clear in 'Wollheim's Paradox: Comment', *Political Theory*, 1 (1973), 317–22.

[27] A. K. Sen, 'Utilitarianism and Welfarism', *Journal of Philosophy*, 76 (1979), 463–89, at 463–4.

where I have no duty to do one thing *or* the other. If this is the intention lying behind condition *L* then it seems to me misguided. For there is a much more direct way of getting rid of the problem of a vanishingly small sphere of moral indifference if that is the worry, namely abandoning strict consequentialism. And Sen's attempt to incorporate a condition guaranteeing a sphere of moral indifference into a consequentialist morality has the unfortunate effect of undermining the judgements of outcomes that we should actually be prepared to make.

We can see how this happens by following Sen's development of condition *L*. His informal statement of the principle of 'personal liberty' runs as follows: 'There are certain personal matters in which a person should be free to decide what should happen, and in choices over these things whatever he or she thinks is better must be taken to be better for the society as a whole, no matter what others think.'[28] Now the first half of this is fair enough. And it is precisely what is guaranteed by a set of liberal rights. The second half could scarcely be said (as Sen claims) to be one of the 'more widely used principles in evaluating social states',[29] since it is not even intelligible as it stands. The assertion has to be interpreted within the framework of social choice theory.

'Socially better' means 'picked out by the social welfare function', and condition *L* means that over certain pairs of choices (at least one pair) each person should be decisive in determining what is picked out by the SWF. Clearly, the question to be raised here is: why should it be supposed that a liberal (or indeed anyone else) would wish to endorse Sen's condition *L*? Why should I wish to insist not only that I should be able actually to decide what happens, e.g. whether my kitchen walls are pink or crimson, but also whether or not it will be 'socially better' that my walls be pink rather than crimson? On the face of it, the latter has less to do with individual autonomy than with megalomania. Surely it ought to be enough that I can decide what colour my kitchen walls are. To ask to be 'socially decisive' in the recondite sense given to that term by social choice theory seems ridiculously presumptuous.

Why would we want to make such a claim? The only explanation I can think of is that, given consequentialism, this is a way of squeezing in an area of moral indifference. But the trouble with this is that, while we may not want to insist that people have a *duty* to (say) act in accordance with the Pareto principle, we may often want to say that it would be a better state of the world if they did, and this possibility is denied by condition *L*.

---

[28] Sen, 'Liberty, Unanimity and Rights', p. 217.   [29] Ibid.

Thus, Sen has written that it could be that

while I would prefer you to read what I consider to be good literature as opposed to what appears to me to be muck, I do not want my preferences to count in the social evaluation as to whether it is better that you read good literature or bury yourself in muck. I might accept taste differences as legitimate and accept the greater relevance of your taste in matters that I agree are essentially your 'concern'.[30]

But the notion that what you read is your business does not entail *de gustibus non est disputandum*. Your taste should, if you insist on following it, have not merely greater but exclusive relevance to the question of what you actually do. But surely I must, if I believe that I have any judgements of taste about literature or colour schemes (as against merely 'knowing what I like'), apply *my* standards to your reading matter or your kitchen walls. If I believe that *Lady Chatterley* is muck, or that crimson walls are inappropriate to a kitchen, then that is what I think. I cannot be expected to change my mind merely because you happen to think otherwise.

Perhaps the underlying problem here is that the word 'preference' is being grossly overworked. Part of the logical positivist baggage that orthodox welfare economics carries around with it is the idea that judgements of better and worse have no cognitive content but are simply expressions of attitudes. Hence, they can be assimilated quite properly to other forms of preference. When we combine this with the other dogma derived (incorrectly) from crude verificationism to the effect that 'interpersonal comparisons of utility' are 'meaningless' (or themselves express a 'value judgement' construed as something without cognitive content), we get the characteristic form of post-Arrow welfare economics in which 'social welfare' is derived from some process of aggregating preferences.

Sen wants to challenge this kind of 'welfarism', but he is insufficiently iconoclastic. The conclusion he wishes to draw from the Paretian liberal dilemma is that we need more than utility information (i.e. in this case preference information) in order to assess social welfare. We need, for example, to know the source of the preference: why does the lewd prefer that the prude read *Lady Chatterley's Lover*? But what he does not challenge is the idea that moral or aesthetic judgements should be treated as preferences and put into an SWF. The only question he raises is whether all preferences should 'count in determining social choice'.[31] So, he implies, nosy (or at any rate

[30] Ibid. 236.   [31] Ibid.

nastily nosy) preferences should count less than 'personal' ones, or perhaps they should not count at all.

This, however, is an attempt to stop the mischief at too late a point. The move that should be blocked is the one that treats moral or aesthetic judgements as preferences to be cranked into an SWF along with other preferences. If I believe that *Lady Chatterley's Lover* is muck, or that crimson walls are unsuitable for a kitchen, then I presumably think it would be a better state of the world if you did not read *Lady Chatterley* or paint your kitchen walls crimson. But the fact that I believe that is not *itself* what makes it better—nor does it contribute even a tiny bit to making it better. If we add strict consequentialism, so that you have a duty to go for the best state of affairs possible, it will follow from my beliefs that you have a moral duty not to read *Lady Chatterley* or paint your kitchen walls crimson. But the ground for the duty is that (I believe) doing those things would bring about an inferior state of affairs to some other that it is open to you to bring about. The ground is *not* that I would 'prefer' you to refrain—or that I and many other judges of literature or colour schemes share the same 'preference'. I may not, indeed, have any preference in the matter at all, in any ordinary sense of the term. I may simply have formed a quite disinterested aesthetic judgement on the question of *Lady Chatterley* or crimson decor. I may not care a bit what you do, but that obviously doesn't give me any reason for withdrawing my judgement.

We might do better, if we are going to assimilate moral and aesthetic judgements to any other kind of thing, to assimilate them to beliefs about matters of fact. If I believe that the Sears Tower in Chicago is taller than the Eiffel Tower, we are presumably under no temptation to turn that into a statement of a preference. And if I have the (fairly incontrovertible) view that it is better that people believe what is true than what is false, it will follow that I think it would be better for people to believe that the Sears Tower is taller than the Eiffel Tower. But surely it should be plain here that they should (in my view) believe it because it is (in my belief) true—not to please me by falling in with my 'preference in the matter'.

Thus, the belief that it would be a better state of the world if you didn't read *Lady Chatterley's Lover* is itself a social welfare judgement, which I arrive at after taking account of the fact that you would like to read the book (and giving that whatever weight I think appropriate), the effects I think the book would have on you, and anything else that seems to me relevant. My belief is just that, and there is no reason on earth why anybody else (or I myself) should treat it as a preference and put it in with other preferences to determine what would advance 'social welfare'. I have already, *ex hypothesi*, taken account of everything I consider relevant in arriving at my judgement about where the social welfare lies. If somebody else were trying to form a judgement on this point, he too would have to form an opinion of what the book would do to you, find out if you wanted to read it, and so on. But he would be rather eccentric to take account of *my* judgement as an ingredient in *his* judgement about social welfare. (He might of course regard me as a literary, or moral, authority, but then he would follow my judgement in reaching his own, not incorporate it as a 'preference'.)

If Sen's concern is with the construction of SWFs out of ill-assorted materials, it is entirely well placed. Indeed, I hope it will not be too self-indulgent to point out that I said this myself, five years before Sen published his Paretian liberal paradox, in my *Political Argument*. In discussing majoritarianism—the idea that things should be done if a majority wants them done—I suggested that we should, if we apply the principle at all, count only privately orientated wants:

> The justification for counting only privately-oriented wants is that it avoids at one stroke the most objectionable feature of the majoritarian principle, namely the way in which it commits one to handing over questions of right and wrong, justice and injustice, to the majority of a group in which one's own voice counts only as one. Yet at the same time the amendment leaves one free to take account of desires which are put forward simply by people as wants in matters affecting themselves. This may seem high-handed at first sight, but further reflection suggests that what I have called 'publicly-oriented wants' are not actually put forward as wants at all. To treat them as wants is to degrade them and to fall into absurdity.
>
> Suppose that I am making up my mind whether it is fair for the *A*'s to get more of something than the *B*'s; and the *A*'s and the *B*'s are the only people directly affected by the division, in the sense of 'affected' which I have defined. Should I, in making up my mind, take account of the opinions of the *C*'s in the matter? I may, of course, let them weigh with me as having a certain authority, but surely it would be ridiculous to mix in the wants of the *C*'s for, say, the *A*'s to win, consequential on their belief that the *A*'s have the best case, on an equal footing with the privately-oriented wants of the *A*'s and *B*'s.[32]

The relevance of this for social choice theory is fairly radical, because it entails that we should reject the whole idea of aggregating preferences —including individuals' judgements about social welfare—into some

---

[32] B. M. Barry, *Political Argument* (London: Routledge and Kegan Paul, 1965), 63–4.

sort of *social* SWF. The error of supposing that this is a sensible thing to try to do goes back to Kenneth Arrow's book *Social Choice and Individual Values*[33] (though, as far as I can tell, no further). And a devastating criticism of it was made as early as the next year by Ian Little, who wrote:

[Arrow] calls his function both a social welfare function and a decision-making process. He believes that 'one of the great advantages of abstract postulational methods is the fact that the same system may be given different interpretations permitting a considerable saving of time.' Yes, but we must be careful not to give such a system a nonsensical interpretation, and it will be my contention that to interpret it as a social welfare function *is* to give a nonsensical interpretation.

Imagine the system as a machine which produces a card on which it is written '*x* is better than *y*,' or vice versa, when all individual answers to the question 'Is *x* better than *y*?' have been fed into it. What significance are we to attach to the sentence on the card, i.e. to the resulting 'master'-order? First, it is clear that the sentence, although it is a sentence employing ethical terms, is not a value *judgment*. Every value judgment must be *someone's* judgment of values. If there are *n* people filling in cards to be fed into the machine, then we have *n* value judgments, not *n* + 1. The sentence which the machine produces expresses a ruling, or decision, which is different in kind from what is expressed by the sentences fed into it. The latter express value judgments; the former expresses a ruling between these judgments. Thus we can legitimately call the machine, or function, a decision-making process.

But what would it mean to call the machine a social welfare function? One would be asserting, in effect, that if the machine decided in favour of *x* rather than in favour of *y*, then *x* would produce more social welfare than *y* or simply be more desirable than *y*. This is clearly a value judgment, but it is, of course, a value judgment made by the person who calls the machine a social welfare function.[34]

There is only one point on which I would like to modify what Little said. I do not think that it makes any more sense to say that individual judgements are aggregated into a ruling or decision than it does to say that they are aggregated into a social welfare judgement. What goes into a social decision (that is to say, a real decision with real effects) is votes, not expressions of views about social welfare. What comes out (say of referendums) are decisions but on what is to be done, not a ruling between competing judgements about what social welfare

[33] Kenneth J. Arrow, *Social Choice and Individual Values* (New York: John Wiley and Sons, 1951).
[34] I. M. D. Little, 'Social Choice and Individual Values', *Journal of Political Economy*, 60 (1952), 422–32, repr. in Brian Barry and Russell Hardin (eds.), *Rational Man and Irrational Society? An Introduction and Sourcebook* (Beverly Hills, Calif.: Sage, 1982), 269–82, at 275–6.

requires. To tie this together with the earlier discussion of (legal) rights, we may say that rights and votes go together in one box (the box marked 'control over actions') while judgements of social welfare go into another box. And this second box does not in addition contain anything corresponding to a vote tally. There simply is no such thing as a social welfare judgement compounded out of social welfare judgements. The thing is a logical monstrosity. As Little said, if you feel you should take account of other people's judgements of social welfare, not merely as suggesting where the truth lies but as preferences to be incorporated into your own 'social welfare function', that is logically possible—though, I would immediately wish to add, morally obtuse. But then the result of that process is *your* judgement about where the social welfare lies. It is not some sort of superordinate judgement that is nobody's judgement and everybody's judgement at the same time.

It may then be asked 'But what happens if the people in a society reach different conclusions about the social welfare?' The answer is, of course: what happens now. Different people do, indeed, disagree about what would make the world better. They argue about it, but there is no guarantee that they will finish up by agreeing. What we neither have nor could have is some algorithm for taking these divergent judgements and producing some 'social' judgement.

What we do need, in order to have a stable society, is a constitution that specifies how collectively binding *decisions* are to be taken. And if the society is to be liberal as well as stable, either the constitution or the legislation enacted under it should set out individual rights. But this is, again, in the sphere of control, not the sphere of judgement.

These rights, since they specify what actions people will be allowed to take without being exposed to legal or (in Mill's extension) social sanctions, have no direct connection with anybody's judgements about what makes a better or worse state of affairs. What Sen offers as his liberal principle—condition L—has no connection with rights, and thus no connection with liberalism à la Mill or Hayek. It is concerned with the relation between individual preferences and the SWF. There is, undeniably, a conflict between condition L and the Pareto principle, because they both deal in outcomes and set up contradictory criteria for a 'socially better' state of affairs. But this merely reinforces the point that condition L is not a liberal principle.

I fear that all this may appear like a minor skirmish on the borders of social choice theory, the details of which can be of no possible interest to anyone except Sen and myself. I want to emphasize that this is not so. If I am correct, the implication is that we cannot expect to get any help from social choice theory in analysing rights because the whole concept of social choice or social preference is too simple to accommodate the concept of a right. Sen's proffered translation of Mill and Hayek into the language of SWFs comes up with altogether the wrong kind of thing.

Since the world is full of social choice theorists and many of them are very clever, I had better be more specific. I do not see how one could deny in advance that it may be possible to carry out some complicated translation of what we actually want to say into some extension of the language of social choice. What I do feel fairly safe in denying is that the result will illuminate any significant problem in moral or political philosophy. Rather, it will continue to generate its own internal puzzles out of its own inadequacies.

The reason for this is that social choice theory is a theory producing orderings of outcomes (states of the world). But the theories we require must include concepts such as the right of an actor (which might be an individual or a collectivity like a governmental sub-unit or a country) to make certain choices, and the notion that an actor ought or ought not to do certain things within the range of things it has a right to do. These simply cannot be connected directly to a system for generating rankings of outcomes, which is what social choice theory is.

Thus, Sen's idea that the solution lies in changing the utility information (so that the lewd and the prude might choose not to have their nosy preferences counted in the SWF) is fundamentally misguided. For the question of the socially preferred outcome (according to the SWF) is different in nature from the question of the rights people should have. There is no need to mess about with the SWF. It may really be that the world would be a better place if the prude widened his horizons and the lewd did not skim novels for the dirty bits and that they are quite right in agreeing this is better than the reverse. But it does not follow that it is morally permissible for them to bring it about if that can be done only by interfering with one another's freedom. The whole idea of anti-paternalism is, after all, that some consequences admitted to be superior should not be brought about if the means are a reduction of freedom of choice. I believe myself that anti-paternalism has got completely out of hand when it issues in objections to the mandatory use of seatbelts or crash helmets. But hardly anybody would wish to say that a reduction in freedom of choice is *always* permissible (still less required) whenever it brings about better outcomes, and that is all we require for the present case.

The second claim mentioned at the beginning of this section is more substantively interesting, and is one that Sen himself has not explicitly defended, though, as I have noted, he has said that he thinks it can be defended. This is the claim that, when rights have been assigned in an ethically acceptable way, it may be wrong for one person to offer to use his rights in a certain way with the object of inducing another to use his rights in a way he would not otherwise choose. I have suggested that such cases can arise, but they all seem to be subsumable under the objection that the freedom to choose is more apparent than real.

It should be emphasized that a positive response to the second claim in no sense rehabilitates the 'liberal paradox'. Suppose we conclude for some reason that I ought not to offer you $10 never to wear that tie again even though I am clear that it would be worth it to me and even though you would be happy to close with the offer. We should not rush to the conclusion that Pareto optimality fails *because* it conflicts with the liberal principle establishing (among other things) your right to wear whatever tie you like. All that can be deduced is that not every Pareto-optimal outcome available under the system of designated rights should be brought about. But the rejection of the view that all Pareto-optimal moves are desirable is a position with respect to the use people ought to make of their rights. It is logically quite independent of the case for establishing rights. We could equally well support exactly the same system of rights and at the same time maintain that the more Pareto-optimal deals that are consummated the better.

If we support a set of rights but believe that not all Pareto-optimal moves are desirable, we will be committed to saying that sometimes people do things they have a right to do but that they should not do. If we support a set of rights and believe that Pareto optimality is one criterion of a desirable outcome, we will find ourselves saying that sometimes it would be better if people were to make some Pareto-optimal deal but that they have a right not to if they choose not to. Both positions are consistent.

Even if there is no logical connection there, it may be asked how my rather indulgent views of trades conforming to the Pareto principle can be reconciled with my earlier-expressed view that judgements about better or worse states of affairs (e.g. that it would be better if you did not read *Lady Chatterley*) should not be treated as preferences and cranked into an SWF. My answer is that there is no inconsistency here because the second question is not whether the fact that the prude thinks it is socially better for the lewd not to read *Lady Chatterley* provides a reason for somebody else (the lewd or anybody else forming a social welfare judgement) to conclude that it would be better for the lewd not to read it. (The prude must of course think it better, but not that it's better *because* he thinks it's better; rather that he thinks it's better because it *is* better.) The second question that I took up is, instead: given that (on the basis of the contingent offers) the prude wants to read *Lady Chatterley* and the lewd does not, is there any reason for us (or them) to conclude that they ought not to do so? In other words, this is a case where, *ex hypothesi*, each does have a preference for what the other does, and these preferences are so strong that each cares more about what the other reads than he does about what he reads himself. Given this highly unusual situation, the question is whether there is anything wrong in their doing what they both prefer, so that the prude reads and the lewd does not. My answer that this is probably all right, given the preferences, does not conflict with my view that the assignment of rights should be done on quite separate criteria from those on which we judge the use people make of them, and my view that in general judgements of social welfare should be distinguished from preferences. The lewd and the prude *do* have strong preferences as regards one another's behaviour; but that is no reason for concluding that beliefs about what is better or worse are usually no more than weaker preferences (or, as Hume might have said, calmer passions) than the kind of preference we may have for vanilla over strawberry ice-cream.

IV   PARADOX LOST

Those who have thought at all about the liberal paradox fall into two groups. There are those who are firmly convinced that it constitutes a serious problem for liberalism, at any rate if one accepts the principle of Pareto optimality, and find it hard to imagine how anyone can think otherwise; and there are those who do not see any incompatibility between liberalism and the Pareto principle, and find it hard to see how anyone could think that there is. As a result of hearing the arguments contained in this chapter, a number of people whose acumen I respect have moved from the first group to the second, but the point of interest here is that the process of conversion has in all cases been swift and painless, without any intermediate stage of doubt.

The explanation for this phenomenon is, I suggest, that everything depends on where you start from. If you begin by rejecting the premiss that individual decisiveness over the social welfare function is an inherent element in liberalism, you can accept the validity of Sen's proof without suffering a pang. From this point of view, the impossibility of reconciling condition *L* (or any variant on it) with Pareto optimality is of no concern, because condition *L* has no ethical significance in the first place.

If, however, you start from the premiss that liberalism requires individual decisiveness over the social welfare function, you are trapped in the labyrinth. The only means of escape appears to be to modify condition *L* in some way so as to render it compatible with Pareto optimality. Sen reviewed a number of these attempts at solving the problem in its own terms in 'Liberty, Unanimity and Rights'. Hardly surprisingly, he found them wanting. Every failed attempt at escape, however, reinforces the conviction that one has uncovered some deep contradiction in social choice theory.[35] Thus, in the commentary which Sen wrote on the original version of this chapter,[36] he incorporated chunks of boilerplate from earlier reviews of the literature which consisted of long series of references to articles related to the liberal paradox. Their function was, I think, intended to be to suggest that the liberal paradox must be a real problem to have collected such a large bibliography around it.

Another occupational risk from immersion in the literature is a tendency to assimilate a new criticism that challenges the framework to an old one that presupposes the framework. Sen's commentary also provides an example of this, and I think the point is worth pursuing, since it will enable me to set out as clearly as possible the distinctive nature of my line on the liberal paradox.

According to Sen, what I have done is to offer a solution to the problem that is similar in essence to that proposed by Robert Nozick.

---

[35] A parallel, and much more important, case is that of Arrow's General Possibility Theorem. Enormous efforts have gone into trying to modify Arrow's conditions so as to make them consistent with one another, and the negative results have reinforced the sense that Arrow's theorem is a major stumbling-block for the concept of social welfare. Yet, as I pointed out in section III of chapter 2 above, even if all of Arrow's conditions were fulfilled simultaneously, this would do nothing to guarantee that the outcome would increase social welfare on any interpretation of the words that was evaluatively significant. Thus, from Arrow's point of view, we have a determinate outcome whenever there are only two options to choose among and also whenever there are more than two but the preferences happen to be single-peaked. But the outcome preferred by a majority to the other(s) might be to exterminate all the members of the minority—scarcely a contribution to social welfare in any interesting sense of the expression!

[36] Amartya Sen, 'Foundations of Social Choice Theory: An Epilogue', in Jon Elster and Aanund Hylland (eds.), *Foundations of Social Choice Theory* (Cambridge: Cambridge University Press, 1986), 213–48, esp. 223–32.

Nozick's position is that, once a set of rights has been assigned to individuals, there is no room for a social welfare function. People must be allowed to do whatever they choose to do with their rights, and any authoritative social decision to the effect that one outcome is better than another must involve an interference with that free exercise of rights.[37]

Now it should be evident, even from this brief exposition, that Nozick implicitly accepts the premisses from which the liberal paradox is generated, in that he assumes an incompatibility between rights and a social welfare function. His 'solution' simply consists in saying 'So much the worse for the social welfare function'. In total contrast to this, what I am maintaining is that there is no way in which a social welfare function can be a threat to individual rights because the two things have different subject-matters. Rights are about what people should be allowed to do, whereas a social welfare function is about what constitutes a good state of affairs. Even if we endorse individual rights for consequentialist reasons only (because we mistrust the intelligence or goodwill of the state, or are concerned about costs of enforcement), we shall still often be led to conclude that people have used their rights on particular occasions in ways that make for a worse outcome than could have been achieved if they had done something else that was legally open to them. There is absolutely no incoherence in saying both that people should have rights that leave them with several options and also that the results of their using their rights will sometimes be less than optimal. It will sometimes be manifestly clear that a choice other than the one actually made would have brought about a better state of affairs. On occasion, the actor himself or herself may admit this.

To sum up, what I offer is not yet another 'solution' to the problem of the impossibility of a Paretian liberal. Instead, my argument is that there is no such problem. What the liberal paradox calls for is not solution but dissolution.

[37] Robert Nozick, *Anarchy, State, and Utopia* (New York: Basic Books, 1974), 165–6.

5

THE LIGHT THAT FAILED?

Alasdair MacIntyre's *After Virtue*[1] mounted a broad-ranging attack on modern liberal societies and their characteristic institutions such as bureaucracies and universities. The defects of liberal civilization were to be traced, according to MacIntyre, to the defects of its underlying philosophy, the doctrine of liberal individualism. In the preface to his recent *Whose Justice? Which Rationality?*[2] MacIntyre does such a good job of summarizing his conclusions and showing how the new book is intended to support them that I can do no better than quote from it. He tells us that in *After Virtue*

I concluded both that 'we still, in spite of the efforts of three centuries of moral philosophy and one of sociology, lack any coherent rationally defensible statement of a liberal individualist point of view' and that 'the Aristotelian tradition can be restated in a way that restores rationality and intelligibility to our own moral and social attitudes and commitments.' But I also recognized that these conclusions required support from an account of what rationality is, in the light of which rival and incompatible evaluations of the arguments of *After Virtue* could be adequately accounted for. I promised a book in which I should attempt to say both what makes it rational to act in one way rather than another and what makes it rational to advance and defend one conception of practical rationality rather than another. Here it is.[3]

It will come as no great surprise to readers of *After Virtue* that the possibility of rational enquiry depends upon 'a conception according to which the standards of rational justification themselves emerge from and are part of a history in which they are vindicated by the way in which they transcend the limitations of and provide remedies for the defects of their predecessors within the history of that same tradition' (p. 7).

The bulk of the book (fifteen of its twenty chapters) is devoted to

---

[1] Alasdair MacIntyre, *After Virtue* (Notre Dame, Ind.: University of Notre Dame Press, 1981).
[2] Alasdair MacIntyre, *Whose Justice? Which Rationality?* (Notre Dame, Ind.: University of Notre Dame Press, 1988).
[3] Ibid., p. ix. Subsequent references will appear in parentheses in the text.

four studies which are intended to substantiate that claim. The first follows through the development of ideas about justice and rationality from the Homeric period to Aristotle. The second analyses the new conceptions introduced by Augustine. The third expounds the synthesis between Augustine and Aristotle achieved by Aquinas. The fourth traces the path of the Scottish Enlightenment from its beginnings in Aristolelianism and Calvinist Augustinianism to the unstable formula produced by Hutcheson and on to the 'anglicizing subversion' carried out by Hume. Although MacIntyre says that other traditions such as the Jewish and Islamic, or those of India and China, might equally well have illustrated his theme (pp. 10–11), these four narratives, as presented by him, comprise a larger story of rise and decline: a progressive movement in Greek thought culminating in Aristotle; a new and necessary beginning incorporating Biblical elements in Augustine; a triumphant overcoming of the emergent problems of both Aristotelian and Augustinian traditions by Aquinas; and the degeneration of those same elements in Scotland (pp. 402–3).

In the course of these historical narratives, MacIntyre offers a number of controversial interpretations of the figures he discusses. His usual way of approaching some controversial point is to cite the adherents of the opposing positions and then to plump for one or the other position with very little in the way of independent argument for it. Given the scope of the enquiry undertaken in the book, this way of proceeding is reasonable and probably inevitable. But it does mean that, apart from whatever force MacIntyre's *ipse dixit* may have, a scholar who prefers the road not taken is given no reason for changing his or her mind. Disputes may of course occur about whether or not MacIntyre has taken the right side, but they are disputes to which MacIntyre himself has little to contribute.

For the purpose of this discussion, I think that the best way of dealing with these issues of scholarship is to stipulate that everything MacIntyre says on points of interpretation in the fifteen narrative chapters is correct. This will enable me to focus without any distractions on the issues that MacIntyre himself identified as central to his purposes in writing the book: the bankruptcy of 'liberalism' and the superiority of the 'Aristotelian tradition' as developed by Aquinas. If MacIntyre's conclusions on these points are found wanting while giving him the benefit of every possible doubt elsewhere, the case would presumably only be strengthened if MacIntyre were also found deficient in his interpretations.

Before getting to the main business, however, I should like to make a few general observations about MacIntyre's four studies. One is that, with the exception of some material on the origins of the Scottish Enlightenment that is rather slow going, the whole thing is written with the panache that we have come to expect of MacIntyre. Whether right or wrong he is constantly thought-provoking. An excellent example comes early on, when MacIntyre discusses alternative translations of a passage in the *Iliad* in which 'Achilles is poised for the moment between on the one hand drawing his sword in order to kill Agamemnon or on the other curbing his *thumos*' (p. 17). MacIntyre then quotes from George Chapman's translation of 1598 which so impressed Keats, Pope's translation of 1715, and a modern one by Robert Fitzgerald. As he points out, each renders the passage in terms of the psychology prevalent in his own time: Chapman 'ascribes to Achilles a "discursive part" and rival "thoughts" in his "mind".' According to Pope, Achilles is torn in eighteenth century fashion between reason and passion. And Fitzgerald portrays Achilles in the psychological style of the present age as subject to alternating impulses of passion' (p. 17).

As an illustration of the point that all language carries with it presuppositions, this could scarcely be bettered. But what implications, if any, does it have for the possibility of making one culture accessible to another? A good translation is a creative reconstruction in one language of ideas originally expressed in another and it must, of course, strive to make the original intelligible in terms that will make sense to its readers. The option of leaving a word like *thumos* untranslated and appending a long footnote to explain the underlying psychology would rightly be regarded as a cop-out. No similar inhibitions, however, beset someone who undertakes to explain a passage in one language, taking whatever space is required to do the job, in another language. And in fact MacIntyre seems, here and elsewhere, to perform that task quite successfully.

I mention this because it brings me to my second general observation, which is that there appears to me to be something of a tension between what MacIntyre says can be done and what he actually does. Thus, in his chapter 'Tradition and Translation' (pp. 370–88), MacIntyre argues that there is no reason for supposing that in principle one tradition can be understood by adherents of another unless they immerse themselves in it and learn its language as, in effect, a second first language (pp. 374–5). The general point may be conceded: the elephantine circumlocutions of the Public Orator of Oxford University in attempting to render into Latin the achievements of honorands from the natural sciences are enough to make the point. But, it may be asked, do not contemporary international languages such as English have the resources necessary for making intelligible other traditions?

MacIntyre denies this. Such languages are indeed relatively devoid of social context—this is the price they pay for their availability to people from a wide variety of backgrounds—but just for this reason they cannot but misrepresent languages (including English of an earlier time) that were the languages of definite communities.

In putting his case, however, MacIntyre helps himself liberally to the argument already mentioned about the impossibility of word-for-word translation. Obviously the possession of a list of 'useful phrases' such as 'Have a drink' in Irish and 'Don't shoot' in Vietnamese (MacIntyre's examples on p. 382) falls very short of the command of a language. But the relevant question here is, I suppose, one of whether, with enough time and patience, it is possible to lay out in modern English the conceptions of humanity, nature, and the gods that are presupposed in the particular utterances made in some language which is the bearer of a certain tradition.

There is an evident problem here in that any alleged example of the phenomenon, if once set out in English, refutes the claim. But presumably the longer someone is able to go on without being forced to admit defeat, the less plausible the claim of ultimate untranslatability becomes. Now MacIntyre himself goes on for a very long time. And if we follow MacIntyre's strict rule for differentiating languages, according to which there are not even 'such languages as classical Latin or early modern Irish' but only 'Latin-as-written-and-spoken-in-the-Rome-of-Cicero and Irish-as-written-and-spoken-in-sixteenth-century-Ulster' (p. 373), we may also say that he traverses a great many languages. Yet he never, as far as I can see, throws up his hands and protests that he is unable to explain what somebody had in mind using certain words in his own language.

My third and last observation grows to some extent from my second. As we have seen, MacIntyre insists that every tradition is bound by time and place as the tradition of a particular society. But if this is so, how far are we justified in detaching a tradition from its social matrix and presenting it as having applicability outside the form of society in which it originally flourished? This question is obviously relevant in any consideration of MacIntyre's claim that we would do well to abandon liberalism for Thomism. I shall return to it in that context. For the present, however, I simply want to point out that

MacIntyre gives very different answers for views with which he is in sympathy and those with which he is not.

The clearest contrast can be found between his treatment of Aristotle, the theorist to whom he is most indulgent, and Hume, who gets by far the harshest treatment of any figure discussed at length. There are notorious difficulties in making Aristotle palatable to contemporary sensibilities (sensibilities which are shared by Mac-Intyre), notably Aristotle's view that there are slaves by nature and his conception of the proper position of women. MacIntyre acknow-ledges these difficulties but, like the Scottish preacher, having looked them firmly in the face he passes on, saying that 'it seems clear' that 'such assertions can be excised from Aristotle's thought without denying his central claims about the best kind of *polis*' (p. 105). In this context, he advises his readers that they can 'see for another view' Susan Okin's book, but he does not actually discuss it.[4] Nor shall I. But, bearing in mind how rooted Aristotle's sociology is in biology, it seems fair to say that there is unquestionably a good deal of generosity required in saying that Aristotle's ideas about natural slaves and women are non-essential aspects of his political theory.

In stark contrast, Hume is presented as entirely a creature of his social milieu, or even more precisely that into which he hoped to propel himself. Thus MacIntyre makes much of Hume's discussion of the objects of pride, such as his assertion that 'the first mechanic that invented a fine scritoire, produc'd pride in him, who became possessed of it' (p. 294). But how essential to Hume's overall political theory is the notion that the owner rather than the maker feels pride in a fine piece of workmanship? Suppose the maker were the only one to feel pride in the object, and the owner simply enjoyed having it. Surely this would still be quite enough to underwrite what Hume needs in order to get his theory of justice going, namely, that property is an ever-present source of potential conflict in a society.

It is only, I believe, by using standards very different from those employed in relation to Aristotle that MacIntyre is able to claim that Hume's theory is limited in application to 'the type of social and cultural order . . . constituting the highly specific way of life of the eighteenth-century English landowning class and its clients and dependents' (p. 295). This is not, of course, to go to the opposite extreme and say that Hume's theory is equally applicable to all times and places, a false dichotomy exploited by MacIntyre (p. 295). But

[4] Susan Moller Okin, *Women in Western Political Thought* (Princeton, NJ: Princeton University Press, 1979), ch. 4.

one indication of the way in which Hume's ideas are less limited than MacIntyre alleges is that his arguments in favour of stability of possessions and against desert and equality as alternative criteria are still the staple of conservative thought today. (It could be argued that Hayek's Nobel Prize should have been awarded posthumously to Hume.)

I want now to turn to what MacIntyre has to say about liberalism. This is very much a continuation of the line taken in *After Virtue* that the 'Enlightenment project' of tradition-free rationality was doomed from the start, and that contemporary liberalism is by its nature incapable of reaching definite conclusions on any controversial public policy issue. In his preface, however, MacIntyre says that he wishes 'to emphasize the fact that this book can be read and evaluated without any knowledge of *After Virtue*' (p. x), and I shall follow him in treating the present book as a self-contained entity, if only for reasons of space.

The relevant chapter here is entitled 'Liberalism Transformed into a Tradition' (pp. 326–48), and that is a pretty good summary of its argument. Liberalism, MacIntyre says, could not possibly deliver on its initial promise of providing us with conceptions of rationality and justice that were unfettered by any tradition. For there is no way in which such a promise could possibly be fulfilled. What actually happened in face of its failure to live up to its promises was that liberalism, instead of going away, itself became a tradition. It is, however, a highly unsatisfactory tradition because it contains within itself unresolved conflicts of principle. Not only are these unresolved but, MacIntyre maintains, nobody even expects them to be resolved. The public culture of liberalism is now, therefore, one which is actually defined by the presence of interminable disagreement. This disagreement reassures people that liberalism is still going strong, but actually what it means is that it is incapable of sustaining rational discussion.

If liberalism really depended on the possibility of pulling itself up by its own bootstraps, as MacIntyre suggests, it would indeed be a vastly implausible doctrine. Obviously, no proposed conceptions of rationality or justice could hope to gain adherents unless they made contact with existing conceptions: if they did not, what reason would there be for calling them concepts of rationality or justice in the first place? All we would have would be a mere arbitrary annexation of the words. Moral reformers, however radical, never start completely from scratch. Rather, they reject some existing ideas while at the same time extending the scope or increasing the importance of others. (Thus, for example, classical utilitarianism is what we get by building up the well-established virtue of benevolence at the expense of competing virtues.)

MacIntyre himself says that traditions begin in practice and only later develop systematic intellectual underpinnings. This is true of liberalism too in that its main elements were originally adopted for reasons that made sense to people in terms of existing outlooks. Religious toleration seemed better than religious warfare, constitutionalism arose from the desire of various interests to protect themselves, and so on. Later on people like Kant and Mill came along and offered general theories from which, they claimed, the characteristic liberal prescriptions could be derived. As MacIntyre says, the debate at this level continues in the academic journals, and we can if we like say that liberalism has in this sense been transformed into a tradition.

Taking a tradition to be constituted by a continuity of discourse within which certain premises are taken for granted and certain texts regarded as having special authority, then liberalism surely is a tradition. For example, a submission to *Philosophy & Public Affairs* or *Ethics* that consisted in the derivation of various moral conclusions from some form of religious fundamentalism would be so far from the shared premises of all previous contributors that it simply would not get a look in.[5] This, however, suggests two reflections. The first is that liberalism as a tradition is scarcely as vacuous as MacIntyre claims it is. The second is that it cannot be true, as MacIntyre claims, that liberalism is the overwhelmingly dominant public culture of countries such as the United States. For although the Reverend Jerry Falwell may be wrong in claiming a 'moral majority', it is at any rate true that he does not lack for followers.

These remarks bring me to my most serious complaint against MacIntyre, which is that in contrasting liberalism with his other traditions he does not play fair. He fails to compare like with like. MacIntyre's 'traditions' are highly artificial after-the-fact constructs in which those who are now seen (but were not necessarily seen at the time) as the Big Names respond in sequence to the perceived inadequacies of their predecessors' theories. Liberalism, in complete contrast, is defined implicitly as the sum total of all the ideas going around in contemporary 'liberal societies'—those of North America, Western Europe, and Australasia. Given that these are the terms of

---

[5] I may perhaps add that during my three years as editor of *Ethics* no such issue ever arose because no such submission was ever received.

comparison, it is hardly surprising that liberalism does not make a good showing.

Suppose we were to treat thirteenth-century Christendom on all fours with MacIntyre's treatment of liberalism. The first thing we would have to observe is that the vast majority of the population would never even have heard the names of Augustine and Aristotle. Their beliefs would presumably have been of a local traditional kind tinctured with whatever Christian doctrine they had assimilated. In the universities, meanwhile, I should imagine that exactly the complaint made by MacIntyre against contemporary academic philosophy might equally well have been made then: that the disagreements were apparently unending in that no definite conclusions were ever settled on. It is, of course, true that Saint Thomas was grinding out the *Summa*, but MacIntyre himself calls attention (pp. 206–7) to the failure of the Thomist synthesis to achieve general acceptance either at the time or in the following centuries.

We can also carry out the reverse exercise and ask how liberalism would look if it were given a treatment parallel to that bestowed by MacIntyre on the other traditions. The proportion of Kantians and utilitarians in the total population of a modern so-called liberal society is probably of the same order as the proportion of Aristotelians and Augustinians in thirteenth-century Christian societies. Just as popular beliefs then were a jumble of Christian and pre-Christian ideas, so popular ideas now are a jumble of Christian and post-Christian ideas (plus some pre-Christian survivals such as astrology). But if we follow MacIntyre's methodology we shall disregard all this and concentrate on academic philosophy. Here we might distinguish two variants of liberalism, utilitarianism and Kantianism, in the same spirit as that in which MacIntyre distinguished Augustinian and Aristotelian variants of Christianity in the thirteenth century. We could trace the history of each as a self-conscious tradition, with its own internally generated problems and proposed solutions. We could also analyse the relations between the two traditions, in the same way as MacIntyre does for the Aristotelian and Augustinian traditions. And, finally, we could present *A Theory of Justice* as our contemporary *Summa*.

MacIntyre concedes that the liberal tradition still awaits a treatment on the lines of his accounts of the four traditions he does discuss in depth. I have obviously done no more than gesture in the direction of such an account. But I see no reason for doubting that in sympathetic hands utilitarianism and Kantianism might be made to look like traditions worthy of respect.

For MacIntyre it is of crucial importance whether or not this is so. The final sentence of the book runs as follows: 'The rival claims to truth of contending traditions of enquiry depend for their vindications upon the adequacy and the explanatory power of the histories which the resources of each of those traditions in conflict enable their adherents to write' (p. 403). In speaking in the previous sentence of the 'emerging Thomistic conclusion' which the process of writing histories will 'confirm or disconfirm' (p. 403), MacIntyre presupposes that liberal history is not going to be very impressive. Yet it seems to me that in the chapter devoted to his attack on liberalism he does not really offer much in the way of support for this negative expectation.

In the end, the point that MacIntyre keeps harping on is that liberalism cannot live up to its own claims for itself: there is no way in which its correctness can be demonstrated to the satisfaction of every rational person, where 'rationality' is understood in a stripped-down way that precludes any appeal to tradition. Now I have already said that liberalism developed not as an a priori doctrine but as an attempt (or more precisely as a set of alternative attempts) to rationalize an emergent liberal social order. In the course of offering such rationalizations some liberal thinkers have made claims of the kind MacIntyre describes, and others have not. I see no reason for defining liberalism so that it must include such claims. Rather, it seems to me that we recognize liberal theories by their substantive content. Some writers will call upon natural rights, some will appeal to sentiments of benevolence, some will argue from hypothetical agreements (which need not be between disembodied beings), some will employ the idea of a categorical imperative, while others will eschew any basis of these kinds and start from specific judgements or 'intuitions' that they hope will be widely shared. Some of these formulations lend themselves to claims about the dictates of pure reason but others emphatically do not. It is surely plain that there is no party line on foundations among liberals. Liberalism does not therefore stand or fall with the viability of the 'Enlightenment project'.

Inasfar as MacIntyre homes in on anything in particular as epitomizing liberal political philosophy, it is on the idea of equality plus neutrality explicitly formulated in those terms by Ronald Dworkin but present (with much else) in Rawls's theory (pp. 342–5). MacIntyre identifies this theory with liberalism and fathers it on all prior liberals. This is highly misleading since I do not think that any of the historical figures he mentions (Kant, Jefferson, and Mill—see p. 344) would have endorsed it. Nor would most liberals today share

Dworkin's or Rawls's problems about subsidizing the arts publicly or protecting ancient buildings and areas of natural beauty.

We should recall in this context that for MacIntyre liberalism consists of the whole public culture of modern societies. Thus he says that 'the contemporary debates within modern political systems are almost exclusively between conservative liberals, liberal liberals, and radical liberals' (p. 392). Yet Dworkin, in the article in which he identified liberalism with the formula of equality plus neutrality, made it clear that what he was intending to capture was the underlying principle of New Deal liberalism, which he explicitly contrasted with what is currently called conservatism in the United States.[6] And Rawls, however he may understand his own project, has been understood by everyone since the publication of *A Theory of Justice* to be offering a rationale for the centre left of the Democratic party.

Leaving this aside for the moment, what does MacIntyre think is wrong with liberalism so conceived? His complaint is that 'the principles which inform [the] practical reasoning and the theory and practice of justice within [a liberal] polity are not neutral with respect to rival and conflicting theories of the human good. Where they are in force they impose a particular conception of the good life, of practical reasoning, and of justice upon those who willingly or unwillingly accept the liberal procedures and the liberal terms of debate. . . . The starting points of liberal theorizing are never neutral as between conceptions of the human good; they are always liberal starting points' (p. 345). Suppose that all of this is true (and I think it certainly is). In what way does it constitute a *criticism* of liberalism? MacIntyre can hardly complain about a tradition's imposing its own 'conception of the good life, of practical reasoning, and of justice' on everyone, since the Aristotelian, Augustinian, and Thomist traditions that he thinks well of do exactly that—indeed, that is the point of them. The complaint must therefore be that there is some objection to liberalism in particular having these features, but MacIntyre doesn't tell us what it is, and I am unable to see that there is any. That the formula of equality plus neutrality is incompatible with, say, a theocracy (whether headed by a pope or an ayatollah) is so patently obvious that it would have to be a very fainthearted liberal who was embarrassed by the fact.

I can only assume that in thinking this is a problem for liberalism MacIntyre is once again relying upon the idea that liberalism must

---

[6] Ronald Dworkin, 'Liberalism', in Stuart Hampshire (ed.), *Public and Private Morality* (Cambridge: Cambridge University Press, 1978), 113–43.

include in it the claim that its conclusions can be derived from a contextless notion of rationality as such. This claim I have already rejected in its general form, but I may add that it is quite absurd in relation to Dworkin and Rawls in particular. Thus, Dworkin's paper 'Liberalism' starts from the existence of a 'New Deal settlement' and asks what under contemporary conditions the continuation of that line of policy would be. In order to answer this he extracts from the New Deal settlement the principle of equality plus neutrality, and then proposes that this should be applied to currently controverted issues.[7] The whole procedure is impeccably MacIntyrean: the problem posed is how to continue the tradition. There is no suggestion that every rational being should subscribe to the New Deal settlement; the paper is addressed to those who do subscribe to it but are confused about its current policy implications. Rawls is a more protean figure, but we should recall that in *A Theory of Justice* he made it clear that his object was to provide a coherent basis for a set of essentially liberal convictions.[8] And in his later writings he has made it quite explicit that his work is addressed to modern liberal–democratic societies. I believe that he is excessively optimistic in supposing that his premisses are shared so widely in his own society, but that does not matter here. The point is that Rawls makes no claim that he could demonstrate the correctness of his theory to anyone in the world, irrespective of that person's existing beliefs.

There remains MacIntyre's complaint that philosophy journals do not produce a consensus on issues of public policy. But here again we must insist on making fair comparisons. The kind of question that MacIntyre has in mind is 'Does justice require that I participate in or oppose this war?' 'Is positive discrimination in favor of members of hitherto oppressed and deprived groups in appointing to this job now an injustice?' (p. 393). No doubt liberal philosophers (and members of the same school such as utilitarians or Kantians) would disagree about such questions. But have we any good reason for supposing that the range of disagreements would be any smaller among Aristotelians, Augustinians, or Thomists? It is significant that MacIntyre makes no effort himself to suggest how these traditions might be made to yield definitive answers to questions such as those that he poses. If he did, I predict that he would be forced to conclude that there is always room for some dispute in getting from the general to the particular. For

[7] Ibid. 113–43.
[8] John Rawls, *A Theory of Justice* (Cambridge, Mass.: Harvard University Press, 1971).

there are too many issues of fact and interpretation that come between the principles and the policies to permit all answers but one to be ruled out.

What we should be interested in is the range of disagreement, and here I think that MacIntyre's example of reverse discrimination is actually rather favourable to liberalism. For there is a broad liberal consensus on equal opportunity. The differences of opinion arise over the degree to which background inequalities that affect people's chances in a competition have to be equalized, and over the legitimacy of short-run remedial measures such as reverse discrimination. Seen from a broad perspective in which we think of all the ways in which societies have disposed of desirable positions (heredity, sale, patronage, and so on), the dispute about discrimination looks like a very parochial squabble among people all committed to the ideal of equal opportunity. I wonder if any of MacIntyre's other traditions could narrow down the range of disagreement to anything like the same degree? As far as war is concerned there is no doubt that liberals disagree about the legitimacy of some wars (e.g. the Vietnam War or the Falkland Islands war) but the history of just-war doctrines does not suggest that any other tradition would find these questions any easier.

My conclusion is, then, that MacIntyre has not in the end given anyone attached to liberalism any good reason for faltering. The case for MacIntyre's own 'emerging conclusion' in favour of Thomism rests on its ability to overcome problems within its Aristotelian and Augustinian heritage. But this scarcely seems good enough. We should surely begin by asking whether it makes any sense to suggest that modern societies should be reconstructed on a model that would entail rolling back not only the Enlightenment but the Reformation (Thomist justice, MacIntyre tells us, includes in it the temporal supremacy of the Pope—see p. 201). The problem is akin to that of 'keeping 'em down on the farm after they've seen Paree,' but on a *much, much* bigger scale.

Modern societies are liberal—to the extent that they are—for the extremely good reason that the only alternative would be civil strife that would make the Thirty Years War look like a picnic. MacIntyre observes that it is 'a feature of all those traditions with whose histories we have been specifically concerned that in one way or another all of them have survived so as to become not only possible, but actual, forms of practical life within the domain of modernity' (p. 391). Thus, 'there are religious and educational communities of Thomistic Christians as well as others kinds of Augustinian Christians, both

Catholic and Reformed' (p. 392). This is indeed so. For although liberalism does presuppose a theory of the good, it is one in which freedom plays a central role, and this includes the freedom to create a community based upon non-liberal principles. But the step from Thomism as the basis for a voluntary community to Thomism as the basis for a whole society is an immense one. The possibility of the first tells us nothing about the practicability of the second. It seems to me that, starting with the societies we actually have now, MacIntyre's Thomistic alternative to liberalism is a non-starter.

6

TRAGIC CHOICES

Tragic Choices, by Guido Calabresi and Philip Bobbitt, is an unusually serious effort at relating the principles discussed by political philosophers to real issues in public policy.[1] It continues, with good reason, to be widely cited. I want here to raise two questions that are central to the interpretation and evaluation of the book. First, I shall analyse the notion of a tragic choice. I shall argue that the definition proposed by the authors is methodologically inconvenient and depends on implicit and highly controversial philosophical premises. Second, I shall take up some points in the substantive chapters and argue in particular that the authors give unnecessary hostages to economic orthodoxy by failing to recognize where it has valid arguments and by making errors in economic analysis themselves which, although they are not crucial to their general case, will tend to discredit it with economists. Since I sympathize with the overall thrust of their challenge to the apostles of the market, my aim here is the constructive one of trying to strengthen it by detaching it from various assertions and denials that seem to me unfounded.

I   THE CONCEPT OF A TRAGIC CHOICE

What makes a choice a 'tragic' one? One way in which we can approach this question is by way of ostensive definition. What are the actual examples of tragic choices cited in the book? I have tried to collect together all the references to cases in the book, and, although I cannot claim that the list is exhaustive, I do not think that any example discussed for a full paragraph or more has escaped me.

Because it is given the fullest treatment, is referred to the most often, and is described by Calabresi and Bobbitt as 'paradigmatic' (p. 177), pride of place should go to the provision of haemodialysis machines (artificial kidneys). More generally, scarce medical resources are also referred to a number of times, and occasionally other examples such as iron lungs and cardiac shunt operations are

---

[1] Guido Calabresi and Philip Bobbitt, *Tragic Choices* (New York: W. W. Norton and Co., 1978). Page references in the text are to this book.

mentioned. Following haemodialysis and its attendant medical cases, we can rank roughly level two others: the military draft (including such questions as the right to buy substitutes) and the right to have children. These three cases, or sets of cases, account for almost all the space given to examples. Of the rest, only one gets any extended analysis, namely, immigration policy in the United States, and it is not altogether clear whether this is regarded as lying within the sphere of tragic choices or as illustrating the more general point that in many areas collective choices cannot but display a differential value placed on the characteristics of different people. The others to get at least a little discussion are: the provision of grade crossings as a road safety measure; the death penalty; distributing food in a famine or water in a drought; choosing occupants of a lifeboat if there is not enough space for all; and choosing subjects for medical experimentation. Others are only mentioned in passing: adoption; child custody; quarantine; what to do about hostages; and abortion. Again, however, it may be that not all of these are to be thought of as examples of tragic choices but rather as illustrations of more general features that tragic choices share: not enough is said to make this clear.

Based on this list, and the order of priority given to the examples within it, we might plausibly construct a definition along the following lines:

A 'tragic choice' is one involving life and death (at least probabilistically) or—less centrally—other vital personal goods such as childbearing, where alternative technically feasible policies will have the effect (whether or not they have the intention) of distributing these goods and bads (or the probability of incurring them) in different amounts and/or in different ways among individual recipients.

The various features of this definition are drawn up with an eye on the list so as to get the right inclusions and exclusions. I think that the definition I have put forward would specify a field of enquiry which, while not self-contained (since whatever might be said of things falling within it would also be true of some others outside), has enough interesting special features to be worth picking out for special study.[2] We might denote it by the oversimplified but adequately mnemonic tag 'life and death cases'.

Although I believe that Calabresi and Bobbitt would have done well

---

[2] An illustration of the fact that there is, as it were, a rational core to this way of grouping subjects for analysis is perhaps suggested by the fact that the authors' list has much in common with the list of cases discussed by Jonathan Glover in his *Causing Death and Saving Lives* (Harmondsworth: Penguin Books, 1977).

to adopt some such definition of the sphere of tragic choices as I have just put forward, the course they in fact follow is quite otherwise. According to them there is no such thing, strictly speaking, as a tragic *situation*. Tragedy, rather, is coextensive with the existence of irreconcilable values in some matter. (In spite of this they do in fact quite often talk about 'tragic situations', but I take it that they would say that such talk is to be understood as shorthand, where the unpacked form would be something like 'a situation in which, according to some given set of values, unresolvable value conflicts come into play'.) Since the book is about social policy, rather than individual decisionmaking (e.g. a certain individual's decision as to whether or not to stop smoking or to wear a seat belt), the locus of these conflicts must be 'society'. But such a manner of speaking involves a crucial ambiguity. We might say that a society is subject to irreconcilable conflict when different groups within it have different views and these are held in an absolute way that does not permit compromise (e.g. the 'right to life' vs. the 'right to choose' in contemporary American sloganeering about abortion). But the same phrase might mean instead that the individuals within the society hold irreconcilable values. And, of course, there could be a combination of both phenomena at the same time in the same society, with some irreconcilable conflicts between different people and others within some individuals.

Unfortunately, Calabresi and Bobbitt do not address this issue frontally, and I think that their analysis gains a certain unwarranted plausibility from their implicitly playing fast and loose with the distinction between distributive and collective sense of the word 'we'. They tend to imply that 'we' are subject to such and such a conflict, where the reality would perhaps more plausibly be put by saying not that each and every one of us is subject to it but that society as a whole is subject to conflict between its members.[3]

---

[3] The most relevant statement comes right at the beginning of the book, where it is said that 'the use of examples may lead the reader to conclude that what we mean by tragic is subjective to each individual, that tragic choices are those that each of us finds appalling. Instead, we intend to discuss the tragedies of cultures; it is the values accepted by a society as fundamental that mark some choices as tragic. The critic of social values may object strongly to decisions his society finds quite acceptable, and readily approve of other choices that his society must make and yet cannot stomach; moreover, he may be right. But it is not with him or with our own imperatives that we are concerned; it is rather with those choices which the society finds intolerable' (pp. 17–18). A contrast is drawn here between what a 'society' or 'culture' finds 'acceptable' or 'intolerable' and what individuals—presumably members of that society or culture—believe about the same matters. This might make it sound as if the societal or cultural conflict is between rather than within individuals. But I think that the more plausible reading is that there are widespread though not universal beliefs held by the members of the society or culture that give

I shall return to this point in a little while. Before doing so, however, I should ask how the author's explicit definition of a tragic choice in terms of value conflicts (pp. 17–19, 22–3, 149–50, 195–6) relates to the definition in terms of 'life and death cases' that, I have already said, fits the authors' actual list of examples. If I am right in thinking that at least some of their illustrations of irreconcilable conflict of values are not intended to be 'tragic' ones, the implication must be that a 'tragic choice' is defined neither simply as a life-and-death case, nor simply as a value conflict case, but as a case of unresolvable value conflict *in the context of* a life-and-death case. If this is so, it of course raises the question of why the intersection of these two sets should be taken as the subject of special study and given the special name 'tragic choices'. The answer could be that life-and-death cases provide a particularly convenient context in which to study unresolvable value conflicts because of the extra urgency of such conflicts in these cases and hence the extra effort that is likely to go into trying to cope with them. Such an answer, if given, would seem to me quite reasonable.

Having said that, however, I must return to the question of whether it would not be better to focus on the way in which societies deal with life-and-death problems, leaving it open as to whether (or how frequently) there are irreconcilable conflicts, and studying the process just as seriously whether there are or not. There are two reasons for preferring such a course to the one actually followed in this book. The first is that it seems to me inconvenient to have one's subject matter so liable to come and go depending on what people think. If some particular question (e.g. provision of expensive medical care) is seen in some societies at times as involving a 'tragic choice' but in others as not (because 'everybody' agrees that it should go to those who can afford it, or to a privileged racial minority only), is that a sound methodological basis for studying the allocation in the first set of cases but not the second? I do not see that it is.

My second point about the idea of tragic choices, as formulated by Calabresi and Bobbitt, is that it seems to me to rest on a suspect ethical assumption. Of course, values conflict, in the sense that there are always, say, problems of equitable distribution versus perverse incentives, or between process values (e.g. fair trial, individual liberties) and outcome values (e.g. reducing crime, cutting the accident toll). But why should this everyday fact be taken to give rise to the

rise to conflicts within those individuals, and that these occasion the 'tragic choices' to be discussed in the book.

conclusion that all we can do is 'limit the spreading stain' (pp. 149–50) or that 'we cannot be barred from using flawed methods since they are all we shall have in the tragic situation' (pp. 61–2)? Why cannot we simply determine in some case what is the best thing to do, taking account of the relevant values? The results may indeed excite emotion, but must we accept that, when the decision is to provide some with dialysis but not all, the authors' quotation from an article on Greek tragedy is appropriate? 'We have a prospect of insuperable moral difficulty, a nightmare of injustice in which the assertion of any right involves further wrong, in which fate is set against fate in an intolerable necessary sequence of violence' (p. 18). It is important to recognize that this is not just a matter of rhetorical excess. Unless the 'tragic choices' analysed by Calabresi and Bobbitt really have this property, much of what they say in the book ceases to be convincing.

There is a large problem lurking here. As is well known, some philosophers hold that in any situation, however sticky, there is always a (relatively) best thing to do. There cannot be a situation in which all alternatives are wrong. Even if every alternative conflicts with a 'prima facie duty', there has to be one that is less bad than the others. That is the alternative which one ought 'all things considered' to choose. The competing view is that in some situations whatever is chosen will be wrong. But this claim is quite plausibly qualified by saying that such a situation can arise only because of the wrongdoing of somebody (who may or may not be the agent), so there is no inconsistency in the moral system considered as one of 'strict compliance'. For example, if you promise to do something intrinsically wrong you must either break a promise or do something wrong. If you make two incompatible promises you must break one. But you are at fault for getting into the situation in the first place. If you are forced to choose between complying with a hijacker's demand or allowing innocent people to be killed, it might be held that either choice is wrong; but you would not be faced with the choice except for the unjust acts of the hijacker. And so on.

It appears to me that the strongest reason for adopting the second view is an unwillingness to concede that one can lightheartedly do something terrible if it is the best thing in the situation. But there is no need to be lighthearted about it. Someone who says that there is always a best thing to do can perfectly well still feel remorse if the choice is between bads but the situation could have been avoided by different action earlier, or regret if the choice is forced by the wrong action of another. But suppose we have a 'trolley case'[4] where none of this applies (the runaway trolley is not due to poor maintenance or a malicious attempt at homicide), then should one feel guilty about switching the trolley from a track that kills six to a track that kills one? It seems not. Remorse or even regret seem out of place—only the feeling that the situation is unfortunate though nobody's fault.

Calabresi and Bobbitt create the impression that life-and-death situations are liable to involve tragic choices in their sense by making a move that seems to me illegitimate. This is the claim, frequently repeated in this book, that there is a widespread social or cultural value to the effect that human life is priceless and should be saved at any cost, however high. 'Our values and institutions depend on the notion that life is beyond price' (p. 39). But we surely ought to ask whether there is any such commitment to the infinite value of life, that no sacrifice is too great to save life, and so on. We do not act as if we thought so, and, although this is more difficult to prove, I do not believe that we think it either. I am inclined to think that the idea is a piece of sentimentality that simply will not stand up to scrutiny.

Since Calabresi and Bobbitt offer no evidence in favour of the claim that there is such an absolute value in 'our' society and culture, I shall not try to assemble any evidence to the contrary. But I do want to point out how central it is to their argument. Thus, to return again to the statement (pp. 61–2) that 'we cannot be barred from using flawed methods since they are all we shall have in the tragic situation', we may ask: Why so? In my view this has not been established by any argument of a specific nature. For anything specific said to the contrary, one is free to believe that the right method can be used in the right kind of case. No: the assertion is really a dogma derived from the idea that no outcome can be justified if it causes some to live and some to die, because life has 'infinite value'. If we drop this assumption, there will still indeed be tough choices to be made, but it does not follow that any procedure for carrying them out must be flawed.

This point can be pursued further in the context of the authors' summary (on pp. 49–50) of what is wrong with each of the 'pure' allocational procedures. In each case, the notion of the 'infinite value of life' is pressed into service—and since no procedure can possibly

---

[4] 'Trolley cases' involve the dilemma of someone standing by the switching gear when a runaway trolley comes down the track. The case envisaged in the text is one where, if the points are left as set, six people at the end of the track will be killed; if the trolley is switched to the other track one person at the end of that track will be killed. Those unfamiliar with contemporary moral philosophy may perhaps be surprised to learn that there is an entire literature devoted to 'trolley problems'.

satisfy that without sacrificing every other possible value, this makes it easy to show that each procedure is, when measured against 'our' or 'society's' values, defective. In each case, Calabresi and Bobbitt mention other problems with each method of allocation, but if we subtract the 'infinite value of life' point from each, we have what seems to me a much more tractable problem in which values will have to be traded off against one another.

I wish to suggest that this notion of tragic choices infects the whole analysis with a kind of fundamental irrationalism. For if life and death cases are indeed (at least potentially) tragic in the sense defined—'a nightmare of injustice in which the assertion of any right involves a further wrong'—all we can do in order to escape intolerable psychological pressure is try to pretend that they don't exist. And, much of the time, the book gives the impression that that is what it is about: not how societies cope with tragic choices but how they attempt to deny their existence. It is not very easy to show this by selective quotation, but I think that anyone who has read the book is likely to have come away from it with the feeling that the book is about fudging rather than facing policy choices in life-and-death cases.

There is, however, an apparent difficulty in treating value conflicts as a source of psychic strain or discomfort. If what really drives social policy is cognitive dissonance reduction, why should societies go to such lengths to accommodate the conflicting values or to arrange institutions so that the conflict is not too overt? Surely it would have been much easier (not to mention cheaper) to change one's values so as to avoid the discomfort in the first place.

If this move is resisted (and I agree that it should be) this is presumably because people not only want to avoid discomfort but really do hold the values. But then we can ask whether they *ought* to hold those values. It may be possible to convince them not to hold a value such as that of the infinite value of life, but to accept that trade-offs are unavoidable and should be faced rationally. Institutional changes may still be required to get to a good trade-off, but this is different from trying to make the problem disappear by sleight of hand. The way in which Calabresi and Bobbitt set it up, the principles tend to be rather crude. A lot of room is then left for juggling to accommodate them, and this is presented as a fairly irrational business. For example: *either* we give all lives a single (maybe implicit) monetary value and trade off between intensive care units, ambulance services, biomedical research, elimination of grade crossings, median barriers on highways, safety of nuclear power plants, aeroplane safety (etc.) *or* we simply follow different strategies in different areas and avoid noticing that this is 'irrational'. The alternative which I would prefer is to try to make sense of the relevant distinctions between different kinds of situations, then see if there are still inconsistencies in the ways in which we deal with them. For example, we might conclude that there is a relevant difference between an improbable large catastrophe and the certainty of a small number of deaths, even if the 'expected' loss of life (i.e. number discounted by probability) is equal. Or we might decide that it makes a difference whether people have a choice of assuming a risk in return for a benefit to them or not. Having done this, we might still conclude that in a relatively narrow area (e.g. medical) or even narrower (e.g. the distribution of services in hospitals) there are inconsistencies that cannot be accounted for by invoking any plausibly relevant differences. But we shall have got away from the simplistic idea (common among economists) that a society must be 'irrational' if the value it implicitly assigns to saving a life is different in different areas.

I believe that the appropriate approach is one combining 'interpretative charity' with independent standards of judgement. That is, I think that it is important to try to see what can be made of the discriminations between cases that people (including ourselves in off-duty moments) feel inclined to make, rather than simply imposing some schematic formula and dismissing any distinctions that cannot be fitted in. But at the same time I see no reason for accepting our unreflective judgements as the last word. Surely it ought to be possible by thinking systematically about things to refine our ideas. That is at any rate the minimally rationalistic premiss from which I would start.

II MARKETS AND MORALS

The Pareto principle (see chapter 13) has two interpretations, one broad and trivial, the other narrower and inherently contentious. In the broad sense it says that if everybody in a society prefers x to y, then it is better for x to be the state of affairs than y. Barring external intervention, it is hard to see how this could be controversial, since *ex hypothesi* there would be nobody within the society to disagree. In this sense, however, 'prefer' has to be given a sense that will allow us to say that one prefers x to y for any reason, including thinking as a matter of abstract justice that x is right or wishing to live in the kind of society that has x instead of y. It should be clear that the policy prescriptions characteristic of economists cannot be derived from this interpretation of the Pareto principle. Wherever some programme provides goods in kind (food, clothing, or housing, for example) an economist will normally observe that it would be Pareto superior to give the recipients the cash value of the goods instead. (This of course presupposes that the good in question can be bought on the market.) Similarly, for any scheme that sets quantitative standards to limit, say, air or water pollution by factories, an economist will typically maintain that there exists in principle some Pareto-superior alternative using pricing (effluent taxes). But on the first interpretation of the Pareto principle, it requires only one person to dissent for any reason to stop any such policy in its tracks.

These characteristic prescriptions follow only if the principle is understood as telling people what preferences they *ought* to include in their judgements. Thus, for example, in a sprightly defence of the standard economist's line, Thomas Schelling says of a hypothetical situation in which money originally allocated for airport safety is given as cash and used for something else: 'And I don't care. I'd rather have the money, the lower taxes [than your having it], but if you are entitled to the money and would rather have the money than [airport] lights, I'll get no satisfaction out of making you buy the lights.'[5] This could be treated as a purely autobiographical assertion, throwing a (not altogether flattering) light on the range of things Schelling cares about. But of course in the context what it means is 'I don't care and you shouldn't either.' It is legitimate for me to have a concern for your utility (preference-satisfaction), but not for your safety, except to the exact extent that it forms part of your utility (as *you* judge it). '*You* may have put too low a value on your life, but I don't know why I should feel guilty about that.'[6] Why is guilt the only appropriate response; how about action to ensure that you do spend the right amount?

In the debate between the economists and just about everybody else, Calabresi and Bobbitt are on the side of the angels but are less help to the angelic hosts than they might be, for two main reasons. First, because of the resolutely 'non-judgemental' (to use a hateful expression) character of the book, they make it too easy for an economist to say: 'Yes, unfortunately people are funny like that, but that simply shows they should either be ignored or straightened out.' (Schelling claims that it takes two hours to convert the average public policy student.)

[5] Thomas Schelling, 'Economic Reasoning and the Ethics of Policy', *Public Interest*, 63 (1981), 37–61, at 49.
    [6] Ibid. 47.

Second, I believe that at a pre-analytic level Calabresi and Bobbitt concede far too much to the economists' general approach. At a number of points in the text, the authors come close to accepting the underlying idea that the object of social policy is to produce an equitable and/or efficient distribution of utility. They differ from economic orthodoxy by wanting to talk about the intensity of utility. But to allow that intensity of *desire* is the factor that should ideally enter into policy is already to concede the fundamental idea: that it is utility that matters, rather than the nature of specific actions, relationships, or conditions.

Thus, for example, in their discussion of political allocation, the authors in effect accept that the standard against which you judge any actual procedure is an ideal market (one with equitable or equal incomes). But there is simply no reason for accepting this. That a political allocation will not take account of the intensity of different people's relative desires to live (p. 36) or serve in the armed forces (p. 42) is an advantage rather than a disadvantage. Why should one suppose that intensity of desire should be the relevant feature, rather than something more objective such as relative need, against a background of equal priority for all, or equal priority for those of the same age? For many allocations, the appropriate criterion will refer to the resources directly and not to the utilities that we might conjecture are produced by them. Thus, the 'intensity' issue raised on pages 111–14 seems to me a red herring.

The same point is at issue in another discussion, in which Calabresi and Bobbitt consider a proposal that the length of national service in different branches of the armed services might be adjusted on a 'market-clearing' basis. That is to say, the less popular forms of military service would require a shorter period of conscription. They reject it by saying (pp. 92–3) that people value their time unequally. This objection seems to me either irrelevant or confused. What is the numeraire in terms of which this unequal value is supposed to be expressed? If money, all this shows is that rich people value everything more—expressed in terms of money—than do poor ones. But it is surely no valid objection to a scheme for distributing the burden of national service that it does not equate the money value of different people's time. That the rich value their time more highly in monetary terms than do the poor should be irrelevant here.

If money is not the numeraire, then what possibly could be? Since time is something that everybody has the same amount of, saying that some people value their lives more than others has no obvious meaning. It could be a way of suggesting that some people's lives are intrinsically more valuable than those of others (for example, that the lives of Whites are worth more than those of Blacks). Or it might be a way of suggesting that some people get more pleasure, happiness or whatever out of their lives than do other people. Neither consideration, however, seems to me one that social policy should take cognizance of in any society committed to the proposition that all citizens should be treated equally. The obnoxiousness of the first is patent. But the second also systematically advantages some over others by giving those who experience things more intensely than others an extra claim on resources. Yet as far as I can see, it is precisely this objectionable kind of comparison that Calabresi and Bobbitt have in mind when they speak (p. 92) of 'relative intensity' as something that allocations should reflect. It is, of course, perfectly valid to take into account the relative intensity of desire for different things *within* one person's life. But the kind of global judgement of relative intensity across people that Calabresi and Bobbitt apparently envisage should have no place.

Precisely because time is a resource that everyone has an equal amount of, the proposal for having different lengths of national service established to 'clear the market' seems to me a good one. It is, incidentally, an application of Bernard Shaw's proposal that everybody should be paid the same but that hours of work should be adjusted on a market-clearing basis so that those in jobs nobody wanted to do would work fewer hours. This is open to the objection that some people might prefer to work longer hours for more money or fewer hours for less, and it is hard to see why they should be prevented from doing so. But no similar objection can be made to the proposal for adjusting lengths of military service to clear the market, because the norm from which the bidding starts is clearly one of an equal length of service for all.

Calabresi and Bobbitt also object to queuing as a method of allocation on the same grounds, namely, that people value their time unequally. This is again a misguided objection. In so far as queuing simply measures the amount of time that people are prepared to give up in order to obtain something, it is an excellent way of allocating something scarce where ability to pay is considered an inappropriate criterion. The popularity of queuing as a method of allocation arises, indeed, precisely from its approximating a measure of the amount of time people are willing to give up in order to, for example, see a certain exhibition.

The objections to queuing are quite otherwise. The first is that it is only a rough and ready measure of willingness to give up time. It discriminates against the aged and infirm, and also favours those with flexible schedules over those with inflexible ones. But the most serious drawback is that the queuing itself constitutes a massive deadweight loss arising from the procedure. If willingness to queue could be established without actually making people queue there would be far more to be said for it.

In putting forward their case against allocating certain things such as medical care through the ordinary market mechanism, the authors take on board so much of the baggage of orthodox welfare economics that their argument fails to get off the ground. By accepting value-individualism (or ethereal anti-paternalism) they open themselves to destructive criticism in its own terms from the partisans of Pareto. And their proposal of 'wealth-neutral' markets is I think hard to defend against the kind of criticism Schelling would bring against it without bringing in staunchly paternalistic or 'merit want' considerations that the authors eschew in their discussion.

This requires some clarification, since the authors do make use of the notion of merit wants, but unfortunately they get it wrong, and this makes their discussion rather difficult to follow. According to them, the phenomenon of merit wants arises only from the maldistribution of income. (See p. 89 and n. 3 on p. 202.) Merit wants occur, they say, when the poor buy less of something than they would if they had more money *and* where this generates what the authors unfortunately fall in with the economists in calling 'external costs', which can include simply the fact that some people in the society do not feel that the resultant distribution of the thing is ethically right. However, if we go back to the original introduction of the term by Richard Musgrave, we can see that merit wants should be thought of as arising whenever the amount of something purchased by somebody on the market is thought (by someone) to be too small.[7] Questions of maldistribution of income thus need not come into it at all. The governments of Western Europe that put big subsidies into opera houses do not do so because operagoers enjoy below average incomes, nor is relative income of users the reason for subsidizing public libraries or national parks. These are thought to be things that a civilized society should provide. The case for providing them free or below costs is derived from 'quality of life' considerations, not distributive ones.

[7] R. A. Musgrave, *Theory of Public Finance* (New York: McGraw-Hill, 1959), 13.

Now we can obviously bring such things as health care and housing under Musgrave's notion of merit goods, by saying that they are good things that people should have. From this point of view it is immaterial whether they would buy more at cost price if they had more income or whether they would prefer the cash equivalent of the subsidy to spend on something else. But notice that this does entail an ineluctably paternalistic view. The alternative 'external costs' approach taken up by Calabresi and Bobbitt under the confusing title of 'merit wants' is, by contrast, indefensible. Either (unlike Schelling) I do care about your having medical care (as against having the equivalent in cash to spend as you like) or I do not. If I do, then it should be whatever *reason* I have for caring that should itself be the reason for your getting the care but not the cash. That is to say, I must be prepared to offer some reason for medical care being important and for its being right to provide it for you even if you would sooner take the cost of it in the form of cash instead and use it on drink with which to drown your sorrows. If my only reason for saying medical care but not money should be provided is that I happen to feel bad about your lack of medical care but not about your lack of money, and I think that social policy should be designed to make me feel good, I am justly open to the scorn of a Schelling. Couldn't I—*shouldn't* I—try to train myself to care about your utility rather than your medical care? If it is simply a matter of how I happen to feel about it, then I surely should.

This point can be made concrete by examining briefly the authors' idea of 'wealth-neutral' markets for, say, the right to have children or for medical insurance. The basic notion here is that the prices or subsidies should be set for each income stratum in the population (e.g. each quintile) so that on average people in each stratum will buy the same amount (have the same number of children, take the same value of insurance, etc.).[8] There is an obvious problem here that is glanced at by the authors but not taken seriously enough, namely, that people in different income bands may have different tastes, so that, for example,

---

[8] There is, incidentally, an error in reasoning on pp. 101–2 about the implications of a mixed price and subsidy scheme for children. The authors suggest that, if some have to pay to have children and others are paid not to, there must be some income group that achieves the putative ideal of 2.1 children without incentives. This is not so. What *is* true is that, if some mix of payments from people to have children and payments to people not to have children is used, there may be some group such that at some point the *pay-out* is zero. For example, if $2,000 a year is paid to couples in some income group not to have any children, $1,000 a year for having only one, and zero for having two, while $1,000 a year is to be paid by them for having a third child, $2,000 a year for having a fourth, and so on, there will be no payment for two children, in either direction. But of course such a couple still faces an effective cost of $1,000 for each child from the first to the nth.

the very rich might have to pay less for the right to have a child than the less rich. On the other hand, if there is likely to be uniformity across *individuals*, there is no point in creating anything so elaborate as a wealth-neutral market rather than simply providing everyone with the same amount—and indeed that is in my view the case for publicly provided health services rather than the authors' wealth-neutral market for insurance.

However, the obvious objection, to which Calabresi and Bobbitt do not pay any attention, is that a wealth-neutral market might well be colossally inefficient in the usual Pareto sense. Suppose that, to get the poorest group to buy on average as much health insurance as the richest group, one had to add nine dollars to every one dollar the poorest are prepared to pay themselves. Clearly, in line with standard consumer theory, one would not expect that a poor person who is given an extra nine dollars to spend will spend it all on medical insurance (or indeed on any one thing). Therefore, an economist will always point out, the poor person would get more utility (that is, prefer the resulting consumption bundle) if he were given the nine dollars in cash and left to spend it how he pleased, rather than being permitted to take it only in the form of extra medical insurance. Giving money allows for the attainment of Pareto optimality; giving it in kind generally precludes it.

Now it is true that one could not in practice guarantee that every poor person would gain from a switch to cash. For as a matter of practical implementation we could not actually offer the cash equivalent. It would obviously be open to gross strategic manipulation simply to ask each poor person how much he would have been willing to spend on medical insurance if a scheme to add nine dollars to every one dollar he spent himself had been in operation, and then give him in cash the amount of subsidization he would have received by spending that amount. We cannot therefore say that it would be a Pareto-superior move to take the money we expected to spend on the first scheme (assuming that we could estimate this by sample surveys) and divide it equally among the poor. (A Pareto-optimal situation is not of course Pareto-superior to every non-Pareto-optimal situation.) On the other hand, we can certainly say with confidence that *most* poor people will prefer getting the average amount that the scheme would have cost. Suppose that it would have cost $900 per head of the poorest section of the population. That implies that each would have spent, on average, $100 of his own money on insurance to get a total benefit of $1,000 in insurance. Now it is clear (on the basis of the standard reasoning) that someone who would have spent the average amount ($100) on insurance and got the average subsidy ($900) is no *worse* off by getting the $900 in cash instead, since he can put the cash into insurance if he chooses. He is almost certainly better off, since he almost certainly will not put more than a proportion of it into insurance. *A fortiori*, anyone who would have spent less than the average and got less than the average subsidy is definitely better off with the cash. This leaves those who would have spent more than $100 and would thus have got more than $900 in subsidy, and here the answer is indefinite. But we certainly cannot, of course, say that such people are necessarily worse off (measured in terms of their own preferences) with the $900 in cash. Suppose somebody would have spent $200 of his own money to get $1,800 in free supplementary medical insurance. The question is whether he values $900 in cash more than $1,800 in insurance: had he been offered a choice between those two options, which would he have taken? Some, we can assume, would prefer the insurance to a smaller amount in cash, and they are the losers from the alternative scheme. But their losses will, we can know for certain, be smaller in aggregate than the gains of those who gain. Thus, the alternative satisfies the two criteria of potential Pareto optimality *and* no adverse distributive effects between poor and rich. The redistribution is among the poor from those who have a greatly above-average taste for medical insurance to those with an average or below-average taste for it.

But this way of putting the point raises a deeper question, namely, whether it is possible to construct a coherent ethical rationale for wealth-neutral markets. I am not at all confident that it is. I have already argued against the 'external costs' approach. If we try to find a more secure foundation, it seems to me that it must be paternalistic; but I believe that this is liable to lead us to something other than wealth-neutral markets. Let me explain.

On the one hand, we have something which we shall call X (it may be the right to bear children or to obtain medical insurance, for example) which, *ex hypothesi*, has been judged appropriate for allocation through a market. This means (a) that people are to be faced with a choice between having more of X and spending more on other consumption items such as cigarettes or cinema tickets; and (b) that we will not do anything to stop somebody spending little or nothing on X if he chooses. On the other hand, we are concerned that, with an ordinary market, the poor will finish up with less (on the average) of X than the rich, and we want to prevent that from happening. We therefore arrange things so that, although they do (on the average)' *spend* less, they *get* the same amount (on the average) of X.

The problem of ethical coherence, as I see it, is this. If we take the line that this thing, X, is 'too important to be left to the market', that is, that the amount of X someone gets should not depend on his income, do we not have to say that X has some intrinsic importance over and above its contribution to people's utility? For if it is important only in so far as it conduces to utility, there seems to be an obvious case for taking the money put into creating a wealth-neutral market for X and giving it to people as cash. Then, if they agree that X is as important as you think it is for their utility, they will in any case spend it on X. If they do not agree with you, they will spend it on something else, and (trivially, given the definition) get more utility. But if we say that X has some special virtue over and above its conduciveness to utility, why should the amount of it that people get be related (even via a modified market) to their willingness to give up other marketed things for it? If we once say that X has an importance not measured by utility, does this perhaps commit us to saying that people ought to get it whether they are willing to pay for it or not? If so, it looks as if we can justify a move away from a straight market only if we adopt a paternalistic position and attribute a virtue to X that is not reducible to its conduciveness to utility (i.e. its tendency to be chosen). But once we adopt that position we seem to be committed to going beyond a wealth-neutral market and saying that the allocation should not be related to tastes at all. The authors' halfway house between an ordinary market and a paternalistically based overriding of individual preferences thus seems to me to be insecurely founded.

This discussion bears on a related policy question that arises at the level of collectivities rather than individuals. Periodically the idea surfaces that the level of educational expenditures (and perhaps other 'essential services') should be related to 'tax effort'. That is to say, within some wider area (e.g. the State of California) each taxing authority (e.g. school district) should be provided with supplemental funds so that the product of a mil (a tenth of a cent) in property tax (or it could be a given rate of income tax or sales tax) is an equal per capita amount of revenue. So, somewhat parallel to the medical insurance case, a district which raises ten times less than the most prosperous one per mil will get nine dollars added to every one it raises. Then an equal 'tax effort' will give rise to an equal per capita expenditure.

But surely the problem just set out for the wealth-neutral market arises here. If education is simply another public good, producing utility for its consumers, why doesn't Schelling's analysis of the municipal airport lighting apply? That is to say, why not estimate the cost of the scheme and give the money as a block grant to school districts or municipalities so that the poorest ones get the most and so on, leaving them to spend it on anything they like? On the other hand, if education is a 'basic right', why should a child's educational opportunities (inasfar as these are affected by money spent on schools) depend on the willingness to pay of the voters in its school district, any more than it should depend on their *capacity* to pay? Once again, it seems hard to rationalize the intermediate stage between (*a*) adjusting incomes (not necessarily to the 'right' level but to the extent implied by a Calabresian wealth-neutral scheme) and then letting things rip, or (*b*) providing a uniform level of service regardless of either capacity *or* willingness to pay.

It may be that the wealth-neutral pricing idea can be revived not to carry the main burden of allocation of some merit good but to trim demand for it at the margin so as to reduce congestion. Suppose that we have made art galleries free or have provided a national health service without any user charges. We now find that there are too many people in front of the pictures and too many people in the doctors' waiting rooms. We might then be tempted to introduce some modest price arrangement to reduce the burden on other mechanisms (mainly queuing and administrative selection) that will be needed to control numbers. Clearly, the ideal would be to set before each person an equal-sized hurdle (a difficult idea to make precise let alone operational, but I take it as intuitively intelligible) so that two people with a sore throat of equal severity or an equal yen to see the treasures of King Tut will be deterred to just the same degree by the price levied. This could obviously be done only by making the price sensitive to income, and this is the basic notion of the wealth-neutral market. In practice, of course, nothing very refined is ever done along these lines. Art galleries with charges for admission have a regular rate and then lower rates for members of groups with low average incomes—the young, the old, and the unemployed. Prescription charges under the National Health Service are waived for those already certified as poor and receiving cash benefits. There are also 'season tickets' for the chronically sick and usually for art museum enthusiasts, in order to work in 'special needs'. Since this structure of pricing is obviously far too crude to present anything like equal deterrence (especially among those who pay the standard price) it cannot be relied on to do much: in practice other restrictions have to be used, and we in fact find queues for popular exhibitions and congested doctors' waiting rooms.

This analysis suggests that the most plausible case for wealth-neutral pricing is to deter. The obverse of deterrence is inducement. And I think that my argument about the relative suitability of wealth-neutral markets for deterrence can be strengthened by noting that the use of such markets seems especially unattractive for inducement. Consider the idea tossed out in passing by the authors (p. 140) for a 'wealth-neutral market for subjects in medical experimentation'. This might involve paying people in the top tranche (those with an income of over, say, $100,000 per annum) several thousands of dollars to get enough of them to undergo some experiment that an equal proportion of people in, say, the poorest 10 per cent of the population could be induced to undergo for less than $100. Since a wealth-neutral market is by definition one in which each income group has to be induced to produce an equal proportion of 'volunteers', the richest segment of the population can in effect hold out for being paid a great deal just because they do not need the money and thus have to be bribed heavily to accept some given degree of inconvenience, discomfort, or health risk. Conversely, the very poor, just because they desperately need the money, lose out. The willingness of many of them to become experimental subjects in return for a relatively small amount of compensation means that they will in fact get paid only a little.

Again, consider the all-volunteer army. A lot of people in the USA are worried about the fact that this (inevitably) attracts disproportionate numbers of Blacks, since they are the people to whom the jobs, given their actual alternatives, look most attractive. This concern is partly political—especially for those who hope to see American troops fighting Communism in Africa in the next few decades—but there is also a rather fuzzy moral sentiment about Blacks carrying an 'unfair share' of the risks involved in defending the country. The obvious 'Calabresian' response would be to have low pay rates for Blacks and high pay rates for Whites, adjusted until Whites and Blacks are proportionately represented in the army. (Not too appetizing as a piece of public policy!) Similarly, an objection to paid blood donation on the line that the poor (and racial minorities) will finish up by giving most of the blood could be met by paying more to middle-class Whites.

My own view is that the fundamental issue in these cases is whether to recruit by appealing to pure self-interest ('Do it if, consulting your own private preferences, the price makes it worth it') or whether to make it a matter of social obligation, either giving rise to appeals to altruism (British blood donorship or volunteering for the British Expeditionary Force in 1914–16)[9] or to authoritative political decision (the draft or perhaps a lottery for experimental subjects). If you opt for the market approach to recruitment, then it seems to me you must accept that the effect will be to attract disproportionately those to whom a given amount of money in return for a given obligation looks most attractive, that is to say, those with fewer alternative opportunities. If you are queasy about that outcome, you should prefer an alternative method of recruitment.

[9] There is a subtle but all-important difference, which could not be captured in any standard economic analysis, between paying people *who* volunteer and paying people *to* volunteer. Volunteers are always paid by the army: the question is whether the pay is (and is supposed to be) the sole motivation. Thus, the evidence from the time makes it clear that the overwhelming majority of those who joined the British Expeditionary Force in the first year of the First World War did so because they saw it as a patriotic duty, not because the career prospects looked attractive in relation to civilian alternatives. I doubt if any major country has come as close this century to regarding its regular army as a collection of mercenaries who just happen to be citizens as has the contemporary USA. One might speculate that this can occur only in a country that never expects to use its army to repel an invasion: the French had the Foreign Legion for fighting overseas but assumed that direct threats to *la patrie* would be met by the draft.

7

CHANCE, CHOICE, AND JUSTICE

I TWO PRINCIPLES OF JUSTICE

The proposition that I want to examine in this chapter can be stated quite simply as follows. A just society is one whose institutions honour two principles of distribution. One is a principle of compensation. It says that the institutions of a society should operate in such a way as to counteract the effects of good and bad fortune. In particular, it says that the victims of ill luck should as far as possible be made as well off as those who are similarly placed in all respects other than having suffered this piece of bad luck. The other principle is one of personal responsibility. It says that social arrangements should be such that people finish up with the outcomes of their voluntary acts.

Let me say this at once. There is no suggestion that these two principles constitute a complete specification of principles relevant to the distribution of benefits and burdens within a society. In fact, it is fairly evident that these principles could not get going at all without other principles to lay the groundwork. The first principle depends for its application on our having as a benchmark for the compensation of victims of bad luck some idea of the welfare level appropriate to those similarly placed except for having suffered the bad luck. And the second principle presupposes an assignment of rights to act (e.g. a principle of equal civil and political rights) so as to provide a legitimate sphere of choice. I should also say that the application of these two principles of justice would always have to be modified by the operation of a principle of expediency, which is I believe accepted in every society. According to this, which I shall call the principle of common advantage, an inequality is justified if it works to the benefit of everybody. It is perhaps worth noting here that utilitarianism consists of offering a particular interpretation of what it means to say that something is to everybody's advantage and then dumping all other principles. In putting forward these two principles of justice I am therefore rejecting utilitarianism.

The problem that I want to concentrate on is this. Let us suppose that we find ourselves initially attracted by both the principle of compensation and the principle of responsibility. How do we fit them together? On the face of it, they fit together very nicely. Indeed, they can be seen as two aspects of a single principle: that it is 'inequitable if an individual is in a worse situation than another because of factors beyond his control'.[1] If something is a matter of luck, that means it is beyond your control; if it is a matter of choice, that means it is within your control.

Unfortunately, however, this verbal resolution of the problem falls apart as soon as we press on it. I can illustrate the difficulties most dramatically by showing that it is possible to extend the scope of choice so that it leaves very little room for chance and conversely that it is possible to extend the scope of chance so that it threatens to engulf choice completely.

II CHOICISM

Let us begin with the first case. I am not concerned here with the possibility that someone might simply accept the relevance of choice and deny that of chance, as a matter of principle. This is a possible position, and indeed it is in general terms that taken by Robert Nozick in *Anarchy, State, and Utopia*.[2] Nozick postulates a framework of rights and then says that just outcomes are those arising from the choices made by people in the exercise of those rights. You might have the bad luck to starve to death under these arrangements because you have not been so fortunate as to inherit or be given enough to live on, and for reasons beyond your control (e.g. disability or inability to find work) cannot earn enough to live on. But Nozick simply has no provision for modifying the outcomes arising from choice so as to deal with bad luck. I am not going to argue with that sort of view, whose unattractiveness seems to me patent. What I am interested in here is the way in which somewhat less extreme versions of Nozick's conclusions can be reached even if both choice and chance are recognized as being in principle relevant.

The best way of approaching this is to consider a simple lottery where people buy one or more tickets for some modest sum like fifty pence, the counterfoils are put into a hat and the winner, who gets everybody's stakes, is the person whose number is pulled out. Nothing could be a better example of an outcome determined by

[1] Julian Le Grand, 'Equity as an Economic Objective', *Journal of Applied Philosophy*, 1 (1984), 39–51, quotation from p. 46, italics suppressed.
[2] Robert Nozick, *Anarchy, State, and Utopia* (New York: Basic Books, 1974).

chance. The principle of compensation would appear to imply that the winner's prize should be redistributed among the participants in the lottery so as to restore the status quo ante. Yet there seems something odd in the suggestion that justice requires this. Why? Fairly obviously the answer lies in the presumptively voluntary nature of participation in the lottery. If people deliberately put themselves in a situation where they have a large chance of losing a small amount and a small chance of gaining a greater amount, isn't it fair that the outcome should stand?

Since a good deal hangs on our returning a positive answer, it will be advisable for us to test the ground carefully before going further. Thus, we should bear in mind that the principle of personal responsibility relates to voluntary actions and that choices may fail to be voluntary in a variety of ways. Conditions undermining voluntariness include coercion, internal compulsion, addiction, provocation, and necessity (the lack of acceptable alternatives). It has to be said that the interpretation of these is itself open to controversy, and hardboiled choicists are liable to construe most of these phenomena as very strong preferences while denying the relevance of necessity altogether. However, even the softboiled might well be satisfied that in some instances the participants in a lottery such as I described were not suffering from such things as social pressure, compulsion, or desperation. So it could still be held that the winner could justly hang on to the prize.

Notice that this answer does not require us to make the claim that any just society must permit gambling. We might accept that a society could justly prohibit gambling either on paternalistic grounds (that some people will become compulsive gamblers and blanket prohibition is the only effective form of protection) or on the Puritanical ground that anything which divorces rewards from efforts is morally enervating. Notice, however, that these grounds do not themselves invoke justice. So long as we accept that a society may justly permit gambling, we can still arrive at the conclusion that, where it is permitted, the winner of a lottery has a just claim on the prize.

This might seem at first glance to be a quite small concession to the idea that choice can trump chance, but it can be used as the thin end of a very thick wedge. I shall invent the word 'choicist' to refer to someone who wants to show that it is consistent with justice to give the principle of personal responsibility a lot of scope at the expense of the principle of compensation, while acknowledging the validity of both principles. I shall now set out what seems to me the best case for choicism. I shall not go as far as some actual choicists but I shall push the case to the limits of intellectual respectability, and perhaps a bit beyond.

A very important weapon in the armoury of the choicist is the institution of insurance. By invoking the possibility of insuring oneself against various misfortunes it is possible to construct an argument that marginalizes the principle of compensation over a wide range of cases. We can connect this to the previous discussion by observing that insurance is simply a form of gambling, where a small loss in the form of a premium is voluntarily accepted in return for the prospect of a large gain in the form of a payout by the insurer. The peculiarity of insurance is simply that what triggers the payment is a piece of specified bad luck. (To the extent that the contingency triggering the payout is not solely due to luck, insurers start talking about 'moral hazard' and getting uncomfortable. Let us leave that complication on one side for now and think of insurance as being against bad luck.) Suppose, then, that your house burns down due to causes completely beyond your control. That is bad luck, straightforwardly enough, as even the most rabid choicist will admit. But, it may be said, whether you suffer financial loss from the destruction of your house depends on your prior decision to insure it fully, inadequately, or not at all. Thus, we can conclude that someone who loses everything in a fire can justly be left destitute because the option of insuring against the loss was available and not taken.

Let us go back to the Nozickian vision of a society in which market-derived outcomes are modified only by private arrangements. How far can it be reinstated by someone who admits the validity of the principle of compensation but wants to minimize its impact? We shall certainly be able to find, consistently with justice, people starving to death. All we need to show is that they had the option of avoiding that fate through insurance and didn't take it. For example, anyone now unable to work owing to sickness or accident but previously in good health could have taken out insurance against loss of earnings. Involuntary unemployment presents more of a problem, unless our choicist has the gall to claim that there is no such thing; but there could be a state-run system of insurance to which individuals could subscribe or not. An honest and intelligent choicist would also have to admit that a purely private system of medical insurance would fail to cover people against the bad luck of being bad medical risks. But again, subscription to the insurance scheme could be made voluntary, so that we could justly have people dying because they couldn't afford treatment. Destitution in old age could obviously be treated as voluntary, in almost all cases.

What about earned income? I think that any serious choicist would have to admit that some people are congenitally unemployable or employable only in jobs whose market value is very low. The principle of compensation would therefore mandate that the results of such bad luck should be modified by transfers, and here we have a clear departure from the Nozickian world. But this still leaves us with most of the enormous disparities in earnings that market systems produce. How far can a choicist defend these against the claim that unequal earnings are largely a matter of good and bad luck—in genes, social background, schooling, or simply being in the right place at the right time?

To some degree the lottery example can be invoked to save the day. Thus, suppose that with given abilities you might acquire the qualifications to go into a high-variance occupation or a low-variance one—become a barrister or a solicitor—then it might be argued that if you do very badly in the high-variance occupation (get very few briefs as a barrister) you have no legitimate cause for complaint. This is a good point for the choicist as far as it goes, but it does not go very far, since the terms of comparison are confined to barristers and solicitors.

An across-the-board justification would require the claim that everybody initially faced the same choice set, and all subsequent differentiation of earnings prospects arises from different choices made along the way. This is on the face of it highly implausible, if we take it that for something to count as a choice it must be a real possibility that it be chosen. (A paraplegic does not have a choice of running or not.) But then everything turns on what has to be true for something to constitute a real possibility.

The classic choicist move here is to distinguish sharply between possibility and probability. For example, it might be conceded that a bright child with well-educated supportive parents will find it easier to do well in school and is, as a statistical matter, more likely to. (It is hard to see how anybody could deny that.) But it may be said that so long as a few children of average brightness and with disadvantageous home circumstances succeed that shows it is possible for all to do so. (This is the sense of 'equal opportunity' in which every private in Napoleon's armies carried a marshall's baton in his knapsack.)

Of course, for even these minimal claims about equal opportunities to be valid, we would already have to be some distance from a Nozickian world, since there would have to be an educational system accessible to all children, whatever their family circumstances, including financial support to enable all children to stay at school through the full term of full-time education, and this school system would have to be set up in such a way as to ensure that all children did actually have the means available to do well if they took advantage of them. This would fairly plainly not be true of contemporary Britain, for example.

Even after all these conditions were met, however, I believe that a sincere choicist would have to admit that not everything is possible to everybody, and concede the case for a somewhat progressive income tax system to deal in a rough and ready way with good and bad luck in relation to the job market. But it would be possible, I take it, to resist the suggestion that an ideally just system of earnings would be one providing everyone with equal final pay after compensating for the disutility of work.

In concluding my exposition of the choicist case, I want to come back to a point I made in connection with lotteries. I said that a just society does not have to allow lotteries to occur. The conclusion favourable to choicism is a purely hypothetical one: that if there are to be lotteries, it is just for the winner to hang on to the prize. The decision whether or not to permit lotteries has to be taken on grounds other than those of justice: protection of the vulnerable or the maintenance of desirable dispositions on one side, and on the other presumably the value of individual liberty to do what one wishes in the absence of compelling reasons to the contrary.

The point can be generalized. Thus, if there are two occupations with the same mean income and different dispersions (as solicitors and barristers might be) then someone who does badly in the high-dispersion occupation cannot complain of injustice, even if failure is attributable wholly to bad luck (including perhaps the bad luck of not having influential connections). But it is not unjust for a society to get rid of high-variance occupations and make barristers part of a salaried legal service. The case for and against will have to be argued on other grounds.

In the same way, the most a choicist can claim on the basis of the principle of personal responsibility is this: *if* a society's institutions make insurance against a whole variety of misfortunes voluntary, and actually provide the insurance (supplementing or superseding privately offered insurance where necessary), then it is not unjust to leave uncompensated the losses suffered by those who have failed to avail themselves of the opportunity of taking out insurance. Considerations of justice will not, however, tell us whether to have a system like that or to have compulsory social insurance and a national health service. That decision will, again, have to be made on other grounds, presumably security and efficiency (since private insurance has high overhead costs) on one side and personal liberty—the opportunity of shaping one's life by one's choices—on the other.

Similarly, a choicist can say that it is consistent with justice for educational outcomes to be heavily dependent on choice, so that pupils who choose not to study are left by the wayside. But it would also be consistent with justice to charge schools with the duty of trying to motivate all their students and require all children to complete their secondary education.

III QUALIFIED CHOICISM

I have tried to give an idea of the way in which choicism works to produce policy implications. Before going further, let me pause for a few general remarks about the presuppositions of the choicist position. Choicism, then, builds upon some simple ideas about choice that appeal to the common sense of a basically liberal society such as ours. Thus, it is assumed that you have a free choice among kinds of fruit if all you have to do is to stretch out your hand and take one from a bowl containing a selection. Similarly, it is assumed that you have the option of acquiring a qualification if you could get it by enrolling in a course you can afford and doing some work that is within your capability. It would be regarded as paradoxical to claim that such choices do not generate responsibility for the outcomes because they flow from preferences that are not themselves chosen.

It is also assumed that if two people have the same choice set they are treated equally, so that two people are equally well treated as consumers if they have the same income, and members of two religious bodies have equal treatment if a uniform, non-discriminatory set of rules applies to both of the bodies. And again it would be thought of as paradoxical to deny this in the first case by pointing out that one person may be able to get more satisfaction from spending the income than the other and in the second case by pointing out that a rule of universal toleration suits a religion that favours toleration more than one that seeks to make everybody conform to it. Yet a case can certainly be made out for these paradoxical claims, which extend the scope of the principle of compensation at the expense of the principle of responsibility.

My main business in the rest of this chapter will be coming to grips with the kind of large-scale anti-choicism that I have just introduced. Before that, however, I should like to show that choicism, as I have expounded it so far, is vulnerable to attack without disputing the common sense premisses about choice and personal responsibility on which it depends. Qualified choicism, as I shall call it for convenience, is the view that the significance (or potential significance) of choice in justifying unequal outcomes has been overstated.

In any attempt to cut choicism down to size, the weakest point in it must surely be the claim that a large proportion of all earnings differentials can be defended as arising from voluntary choice. To maintain this, the choicist claim about equality of opportunity has to be the strong one that at any rate most differences in final educational attainment come about as a result of children making different choices out of steadily divergent choice sets that were at some early stage identical. But if only a few children of average native ability from disadvantaged backgrounds do well educationally, this must cast doubt on the claim that doing well formed a real option for all the rest. It seems more plausible to suppose that we would find some special factors accounting for the exceptions, and that they could not therefore be used to show that the other children could have done the same if they had chosen to.

I deliberately built up the choicist position starting from its strongest case and working down from there. I do not therefore believe that there is any sound objection from the qualified choicist viewpoint to the lottery example. The extension to insurance, however, seems more open to challenge. Much, I suggest, turns on the answer to questions like these: under what conditions would it be rational for someone dependent on employment for an income to decline insurance, if available on reasonable terms, against loss of earnings? If the answer is (as I think it indeed is) that there are almost no circumstances in which this would be rational, the conclusion will have to be that those who do not take the insurance are lacking in foresight, suffer from weakness of will, or are simply too ill-organized to act appropriately. Any of these would be enough to at any rate call into question personal responsibility to the extent of suggesting that destitution is too high a penalty for failure to insure. Where almost all rational choices would go the same way, leaving people the choice is rather like leaving a stretch of dangerous cliff unfenced so as to leave people the option of plunging into the sea.

I now want to turn, as promised, to a more radical critique of the choicist position, which I shall call anti-choicism. It may be recalled that when defining choicism I excluded from consideration those people who simply do not recognize the validity of the principle of compensation. My choicists are people who recognize it but seek to minimize its role in determining just outcomes. I shall define anti-choicism so that it is the converse of choicism. I shall therefore leave on one side those who hold a normative theory that has no room for the principle of personal responsibility from the outset. Examples of such theories would be: that average utility should be maximized, that minimum utility should be maximized, or that some function with equal distribution and average level of utility as arguments should be maximized. Of course, in working out the implications of such theories it will no doubt be found necessary to attach consequences to actions so as to encourage socially beneficial actions and discourage anti-social ones. But this is purely instrumental, justified by its tendency to increase the maximand.

The position I am interested in is one which accepts in principle that choice and chance are both relevant to justice but goes on to claim that when we look carefully we shall find that chance will largely or wholly swallow up choice. To make it plain that I am focusing on only one way of not being a choicist, I might perhaps have done better to call anti-choicism 'chancism', but sufficient unto the day is the neologism thereof.

The issue between choicism and anti-choicism turns on the relevance of tastes, aspirations, and beliefs to personal responsibility for the outcomes of choices made in accordance with them. Choicism, as I am defining it, adopts a robust line on this: naturally people's choices flow from their tastes, aspirations, and beliefs; but this is precisely what endows the choices made on the basis of them with authenticity. (If someone suddenly did something totally 'out of character', that would be more liable to lead us to accept a plea of 'diminished responsibility' for the outcome.)

The anti-choicist position, in contrast, holds that people cannot be held personally responsible for their tastes, aspirations, or beliefs, and this entails that they also cannot be held responsible for the outcomes of actions that flow from them. To save repetition (though at the cost of some violation to the language) let us talk about 'preferences' to refer to tastes, aspirations, and beliefs. Then the anti-choicist view can be explained in this way. Although the principle of personal responsibility is valid as a principle, it does not have any application in the world we actually live in, which is one of universal causality. Personal responsibility depends upon choice, but we do not in general choose our preferences. It is true that it is sometimes possible for us to change our preferences by working on them. But presumably the decision to try to change some existing preference derives from a second-order preference which is not itself chosen. And even if we admitted yet higher-order preferences, we would never get to a radical choice, a choice unconditioned by a preference that was not itself subject to choice.

A more moderate version of anti-choicism embraces the basic anti-choicist premiss by saying that the only preferences to generate personal responsibility are those that were deliberately created by the agent, whether or not they could now be changed, and those that could now be changed by the agent, whether or not they were deliberately created in the first place. The distinctive feature of moderate anti-choicism is that it abandons the dogma that no preferences can ever pass the test and instead settles for a case-by-case approach. Some preferences, it is supposed, will give rise to personal responsibility but many others will not.[3]

Rather than engage in any more preliminaries, let me exhibit anti-choicism, in both of its forms, in operation. I shall take up two questions which, I will note in passing, are usually discussed by quite different sets of people, even though the underlying theoretical issue is the same. For my first example, I shall return to the idea of equal educational opportunity.

In my discussion of qualified choicism, I pointed out that the size of the choice set facing an individual is always problematic. That some alternative is formally open to a certain person—to take an advanced course in physics, say—does not mean that it is a real possibility for that person: it may require capacities he or she simply has not got. Nevertheless, I still assumed that there are real choices open—to take one subject or another, to study hard or not, to stay on at school or not, and so on—and that these at any rate give rise to responsibility for their outcomes. On the extreme anti-choicist view, this is invariably a delusion. For the choice must flow from a preference which is, immediately or at some remove, not the result of choice. In case it seems hard to take this seriously, let me observe that much of the

---

[3] See G. A. Cohen, 'On the Currency of Egalitarian Justice', *Ethics* 99 (1989), 906–44.

literature on the subject presupposes that choices are a source of unequal opportunity on all fours with home environment and quality of school. It is assumed, as an unargued ideal of social justice, that if we factor out differences in native endowment we ought to be able to slice through the population of a society along any dimension—gender, religion, ethnic group, race, social class, region, and so on—and find on each side of the division a perfect microcosm of the society as a whole, as far as levels and perhaps even types of educational attainment are concerned. Since it seems evident that part of the explanation of systematic differences in group achievement is the existence of different patterns of preference among their members, it must be that these are to be regarded as sources of socially unjust inequalities in educational outcome.

The moderate version of anti-choicism would leave it open that some choices were genuine and could properly act as an acceptable basis for differences in outcome. But to just the extent that these choices were patterned, so that girls systematically tended to make different choices from boys, or WASPs from white 'ethnics', this very fact would suggest that the sources of the underlying preferences should be sought in cultural attitudes and thus seen as a matter of chance rather than choice.

It should perhaps be added that the choicist criterion accepts non-culpable ignorance as an excusing condition. (If I put white powder in your coffee, sincerely and reasonably believing it to be artificial sweetener, I am not responsible for your being poisoned when it turns out to have been strychnine.) No doubt some ill-advised educational choices can be brought within the range of that limitation on the scope of the principle of personal responsibility. But it is hard to see how it could be made to cover, say, the tendency for a smaller proportion of girls than boys to study science subjects, or the smaller appetite for a college education among white 'ethnics' as compared with WASPs. The gap between the implications of choicism and the implications of anti-choicism thus remains wide.

The best way into my second example is via a reconsideration of the choicist idea that can be expressed in the words: 'Equal choice sets constitute equal treatment.' It is fairly easy to see that as it stands this must be an incomplete specification. Confronting two people with the same set of options cannot be a sufficient condition of equal treatment. If I like apples and you like oranges, a bowl containing both gives us equal treatment; but one containing only oranges would just as well satisfy the condition of confronting us with an identical choice set.

Similarly, a law permitting the practice of all varieties of Christianity but prohibiting all others is equal treatment among Christians but not between Christians and others; yet all of them face the same choice set.

It looks as if to the condition that the choice sets should be the same we need to add something about their having the same value. But how do we tell when two choice sets have the same value? Choicists are in the embarrassing position of having no general answer to this question. In the case of consumer goods, for example, it can be said that people are treated equally when they have equal amounts of money, because this means that they have an entitlement to the same share of the society's resources: the equality of value is established by the equal cost to the rest of the society. With members of religious faiths, a criterion of this kind gives no help. Equal treatment will have to mean that they all get the same tax treatment, the same treatment with regard to schooling, the same treatment under the blasphemy laws, and so on. The legal framework has equal value for all religious faiths only in this sense: that it does not give special favours to one that it does not give to others.

Anti-choicists, in contrast, offer a simple and comprehensive criterion of equal value: a certain choice set has the same value for two people if the option in it that each most prefers produces the same level of welfare, understood subjectively as 'utility'. (This option may, of course, be a different one for the two people.) Since the same criterion applies in all areas, we can aggregate across them and arrive at the general conclusion that social justice requires equal welfare for all the members of a society. For whatever it is about them that results in their actions yielding more or less utility is a matter of good or bad luck. The principle of compensation demands, therefore, that the effects of this good or bad luck should be cancelled out by an appropriate redistribution of resources.

It may be objected immediately that, if all actions produce the same amount of welfare for the agent as everybody else has, nobody will have any incentive to behave prudently, or to do things that benefit others rather than things that harm them. The average level of welfare of the population, which everyone share in, will be lowered only infinitesimally over a large population. Everyone therefore stands to gain from a move away from guaranteed equal welfare to a set-up that attaches reward and penalties to beneficial and antisocial actions respectively.

Is this simply, then, a return to the principle of personal responsibility? No. It is true that the institutions called for by common advantage will at a number of points be similar to those implied by the principle of personal responsibility. But the rationale will be quite different. Some criminologists, for example, have taken a strong anti-choicist line and argued that all or almost all criminal behaviour is the result of some combination of unfavourable heredity and crime-inducing environment. It is quite consistent with this to say that crime should be punished in order to reduce its incidence. But at the same time it has to be admitted that the deliberately lowered welfare levels of convicted criminals arc a matter of bad luck on their part, and thus unjust. It is simply that the common advantage requires that they suffer in order to provide an example to others (and themselves in future). Thus, if things could somehow be arranged so that prisoners enjoyed the average level of welfare, while everyone (including them when they left) could be induced to believe they were suffering, that would be an ideally just state of affairs. Actual punishment is a concession by justice to expediency.

By invoking the principle of common advantage, then, we can fend off the more disastrous implications of the anti-choice position. But we may still feel that there is something mildly crazy about the idea that an ideally just situation would be one where people who needed champagne and caviar to get to the average level of consumer satisfaction would get more money or where the adherents of some killjoy religion would have to be allowed to bring everybody else down to their own level by stopping others from enjoying themselves.

Let's suppose that we accept the basic anti-choicist premiss that the outcomes of unchosen preferences are a matter of good or bad luck. We could move away from the implication that justice mandated equal welfare if we adopted what I called the moderate anti-choicist position. This, it will be recalled, made room for personal responsibility for preferences provided they had either come about as a result of choice or could now be changed as a result of choice. The claims of a person with below-average welfare for compensation could therefore be resisted if the preferences causing the trouble were subject to choice in either of these ways. It does not seem to me, however, that this move would do much to get rid of implications of the kind I outlined a moment ago. The whole idea of choosing to change one's beliefs is fishy, while tastes for luxuries are notoriously hard to extinguish once established. Religious beliefs are less often deliberately cultivated than acquired in the course of one's upbringing; and although expensive tastes *may* have been cultivated, we certainly cannot assume that all are.

A heroic solution, which has been adopted by John Rawls, is to say that people's tastes, aspirations, and beliefs are always open to modification, so people can properly be held responsible for them. This enables him to adhere to what I have called the basic anti-choicist premiss and yet finish up with the classical choicist conclusion that people are treated equally if they have equal rights and equal incomes—in Rawls's terminology, equal shares of primary goods.

On the face of it, Rawls's claim about the malleability of preferences is an empirical one, and a hopelessly implausible one to boot. He has made it clear, however, that this is a part of a 'model conception of the person' which is presupposed by the theory.[4] An unkind, but I fear accurate, way of putting this would be to say that Rawls wants to salvage liberal conclusions about primary goods as the currency of distributive justice, and can do so without repudiating the anti-choicist premiss only by inserting between them a postulate ensuring personal responsibility for preferences. The justification of this postulate—that all preferences are subject to choice—is not that it is true (or even credible) but that it is needed to get the answer to come out in the right place.

It is easy enough to dismiss Rawls's proposed solution, and I have no doubt that we should not waste time on it. Unfortunately, however, Rawls's ill-fated venture in dogmatic psychology has provided a golden opportunity for theorists antipathetic to liberal conclusions to suggest that they depend on something of the sort. It is clear, however, that this is not so, because these conclusions can be derived quite straightforwardly so long as the anti-choicist premiss is repudiated. The most that Rawls's contortions show is that it is hard to get from anti-choicist premisses to choicist conclusions, and this should not surprise anybody.

V RESPONSIBILITY FOR PREFERENCES: AN ALTERNATIVE APPROACH

We come back, then, to the anti-choicist premiss. If it were to be generally accepted, it looks as if we would have to make fairly drastic changes in our ideas about what justice ideally entails, though problems of implementation would perhaps mean that we should see little change in actual social arrangements. But should we accept it? It seems to me to have appealed to too many people of undeniable

---

[4] See especially the Dewey Lectures on 'Kantian Constructivism', *Journal of Philosophy*, 77 (1980), 515–72.

intelligence to be simply dismissed in favour of the bluff choicist position that the status of preferences is irrelevant to personal responsibility. What I should like to propose instead is that we should divide the spoils between choicism and anti-choicism, accepting the more intuitively appealing part of the anti-choicist premiss but dropping the part that leads to the more unappetizing conclusions.

Let us agree, then, that it is legitimate to look behind choices to preferences before establishing personal responsibility for outcomes. People arc, indeed, responsible for the outcomes of actions only if they are also responsible for the preferences from which those actions flow. But the error in the anti-choicist position lies, I suggest, in the next step which makes responsibility for preferences depend upon their being subject to choice. The alternative I propose is that people are responsible for their preferences whenever they are content with them. How these preferences originated is irrelevant, and the ease with which they could be changed is relevant only in this way: that we would have to question the sincerity of your claim not to want to have the preferences you actually do have if it were easy for you to change them.

I shall call this view 'semi-choicism', since it abandons the choicist resistance to any inquiry into responsibility for preferences, but rejects the anti-choicist criterion for responsibility for preferences. I wish to maintain that semi-choicism has two virtues: it has a certain intrinsic plausibility, and it also gets the right answers (or what seem to me the right answers) on particular problems.

Consider again the case of religious belief. Suppose you were raised in some strict, puritanical sect according to whose tenets most pleasures are sinful, and you continue to believe in those tenets. Now you could, obviously, wish that the truth about the will of God was more accommodating, but so long as you really believe that that is how things are, you cannot regret believing it, even if you recognize that some other set of beliefs would be compatible with choices having more enjoyable outcomes. The difficulty in changing your beliefs is not so much empirical as logical. Let us imagine your saying, 'Of course, it would be hard for me to change my beliefs now, after such a long process of indoctrination, but I wish I had been brought up in some less restrictive faith so that I would now have more congenial beliefs.' In saying that you would, it seems to me, be saying that you no longer did believe in what you had been brought up to believe. Once you thought it through, you would be more honest with yourself to say, 'Of course, I no longer believe that all those pleasures are really sinful, but I still experience powerful guilt feelings about them.' It would be quite reasonable, I suggest, for someone in this position to be offered psychotherapy on the National Health Service in order to be relieved of these irrational feelings of guilt. And this, it may be observed, is precisely what is mandated by semi-choicism. For in this case you have preferences left over from your religious upbringing that you do not identify with and would like to be rid of. So long as you continued to believe, however, you could hardly complain that it was bad luck to have the preferences you had, since you would not have wished things to be any different.

Beliefs raise special issues because it is hard to give any sense to the idea of wanting to believe something other than what you do believe (as against wanting it to be the case that something else is true). However, the semi-choicist approach works equally well on preferences which are not conditioned upon belief in the way that religiously derived preferences are. Consider, for example, sexual preference. Now at present homosexuals are not given equal treatment according to the choicist criterion of having rights with equal value to those of heterosexuals. For example, a homosexual couple is less favourably treated than a heterosexual one by the laws dealing with income tax and estate duty. Suppose, however, that homosexuals and heterosexuals were treated equally according to the choicist criterion of equality, but that for some reason homosexuals tended to be less satisfied with life than heterosexuals. This would not be properly regarded as bad luck in as far as people feel that their sexuality is a central aspect of their personality and do not wish to be changed into some other kind of person.

That such a change is, as an empirical matter, difficult or impossible to accomplish, is not important. If a pill were invented tomorrow that switched people's sexual orientation painlessly and without side-effects, it would (I assume) have few takers, even if it were generally believed that one kind of sexual orientation tended to create more satisfaction with life than the other. To see this, I ask you to engage in another thought experiment. Imagine you were told that somebody who had been and could again be happier than you had suffered a ghastly accident, but that by killing you and attaching his head to your body he could, by a miracle of surgery, be restored to his old self. If you were a dedicated utilitarian, you might reluctantly agree that this was, impersonally considered, the best course of action. But you would surely not regard it as being in your interest. You would not, therefore, go around saying what bad luck it is that such an operation is not actually available. But if you wouldn't do that, why should you feel inclined to say what bad luck it is that you have your character rather than a quite different one?

As before, we can add that the semi-choicist position would call for the National Health Service to provide counselling and then assistance to anyone who genuinely, after careful consideration of all the implications, wanted to try to change sexual orientation—in either direction. But that seems to me perfectly reasonable. Once again, therefore, I suggest that the semi-choicist approach seems to come out in the right place.

What, finally, about tastes? Let us concede (though I doubt if it is invariably true) that a connoisseur gets less pleasure from a bottle of plonk than does somebody who wouldn't notice if it was Château Lafitte, and so on. Does that mean that a connoisseur reduced to drinking plonk wishes he were unable to tell that it is plonk and imagine how much better Château Lafitte would be? I doubt it. The ability to make fine discriminations is, after all, not something to be lightly wished away. But we should notice that where we do find tastes which many people wish they could change, it is considered quite appropriate for the National Health Service to offer help, examples being smoking, drinking, drug abuse, and eating disorders. To the extent that people want to change their preferences and cannot, the semi-choicist agrees with the anti-choicist that this is bad luck, and quite rightly so, it seems to me.

VI CONCLUSION

The issues that have been raised here about the roles of chance and choice are central to so many aspects of public policy that it is hardly surprising to find them surfacing constantly in everyday political arguments. The task of political philosophers in all this is to clarify the terms of debate. My experience in presenting the ideas contained here has been that some of my examples elicit unanimous responses where others give rise to mixed reactions. The conclusion I am inclined to draw from this is that there is more going on in some of these cases than I have yet identified. More work needs to be done to refine the analysis and to apply it.[5] I feel convinced, however, that any adequate theory of distributive justice will have to give a central position to chance and choice.

[5] I hope to contribute to this process myself by presenting a greatly extended analysis of chance and choice in *The Possibility of Justice*, vol. ii of *A Treatise on Social Justice*, forthcoming from the University of California Press and Harvester/Wheatsheaf.

8

CAN STATES BE MORAL?
International Morality and the Compliance Problem

It is quite a mistake to suppose that real dishonesty is at all common. The number of rogues is about equal to the number of men who act honestly; and it is very small. The great majority would sooner behave honestly than not. The reason why they do not give way to this natural preference for humanity is that they are afraid that others will not; and the others do not because they are afraid that *they* will not. Thus it comes about that, while behaviour which looks dishonest is fairly common, sincere dishonesty is about as rare as the courage to evoke good faith in your neighbours by showing that you trust them.

F. M. Cornford, *Microcosmographia Academica*

I

In the last few years I have presented a number of papers to various audiences on issues of international morality and have also conducted several courses for college students and professionals. From experience, I can safely make the generalization that in any such context sooner or later (and usually sooner) the objection will come up that this is merely flailing the air. For, it is said, the conduct of states is not an appropriate subject for moral evaluation or censure. Of course, some people will suggest that there is no point in moral discourse in any sphere of life. This kind of universal moral scepticism raises deep philosophical issues which would be well worth discussing on some other occasion. But for the present purpose I wish to direct my attention to those who do not deny the appropriateness of moral appraisal in ordinary life but who do nevertheless hold that it is inappropriate in the international arena.

Why might someone make a distinction along these lines? Two reasons seem to be most commonly put forward for scepticism specifically about international morality. The first is that governments almost invariably pursue the national interest whenever it conflicts with the interests of other countries, and in any case they have a duty

to their citizens to do so. The second reason has been expressed as
follows by Terry Nardin (although this is not his own view):

> The international system is not to any appreciable extent a society united by
> common rules, but simply an aggregate of separate societies each pursuing its
> own purposes, and linked with one another in ways that are essentially ad
> hoc, unstable, and transitory. The conduct of each state may in fact be rule-
> governed, in the sense that each observes rules of its own choosing. But
> because the decisions of each are governed by different rules, the separate
> states cannot be said to be members of a single society of states united by
> common rules of conduct—rules whose authority is acknowledged by all
> states.[1]

The reasoning that connects the two is, roughly speaking, that if
each state pursues its own national interest, a given state will comply
with common rules only to the extent that it can be made to be in that
state's interest to comply. But, in the absence of 'a common Power to
keep them all in awe', as Hobbes put it,[2] there is no way of ensuring
that most states will comply most of the time with any set of rules. So
there are not, in any real sense, any rules governing international
conduct.

Before going any further, it is worth observing that both of these
points have analogues in common-sense morality as it operates within
societies. This would cut no ice if we were dealing with a universal
moral sceptic. But since we are not this is a potentially significant
finding. Thus, in common-sense morality it is generally held to be
acceptable (and indeed under some conditions praiseworthy) for
different people to have different 'moral aims'.[3] That is, we do not
believe there is a single good that all have an equal moral obligation to
pursue. Instead we believe, for example, that it is right for a given
individual to pay more attention (or give more weight) to the interests
of persons to whom he or she is related by ties of family or other
association and commitment than to the interests of others. (This
includes giving more weight to one's own interests than to those of
randomly selected others.)

In common-sense morality it is also generally thought that there is a
class of social norms to which adherence is morally obligatory only if

---

[1] Terry Nardin, *Law, Morality, and the Relations of States* (Princeton, NJ: Princeton University
Press, 1983), 36.

[2] Thomas Hobbes, *Leviathan*, C. B. Macpherson (ed.) (Harmondsworth: Penguin Books,
1981), ch. 13, p. 185.

[3] Derek Parfit, *Reasons and Persons* (Oxford: Clarendon Press, 1984). For an earlier, simpler,
and clearer exposition, see 'Prudence, Morality, and the Prisoner's Dilemma', *Proceedings of the
British Academy*, 65 (1979), 539–64, esp. p. 559.

enough other people adhere to them. With a practice that is collectively beneficial provided that it is generally observed (the standard
philosophical example is refraining from wearing a path by taking a
short cut across a lawn), the presumption is that fairness requires each
person to observe it on the condition that enough others do so to
achieve the object served by the norm. On the other hand, if the norm
is not efficacious in providing people with a reason that they accept
(and act on) for eschewing their private, antisocial interests, then the
moral obligation on each one to observe the norm tends to evaporate.

I am being deliberately vague about the form of the relation
between compliance by others and the obligation to conform to a rule
oneself because I believe that relation will vary according to the details
of the case. In some instances, just one bit of non-compliance releases
everyone else from an obligation to refrain from doing what the norm
prohibits. If one neighbour shatters the peace of the neighbourhood
by using a power mower early on a Sunday morning, it does not make
much difference if others do so too. But in other instances much of the
collective benefit may be achieved even with a substantial amount of
non-compliance.[4] If only three-quarters of householders in a city
centre comply with a rule against burning garden refuse, the air may
be much less dirty than if there were no restraint, and this might
plausibly be thought to generate an obligation of fairness to comply,
albeit a weaker one than if compliance were closer to being universal.

I should emphasize that the structure of common-sense morality is
not utilitarian, since this may not be apparent from these examples.
The question is not simply which act—compliance or non-compliance—would have the most net beneficial consequences, given
what all the others are doing. It is true that in some cases the dictates of
common sense will coincide with those of utilitarianism. If, for
example, so many people have already walked across the grass that a
path of completely bare earth has been created, utilitarianism and
common sense would agree that there is no moral obligation on
anyone to refrain from taking the short cut. This can be called the
'threshold effect'. Here utilitarianism and common sense unite in
dissenting from the view held by some philosophers that, even when
some threshold has been passed, the right thing to do is unaffected by
the absence of beneficial consequences.

Such a view is characteristically arrived at by taking a framework
for moral decisionmaking that is not unreasonable in itself, but then

---

[4] Brian Barry and Russell Hardin (eds.), *Rational Man and Irrational Society? An Introduction and
Sourcebook* (Beverly Hills, Calif.: Sage, 1982), 108.

applying it too immediately and simplistically, without recognizing the need for institutional mediation between the ultimate criterion and the demands of morality in concrete situations. One way in which this happens is that Kant's formulation of the categorical imperative—that one must be able to will the maxim of one's action as a universal law—is misapplied. (One can with perfect consistency will universal adoption of the maxim that one walks across the grass whenever, because of the actions of others, there is no point in not doing so.) Another route which can lead to the same conclusion is to take ideal rule utilitarianism—the doctrine that the best set of rules is that which would have the best consequences if it enjoyed general adherence—and then to say that the right thing to do in any actual situation is to act on the rules of ideal morality so understood, whether or not others either recognize or act on these rules.

According to common sense it is mere quixotry to feel obliged to do something that is in fact pointless simply because it would have a point in some counterfactual state of the world. And I think the common-sense position will withstand any amount of philosophical scrutiny. There are some who claim to find an argument against utilitarianism (that is, act utilitarianism, not the curious form of ideal rule utilitarianism mentioned above) in that it gets what they regard as the 'wrong answer' in threshold cases. They are, in my view, kicking the ball through their own goal: what they regard as an argument is actually a *reductio ad absurdum*.

Common-sense morality is thus not unconcerned with beneficial overall consequences in evaluating actions. But it differs from utilitarianism in that it is not concerned solely with the production of beneficial overall consequences. The prescriptions of the two will normally coincide in threshold cases, but even then the way in which they reach their shared conclusions is not quite the same. For utilitarianism the decisive point—and the only one that could possibly matter—is simply that, given that others have already worn a path in the grass, there is no collective benefit gained from walking around the edge that can be set against the benefit the agent himself gains from cutting across. There is obviously then a net overall benefit from cutting across. The line taken by common-sense morality includes all of the above considerations, but it does not stop there. It goes on to say that there is no collective benefit that others can help provide: if other people go to the trouble of walking around, they are merely taking gratuitous exercise. Since there is no collective benefit from which one gains as a result of the forbearances of others, there can be no unfairness in not contributing to it oneself, and this is the real reason why it is morally permissible to walk across the grass. To introduce a new metaphor, one cannot properly be accused of being a free rider if the train never leaves the station.

In a threshold case, this extra loop is trivial because there is no way in which one can help provide any collective benefit by one's own action, even if one wishes to. This is precisely the reason for the conclusion of common-sense morality coinciding with that of utilitarianism. Fairness does not enter in because the issue of fairness is pre-empted by the recognition that the 'co-operative' move does not in fact do anybody any good. We might say that the utilitarian conclusion is determined by its own single criterion, whereas the more complex common-sense conclusion is overdetermined.

To see that there really is a difference between the practical implications of common sense and those of utilitarianism, we need only look at a non-threshold case. It does not have to be one in which the net benefit from an agent's contributing to a public good is invariant with respect to the number of others who contribute. That is the simplest case. But the general form of the relation we require is simply that, even when few other people are contributing, there is still a net benefit to be gained from any given agent's contribution (after subtracting the cost to the agent of producing the increment of collective benefit enjoyed by all). Such cases are quite common in real life, though it will often be hard to establish the amount of collective gain from a single contribution in order to compare it to the cost of that contribution to the actor. But Derek Parfit is correct in calling it a 'mistake in moral mathematics' to suppose that a small effect diffused over a large number of people is not a real effect; it may be significant in determining the moral quality of the act that brings it about.[5]

Returning to the example of air pollution, we may observe that there may be no upper threshold in many cases. Even if everyone living in the city centre except me is burning soft coal, it is quite possible that there is still a net benefit from my refraining from doing so: the overall reduction in air pollution outweighs the cost to me of using some alternative means of heating. On the utilitarian criterion, this is enough to generate the conclusion that I have a moral obligation to refrain from adding my smoke to the pall already created by the others. But, according to the dictates of common-sense morality, I have no such obligation. The failure of the others to contribute to the

---

[5] Parfit, *Reasons and Persons*, pp. 78–82.

collective good—clean air—releases me from the moral obligation to do so myself. I cannot reasonably be accused of behaving unfairly if I fail to act on a norm that so many others who are similarly situated are failing to act on.

We can again make the point by using the 'free rider' metaphor. In the previous case there was nothing I could do by myself to make the train go. Here the point is simply that, even if I do not pay my fare, I am not riding at the expense of others. In this case, my fare would suffice to move the train a minute fraction of an inch, but then the others would be free riding at my expense. I have no obligation to give them a free—even if extremely short—ride.

Common-sense morality is capable of discriminating between different kinds of moral judgement. Thus, although in the situation described it would not be morally obligatory to refrain from burning soft coal, it would certainly be admirable. Anyone who did so would be exhibiting the virtue of beneficence. Common-sense morality differs from utilitarianism in that it denies that what does the most good is in general obligatory and that it recognizes other virtues besides beneficence, such as that of behaving justly towards others.

For utilitarianism, then, the relevance of what other people are doing is purely contingent: we need to know what they are doing simply because it may make a difference to the net benefit that a single act of contribution would bring. But once the presence of a net benefit has been established, there is an obligation to contribute, regardless of how few others are contributing. Indeed, we can imagine a case, such as traffic congestion, in which the fewer who contribute by refraining from driving, the larger the net benefit from a single act of contribution. Then, by the utilitarian criterion, the obligation to contribute becomes more stringent the smaller the proportion of others who contribute. According to common-sense morality, however, the obligation of fair play would always diminish as the number of contributors diminished. None the less, if a single contribution would do a lot of good, and particularly if it would alleviate suffering or destitution, then it might be required by common-sense morality as an obligation of humanity. Normally, however, benefits that fit this description are not collective in character.

II

So far I have suggested that the two grounds most often advanced for denying that international affairs can be subjected to moral appraisal have clear analogues in what common-sense morality holds about morality within societies. Corresponding to the claim that political leaders have a right, perhaps even a duty, to pursue the national interest is the notion that people have their own legitimately differing 'moral ends', which will permit or possibly even require them to give more weight to their own interests and to those of people connected to them than they give to the interests of others. And, corresponding to the claim that the lack of assurance that other states will comply with international norms releases states from any obligation to observe them, there is in common-sense morality a complex connection between the degree of compliance by others and the obligation to conform to a norm oneself.

My purpose in pointing out these connections is simply to examine the following question: if these two features of common-sense morality are not usually thought to cause it to self-destruct as a source of moral obligations and other moral phenomena (and I believe that in fact they do not), why should it be supposed that their international analogues must have such devastating implications for the possibility of moral appraisal in international affairs?

Let us take up in turn the two alleged grounds for the amorality of the international order. The relevant implication for states of the notion of different 'moral ends' is that governments have some duties—possibly quite extensive—towards their own citizens that they do not owe to citizens of other countries. (Those who prefer to formulate issues of political obligation in lateral rather than hierarchical terms could express this by saying that citizens of a single country owe one another things that they do not owe citizens of other countries.) But this does not mean that anything goes. Generally speaking, my special obligation to my family does not legitimate lying, stealing, cheating, or killing on their behalf. The special obligation is set in a context of constraints on the morally acceptable means of advancing my moral ends.

It would seem that countries are in a position exactly analogous to this. We can easily allow that a government has duties to its own citizens that it does not owe to people in other countries. But again, this does not mean that the government has a moral licence to do anything to advance the national interest without regard to possible violation of the legitimate interests of others. (Is there anything magical, after all, about one particular grouping—a nation-state—that can dissolve all wider moral considerations? Why should this one level of association be exempted from moral constraints that apply to all others?)

To the extent that we can talk about a common international morality, it takes the form of a belief that there are morally binding constraints on how governments can pursue their national interest. This raises the second alleged ground for the amorality of the international order: how can there be morally binding constraints without a centralized agency of enforcement? In the Hobbesian 'condition of mere Nature' which characterizes the relations of states with one another, would not anyone adhering to moral constraints 'but betray himself to his enemy'? 'For he that would be modest, and tractable, and perform all he promises, in such time, and place, where no man else should do so, should but make himself a prey to others, and secure his own certain ruine.'[6]

The simple answer, which is not complete but is still worth giving, is that the moral norms that govern everyday life in a society are generally not backed by legal sanctions either but are none the less quite broadly effective in restraining conduct. The response will inevitably come that this evades the issue because the security provided by legal enforcement provides the essential underpinnings of a whole system of mutual restraint within a society. This argument undeniably has an element of truth. International relations, in contrast, are fundamentally conditioned by the absence of an agency capable of enforcing compliance. A state normally commands a monopoly on the use of violence within its territory, whereas international law and morality permit the waging of war under certain conditions. However, the notion that in the absence of a core of centrally enforced norms there can be no others that are effective is simply erroneous. Huge numbers of international transactions take place every day on the basis of norms that the parties rely on and, in fact, adhere to—some codified into international law and others developed through custom.

It is true that much of the compliance with these norms can be accounted for by the rational pursuit of interest. It is to a state's advantage to not be excluded from the system of diplomatic relations, to have a reputation as a reliable trading partner, and so on. Hobbes, who is often regarded as an authority by the realists, deduced from the postulate of survival that one should 'seek peace' in the state of nature. He drew up a long list of prescriptions—'laws of nature'—that should be acted upon as long as doing so is compatible with safety. 'He that having sufficient Security, that others shall observe the same Lawes

---

[6] Hobbes, *Leviathan*, ch. 14, p. 196; ch. 15, p. 215.

towards him, observes them not himself, seeketh not Peace, but War; & consequently the destruction of his Nature by Violence.'[7]

In practice, states can often follow the (admittedly quite undemanding) prescriptions of positive international morality without putting their security at risk in the slightest. It is equally true that much of the time there are self-interested motives for sticking to the prescriptions of common-sense morality in everyday life. And ordinary experience shows that, to the extent that others observe the norms, we feel an obligation to do so too. Perhaps the truth is that most of the time we do not inquire too minutely into the reasons for doing what is required. We recognize the general advantageousness of the system and accept its authority in guiding our actions. States are, I would suggest, not very different in this respect. Their standard operating procedures are to adhere to the appropriate international norms; it would actually be unworkable to have to determine on every occasion where the exact balance of long-term and overall interest lies before taking action.

I have conceded, however, that because common international morality does not ask a lot, the question of reasons for adhering to it is not a very pressing one. Nardin has summed it up as follows:

The moral element in international law is to be found in those general principles of international association that constitute customary international law, and above all in the most fundamental of those principles, such as the ones specifying the rights of independence, legal equality, and self defense, and the duties to observe treaties, to respect the immunity of ambassadors, to refrain from aggression, to conduct hostilities in war in accordance with the laws of war, to respect human rights, and to cooperate in the peaceful settlement of disputes.[8]

When we look at economic affairs, what is striking is the absence of any international system comparable to that within nations to tax those who can afford it to provide assistance to those who would otherwise be destitute. This does not mean that there is no mechanism for international redistribution: the World Bank does after all make loans on favourable terms to poor countries. But these are discretionary and in any case do not represent a sizeable transfer. The domestic analogue would be closer to a system of soft loans from the government to small businesses than to a welfare system. Here, no doubt, the absence of coercion makes itself strongly felt. If contributions to government coffers were raised by voluntary subscription, even tax

---

[7] Ibid., ch. 15, p. 215.   [8] Nardin, *Law, Morality, and the Relations of States*, p. 23.

rates of 10 per cent would be regarded as visionary and utopian, as they are in the international context. We would hear that it asks far too much of human nature for the wealthy to tithe themselves to benefit the poor. The affluent countries are committed in principle to give 0.7 per cent of gross national product as official aid, but even that rate greatly exceeds the amount that almost any country actually provides.

III

Is this an inevitable consequence of the lack of an international sovereign? The best way to approach this question is indirectly. Let us first ask what the ideal would be if we were to ignore the problem of compliance, and then see what adaptations would be required. We must know our aim before we can tell how far short of the target we are bound to fall.

What exactly do we mean by 'ideal morality'? Derek Parfit, who makes heavy use of the notion, defines an 'ideal act theory' as one that 'says what we should all try to do, simply on the assumptions that we all try, and all succeed'.[9] This is not quite right, because ideal morality should not include prescriptions to attempt things that we have good reason to believe people, or collectivities such as states, could not succeed in doing if they tried. We are interested here in utopian thinking—not science fiction. In constructing a 'full compliance' theory of morality,[10] we should look for one that abstracts from what I have called the 'compliance problem'. This is the problem that people may not act on the prescriptions embodied in a normative system that covers them, even though they could do so perfectly well if they chose. We normally focus on the prospect that people will fail to comply because prescriptions of morality ask them to act in some way that runs contrary to (what they perceive as) their self-interest. But we must also allow for the prospect that people may simply not accept as valid the particular set of prescriptions with which we are concerned.

Since many people are familiar with the concept of 'ideal theory' as introduced by John Rawls in *A Theory of Justice*, it may avoid confusion if I discuss the ways in which my notion of ideal theory agrees with or departs from his. The point of similarity is that Rawls equates ideal theory with what he calls 'strict compliance theory',[11] by which he means a theory of justice constructed on the assumption that

---

[9] Parfit, *Reasons and Persons*, p. 99.
[10] Ibid.
[11] John Rawls, *A Theory of Justice* (Cambridge, Mass.: Harvard University Press, 1971), 8, 9.

'the parties can depend on one another to conform to them'.[12] But my conception of ideal theory diverges sharply from that of Rawls in an important way.

In constructing an ideal theory we must, Rawls says, address what he calls 'the strains of commitment'. By this he means that people may find it difficult or impossible to adhere to some sets of principles.[13] This might be interpreted as being equivalent to my demand for utopia rather than science fiction: we do not want principles that require people to do what is impossible or even difficult if this implies that people are liable to fail if they try. But this is not what Rawls has in mind.

Rawls says that, even when designing an ideal theory, we should throw out 'principles which may have consequences so extreme that [people] could not accept them in practice'. And his example of an 'extreme' principle is the utilitarian principle that people should act to maximize overall well-being. For this requires some people 'to accept lower prospects of life for the sake of others'. (By lower prospects Rawls presumably means lower than the prospects under some alternative principle.) Thus, the utilitarian principle as a basis for a social ethic 'is threatened with instability unless sympathy and bene-volence can be widely and intensively cultivated'. Without a word of discussion, Rawls assumes that this cannot be done, and immediately concludes that we should 'reject the principle of utility'.[14]

This cavalier disposition of an important and difficult psychological question illustrates precisely what is wrong with Rawls's conception of ideal theory. By incorporating the problem of compliance (as I have defined it) under the description of 'the strains of commitment', Rawls moves too fast in the direction of practicality, while at the same time stopping short of it. His 'ideal theory' is an unsatisfactory hybrid of ideal and practical considerations—and is neither really ideal nor really practical.

The theory makes large concessions (perhaps too large) to the fact that people may not be willing to do things that are perfectly within their power but which would require them to make sacrifices. At the same time, the theory assumes that, provided some threshold of 'non-demandingness' is passed—Rawls supposes that his own theory passes this threshold—we can assume absolute and invariable compliance with the dictates of the theory. It is hard to know what to do with such a theory. It seems better to start from an ideal uncontaminated by the

---

[12] Ibid. 145. [13] Ibid.
[14] All quotes in this para. are from ibid., p. 178.

compliance problem and then, moving away from that point, to introduce *all* the problems of compliance in their awful variety and complexity.

In thinking about the dimensions of the compliance problem, we should notice that there are two ways in which an ideal theory may run into difficulties with compliance. These two ways do not invariably go together and there is some reason to believe that they tend to be inversely related. First, an ideal theory of morality may run into practical difficulties because it is excessively *liable* to non-compliance. Second, it may run into difficulties if it is excessively *vulnerable* to non-compliance.

Other things being equal, a rule will be less liable to non-compliance the less that conformity with it entails a conflict with some strong desire, the more readily that non-compliance can be monitored by others, and the more incentive that others have to react to non-compliance in a way that reduces or eliminates the advantage gained. Other things being equal, a rule will be less vulnerable to non-compliance the less any level of non-compliance affects the value of the rule. In particular, it is important that the point of the rule—the ends that justify it—should not be frustrated by a small number of cases of non-compliance.

IV

I shall return to non-compliance later. For now let me relax the constraint imposed by problems of compliance and ask what an ideal set of international norms would look like, focusing particularly on the question of international economic distribution.

There is an influential view (put forward by among others John Rawls in *A Theory of Justice*) that distributive justice can be predicated only on relations within a society, where a society is understood as a scheme for mutual advantage through joint participation in co-operative undertakings. The idea is that distributive justice concerns the distribution of gains from social co-operation. This seems mistaken if it is seen as setting the limits of distributive justice.

If one country builds tall smokestacks and pumps sulphur into the atmosphere, which descends on another country downwind in the form of acid rain, then it has injured the other and, as a matter of justice, should either clean up its industry or compensate the other country. There need be no reciprocal advantage or even any other form of relationship between the two. Not all economic value is created by the co-operative effort that goes into it; production requires a production site, capital, and usually raw materials. The notion that claims of justice can arise only among those engaging in a co-operative enterprise puts things backwards. Before co-operation can occur, distributive questions must have already been answered about rights over land, resources, and other advantages that would-be co-operators did not themselves create. As a matter of ideal morality, the answer currently accepted in the international community—that each state has an absolute right to everything within, under, over, and extending two hundred miles beyond its national boundary—is a rotten one. But my present point is simply that an answer must be given to these distributive questions, and that that answer will establish a global distribution of some kind among countries that need have no co-operative relations at all.

The insistence on co-operation as a condition of morality stems from a conception of morality as a scheme of mutual advantage from mutual restraint. This, however, introduces the compliance issue too soon and too strongly. It provides a self-interested motive for compliance with moral norms by making the content of moral norms entirely coincident with what a sophisticated calculation of self-interest would require.

There is an alternative conception of morality that can be found in Rawls, sitting uneasily alongside the one discussed above—one which has been put forward most clearly by Thomas Scanlon,[15] although it was anticipated by, for example, David Hume and Adam Smith. According to this tradition of thought, there is a strong connection between morality and impartiality. A moral position is one that can be accepted from any viewpoint. It is not enough for me to say, 'This arrangement suits me.' The arrangement must be capable of being defended to all those affected; if any other person affected could not reasonably be expected to accept it in the absence of coercion, then the arrangement cannot be morally justified. I have already pointed out that much of the time there are good reasons of self-interest for doing what the moral norms of one's society require. According to this alternative conception of morality, the primary motive for behaving morally for its own sake is simply 'the desire to be able to justify one's actions to others on grounds they could not reasonably reject', where

---

[15] Thomas M. Scanlon, 'Contractualism and Utilitarianism', in Amartya Sen and Bernard Williams (eds.), *Utilitarianism and Beyond* (Cambridge: Cambridge University Press, 1982), 103–28.

the basis for others' reasonable rejection of one's actions is given by *their* 'desire to find principles which others similarly motivated could not reasonably reject'.[16]

This may appear to be a circular definition of morality and the moral motive because the notion of 'reasonableness' already presupposes that people have some moral ideas. I am not sure how Scanlon would reply to this charge, but I believe it ought to be admitted. There are two ways in which we can avoid giving reasonableness a moral tinge, but both of them mask the central idea of the theory in the process of tidying it up.

One possibility is to impute to the parties purely self-interested motivations, so that each will agree only to whatever will best serve his or her interests. Reasonableness is thus construed as if it corresponded to the 'rationality' of game theorists and decision theorists, and indeed, this interpretation of reasonableness would make moral theory a subject for one or the other of those disciplines.

If we set things up so that the parties have conflicting ends (as they usually do in real life) we get a problem for game theory. It seems plausible that there must be some arrangement that is better for everybody than a free-for-all. The problem is to identify the pay-offs offered by a free-for-all and then to devise some rule for distributing the gains that can be achieved by moving away from a free-for-all towards this other arrangement. We thus arrive at a theory like that of David Gauthier,[17] behind whom stands the sardonic figure of Hobbes.

If, on the other hand, we eliminate conflicting interests by introducing constraints on the information available to the parties about their respective positions—a 'veil of ignorance', as Rawls calls it—we get a decision-theoretic problem. Since the veil of ignorance, whatever the precise details of its construction, gives each party identical information to work with—information laundered of any clues that would enable them to differentiate among themselves—they are all faced with the same set of calculations. Hence, we can represent the problem as one presented to a single decisionmaker. This produces theories such as Harsanyi's derivation of utilitarianism from the maximizing of expected utility,[18] or one strand of Rawls's theory of justice, where a conservative, risk-aversive (maximin) rule for making choices under uncertainty is seen as leading to the difference principle, which

---

[16] Ibid. 116 and n. 12.

[17] David Gauthier, *Morals by Agreement* (New York: Oxford University Press, 1986).

[18] John C. Harsanyi, 'Cardinal Welfare, Individualistic Ethics, and Interpersonal Comparisons of Utility', *Journal of Political Economy*, 63 (1955), 309–21.

prescribes that the position of those who are worst off should be raised to as high a level as possible.[19]

The other method we could use to purge the notion of reasonableness of any moral content would be to take Scanlon's formula literally and suppose that the parties are *solely* motivated by the desire to reach agreement. Under this version we would not impute to them any substantive views at all about the acceptability of one outcome over any other. This line of thought would bring the problem of the terms of agreement under yet a third branch of formal theory. We would look to the work on pure co-ordination problems pioneered by Thomas Schelling in *The Strategy of Conflict*[20]—the sort of problem that arises when two people want to meet in a town without having made prior arrangements, and therefore each tries to decide where he will have the best chance of meeting the other, given the knowledge that the other is trying to make the same decision.[21] The moral theory that arises from this is conventionalism: the content of morality is arbitrary, but it is still binding because it matters that we all act on the same rules, whatever they may be. Morality, in this view, becomes the search for 'prominent solutions' (or 'Schelling points', as they have come to be known) in situations where some rule is needed.[22]

The youthful David Hume, ever on the look-out for paradoxes with which to jolt the world of polite learning into paying him some attention, came close in the *Treatise* to maintaining that rules governing property are conventional in this way. The operations of the 'fancy'—the disposition of the human mind to make associations between different ideas where there is no connection in reality—were invoked to explain why the details of the rules about property took the form they did.[23] But by the time he wrote the *Enquiry*,[24] Hume had modified his position and maintained only that fanciful analogies or associations of ideas might come into play in order to settle the issue between two or more alternative rules that were equally beneficial.

---

[19] See Brian Barry, *The Liberal Theory of Justice* (Oxford: Clarendon Press, 1973), ch. 9, pp. 87–107; and Rolf E. Sartorius, *Individual Conduct and Social Norms* (Encino, Calif.: Dickenson, 1975), 122–9.

[20] Thomas C. Schelling, *The Strategy of Conflict* (Cambridge, Mass.: Harvard University Press, 1960), ch. 4, pp. 83–118.

[21] See also David Lewis, *Convention* (Cambridge, Mass.: Harvard University Press, 1969).

[22] See Karol Sołtan, *The Causal Theory of Justice* (Berkeley and Los Angeles: University of California Press, 1987).

[23] David Hume, *A Treatise of Human Nature*, L. A. Selby-Bigge (ed.), 2nd edn. by P. H. Niddich (Oxford: Clarendon Press, 1978), vol. iii. sec. 3, pp. 501–13.

[24] David Hume, *An Enquiry Concerning the Principles of Morals*, in *Enquiries*, L. A. Selby-Bigge (ed.), 3rd edn. by P. H. Niddich (Oxford: Clarendon Press, 1975).

This is surely much more plausible. The rule, for example, which assigns the lambs to the owner of the ewe stems not merely from a tendency for the 'fancy' to run from the one to the other but also from the rule's convenience and its avoiding the creation of perverse incentives.[25] The rule of the road—to drive on the right or to drive on the left—is scarcely the paradigm of a moral rule. Usually it does make a difference what the content of the rule is.

I have spoken of two ways to construe the notion of reasonableness so as to purge it of distinctly moral content. If we assimilate reasonableness to the rational pursuit of self-interest, we get a problem in game theory or in decision theory, depending upon what we do about information conditions. If we press to the limit the idea of seeking an agreement with others who are also seeking one, we get a problem of co-ordinating expectations. I have mentioned in passing the great implausibility of the second approach. Regarding the first, I shall only say that seeking to transform what was intended as a guide for thinking about morality into a calculus capable of deriving moral conclusions from premises devoid of any moral content seems to me to miss the original point.

The notion of reasonableness is admittedly indefinite, but it is not devoid of content. What we need to do to build up the theory is to specify it further, not substitute some simpler and more tractable notion. Thus, if we say that somebody has made a reasonable offer, we generally mean that it is an offer that the other party would be reasonable in accepting. A reasonable person is one who has a tendency to make—and accept—reasonable offers. We will have to tighten this definition if we want to characterize further the range of reasonable offers in some specific situation (and it is likely to be a range rather than a unique position). But even without going further, we can be quite sure that a reasonable offer will not be identified with a rationally maximizing offer, either with full information or behind some kind of veil of ignorance.

I do not now have the fully developed theory in hand, though I hope to in a few years' time.[26] For now I must press on with the problem of this chapter. So far I have only pointed at the way in which morality might be understood as that which it would be reasonable for all to accept. Let me suggest, without filling in all the steps, how evidence

---

[25] Ibid. 195–6.

[26] The first instalment of what is promised here is *Theories of Justice* (Berkeley and Los Angeles: University of California Press, 1989). This is the first volume in a 3-volume *Treatise on Social Justice* which will, taken together, constitute my attempt to give substance to the approach laid out in this chapter.

from the real world can be brought to bear in order to establish what this conception of morality dictates for international distribution.

As the theory stands, it sets up an ideal decisionmaking context of uncoerced agreement that is found only rarely and, it seems safe to say, never in large groups such as states.[27] Nevertheless, societies approach the ideal to varying degrees, and it is not mere sentimentalism or unreflective submission to the local ideology to suggest that the modern, Western liberal-democratic states are, by comparative and historical standards, relatively high on the criterion of unforced agreement. With obvious exceptions such as Northern Ireland, the gaols do not contain many political prisoners, and no sizeable section of the population is thoroughly alienated from the society's major institutions. Suppose, then, that we look for invariant features of these societies. If we find them, can we not at least say that we have a presumption in favour of assuming that these features are ones that arise in conditions of uncoerced agreement? There are two features that are common to all liberal-democratic societies. They may not be equally well-developed in all of these societies, but there is a positive correlation between the degree to which these features are present and the extent of universal, uncoerced consent.

The first feature is this: these countries are all to some extent market societies, and wherever the operations of the market cause people's incomes to vary widely from year to year, owing to factors outside their control, the state will suppress or heavily intervene in the market to mitigate or eliminate these effects. An obvious and striking example is responses to the income levels of the agricultural sector. The United States—that bastion of the free market—no less than the countries of the European Economic Community (EEC) has an elaborate system of quotas, subsidies, and price supports to cushion farmers from the rigours of the market.

The second invariant feature of these countries is that they have some kind of system for the relief of indigence caused by illness or injury, unemployment, age, or youth. The well-being of those who, for some reason beyond their control, are unable to maintain themselves

[27] It is commonplace in the literature that Rawls's 'original position' has some similarities to Habermas's 'ideal speech situation'. More interesting are their dissimilarities. The spirit of the present enterprise is I believe closer to Habermas, who writes: 'it is a question of finding arrangements which can ground the presumption that the basic institutions of the society and the basic political decisions would meet with the unforced agreement of all those involved, if they could participate, as free and equal, in discursive will-formation'. See Jürgen Habermas, 'Legitimation Problems in the Modern State', in *Communication and the Evolution of Society*, Thomas McCarthy (tr.) (Boston, Mass.: Beacon Press, 1979), 186; see also Joshua Cohen and Joel Rogers, *On Democracy* (Harmondsworth: Penguin Books, 1983), ch. 6, pp. 146–83.

at a certain minimum standard is regarded as the responsibility of society, with the state collecting the taxes necessary to make the required payments. That a mechanism of this kind is crucial for the uncoerced acceptance of basic social institutions is evidenced by the way in which such schemes have typically expanded as suffrage has been extended to new groups further down the social hierarchy. It is particularly significant that in some cases welfare legislation was introduced by a conservative government as a concomitant of the extension of the franchise precisely in order to forestall destabilizing demands on the system (Bismarck's Germany being the famous example).

When we turn from this domestic intervention and redistribution to the world economy, we are immediately struck by the absence of anything remotely comparable to either feature. Countries with one-crop or one-mineral economies are at the mercy of the ups and downs of the international market with only very spotty exceptions (e.g. the STABEX scheme for certain primary commodities operated by the EEC countries and their former colonial dependencies). There is no scheme for the systematic transfer of funds from affluent countries to poor ones, although there have been proposals: the demands of Third World countries for a New International Economic Order centre around the attempt to bring commodity markets under some kind of international control, and proposals for the continuous creation under the International Monetary Fund of Special Drawing Rights for poor countries might be seen as an imperfect way of easing the constraints on their economies.

Both lines of initiative have foundered on the unwillingness of rich countries, led by the US, with Japan, Germany, and, lately, Britain in support, to countenance any steps towards a new deal for the poor countries. It seems clear that this refusal sticks only because the rich countries have the power to make it stick. The poor countries do not accept the reasonableness of the status quo, and neither would we if we were in their position. I have argued that it is a basic presupposition of the domestic politics of all countries in which the basic institutions achieve a fair level of popular consent that people should not face ruin and destitution as a result of circumstances beyond their control. This presupposition should also apply in international situations, where people's life chances are set primarily by their having been born into a particular social position in a certain country, and where no plausible amount of personal exertion can raise the majority of people in a desperately poor country above poverty.

It is not necessary to argue here the precise implications of these ideas for the amount and nature of international redistribution that is called for as a matter of ideal morality. I shall assume, however, that it is very much larger than the current level of transfers, including the maximum of 1 per cent of GNP currently given by any of the relatively wealthy countries. There must be practical limits on what the poorer countries can absorb, and these might well limit transfers. But the point is that there is no need to settle these questions in order to see the direction in which things ought to go.

V

Let us now return to the problem of compliance. The immediate question is: wherein does the compliance problem actually reside? It would be easy to assume that we need to come up with a scheme that all actors—in this case states—find to be in their interest to comply with. But this was not how we approached it in discussing compliance in everyday life. There it was argued that the system of obligations should not be too prone to subversion by non-compliance. The analysis had two components. First, I suggested that liability to non-compliance is a function of the sacrifice demanded and the degree to which non-compliance could be monitored and sanctioned by others. Second, I treated vulnerability to non-compliance as a matter of how serious a threat was posed to the achievement of one's 'moral ends' by the non-compliance of others.

If we relate this approach to international affairs, we can conclude, perhaps surprisingly, that the problem of compliance is not a serious impediment to moving towards a much greater degree of international co-operation on economic matters and a greater international redistribution of income. Looking first at vulnerability, it seems clear that no government's moral ends would be gravely jeopardized if it co-operated in an international scheme (say, that proposed in the Law of the Sea Convention) with which there was some non-compliance. The state can cease to comply or pull out if enough others do so, and in the meantime the relative disadvantage from complying where others do not is unlikely to be of disastrous proportions. Similarly, for countries that pay their share in some redistributive arrangement (say, a percentage of GNP into some international fund), it is irritating but not a major setback to their interests if some countries pay less than their share. We might say that the self-sufficiency of states, in comparison with individuals, has the implication that norms for states are generally less vulnerable to non-compliance than norms for individuals.

Of course, it might be thought that international norms would for the same reason be particularly liable to non-compliance. Because states are less dependent on the co-operation of others to achieve their moral ends, they have less of a self-interested motive for observing any set of international norms. I have already noted the obvious point that legal sanctions of the centralized kind available within countries do not exist internationally. But that should not blind us to the ways in which states already feel constrained, not by fear of military force directed against them, but simply by the anticipated consequences of violating international norms. The standard case is the reluctance of governments to repudiate loans, even when the regime has changed and the previous regime's loans were misappropriated (as in Nicaragua). A more complex example is that of the EEC, which has a system of taxation and a body of economic regulations but has no sanctions except the disadvantages to a member state of withdrawing or being expelled. In other words, to the extent that interdependence exists, it tends to make compliance with the norms defining that interdependence more reliable.

The number of states in the world is small enough for there to be some real chance of monitoring compliance with a set of norms which have been defined as states' obligations, and of making continuation of the arrangement dependent on the achievement of a certain level of compliance. There is nothing in the problem of compliance to prevent governments from looking for ways of implementing the requirements of ideal justice by setting up international schemes. What makes such moves so difficult is not compliance but motivation, and one of my major aims in this chapter has been to try to avoid confounding the two. The problem of compliance, as I have presented it, presupposes some willingness to act morally simply for the sake of acting morally, but allows for a legitimate concern about the performance of others. The structure is, in terms of game theory, an assurance game rather than a prisoner's dilemma: so long as others co-operate, co-operation is preferred to non-co-operation.

F. M. Cornford, in his classic analysis of academic politics, *Microcosmographia Academica*, remarked that there is only one argument for doing something—that it is the right thing to do—and all the rest are arguments for doing nothing.[28] It sounds much more portentous to

---

[28] F. M. Cornford, *Microcosmographia Academica* (London: Bowes and Bowes, 6th edn. 1964), 22.

say that a desirable change is unfeasible because it depends on too many other people doing the right thing than to confess simply that you choose not to make the change because, although it is the right thing to do, by doing it you would incur some cost.

The current celebration of selfishness at home and chauvinism abroad that is apparently electorally popular in both Britain and the US may mean that hypocrisy—the tribute paid by vice to virtue—is no longer in fashion. The pure assertion of naked national self-interest may not raise a blush. Unfortunately, in the account of morality I have relied on here there is no way of making logically coercive arguments to get people to behave morally. I cannot, for example, maintain that those who violate the requirements of morality are engaged in some kind of self-contradiction. In the view I have advanced, people must want to behave in a way that can be defended impartially—in a way that has a chance of being accepted by others without coercion—for moral motivation to take hold. This is a psychological phenomenon rather than a logical one. Once people have moral motivation, rational argument has a place in helping to determine what the concrete requirements of morality are. But people cannot be persuaded into having moral motivation if they lack it. Psychopaths are not necessarily lacking in ratiocinative capacity.

If this is correct, it is natural to ask what conditions predispose people to acquire moral motivation, or, in other words, what conditions arouse the moral motive. I speculate that part of the answer is that the experience of dependence on others is an important predisposing factor. Those who are in a position to control the lives of others commonly become tyrannical. They behave in ways that they would not voluntarily accept if they were on the receiving end. It is in situations where one must gain the co-operation of others in order to achieve one's own ends that one cultivates the habit of looking at things from the other person's point of view and considering what type of conduct the other person might reasonably find acceptable.

As a proposition of speculative moral psychology, the suggestion is that equality of power—or at least not too extreme an inequality of power—is conducive to the formation and elicitation of moral motivation. But I do not mean to reinstate the Hobbes/Gauthier conception of morality through a back door; I am not saying that the *reason* for acting morally is that, under conditions of approximately equal power, it is necessary for the pursuit of one's own advantage to co-operate with others on terms that can be mutually accepted as reasonable. The motive for acting morally remains what I have said:

the desire to be able to justify our conduct. And that desire is more likely to come to the fore in conditions of approximately equal power than in conditions of serious inequality.

If there is anything to all of this, the application at the international level is fairly apparent. The world is a place in which states are unequal in power. The question is whether to follow Robert Tucker in rejoicing in this fact, as he did as an adviser to President Reagan in the 1980 election campaign and in his book *The Inequality of Nations*,[29] or whether to regard it as regrettable. Clearly, for anyone who would like to see more moral motivation in the conduct of international relations, the current degree of inequality must be seen as a great misfortune. The problem is not only one of global inequalities of power, but one of extreme regional imbalances of power as well. The Soviet invasion of Afghanistan and the US invasion of Grenada are paralleled by the Israeli invasion of Lebanon and the South African invasion of Angola—all were carried out in the face of virtually unanimous disapproval from the rest of the world. There could be no better illustration of Lord Acton's dictum that all power tends to corrupt than the arrogant reactions of all four of those governments to international criticism, as typified by Reagan's reaction to the UN vote (108 to 9) condemning the invasion of Grenada: 'It didn't upset my breakfast at all.'[30]

The best prospect for the future is the hope that the present extreme inequalities of power among nations will be reduced. And there is some hope for the long run. The period since the Second World War has seen massive decolonization and the creation of new states that, though individually weak, are certainly better placed to defend their interests than they were before independence. The American post-war hegemony has also ended: the economic preponderance of the USA in the world economy was inevitable in the aftermath of the Second World War but was bound to disappear once recovery set in. There seems to be a long-term trend towards a more interdependent world.

Unfortunately, however, it looks as if this evolution will be opposed by the superpowers with all the forces at their command: covert destabilization operations, military aid to regional surrogates, and, if all else fails, direct intervention. It seems doubtful that this will prevent the equalization of power in the long run. But in a world

---

[29] See Jeff McMahan, *Reagan and the World* (London: Pluto Press, 1984), 11; Robert Tucker, *The Inequality of Nations* (New York: Basic Books, 1977).

[30] McMahan, *Reagan and the World*, p. 166.

brimming with nuclear weapons there is the danger that, adapting Keynes's aphorism, in the medium run we shall all be dead. Ultimately, if we are to be saved, it will be by political action rather than by political philosophy.

9

HUMANITY AND JUSTICE IN GLOBAL PERSPECTIVE

This chapter has three sections. The first argues that considerations of humanity require that rich countries give aid to poor ones. The second argues that considerations of justice require transfers of economic resources from rich countries to poor ones. The third picks up the distinction between aid and transfer and argues that, when we get into detail, the obligations imposed by humanity and justice are different, although not incompatible.

I HUMANITY

What is it to act in a way called for by humanity? A humane act is a beneficent act, but not every beneficent act is a humane one. To do something that helps to make someone who is already very happy even happier is certainly beneficent, but it would not naturally be described as an act called for by considerations of humanity.

The Oxford English Dictionary defines humanity as 'Disposition to treat human beings and animals with consideration and compassion, and to relieve their distresses; kindness, benevolence.'[1] In this chapter I shall understand by 'humanity' the relief of distress. As a matter of usage, it seems to me that the *OED* is right to put this before the more extended sense of kindness or benevolence in general. In any case, it is this notion that I want to discuss, and the word 'humanity' is the closest representation of it in common use.

There are three questions to be dealt with. First, is it morally obligatory to behave humanely, or is it simply laudable but not morally delinquent to fail so to act? Second, if it is morally obligatory, what implications does it have, if any, for the obligations of rich countries to aid poor ones? Third, if (as I shall suggest) rich countries have a humanitarian obligation to aid poor ones, by what criterion can

---

[1] *The Oxford English Dictionary*, sub. Humanity, 3b. In the light of the central example to be discussed below, it is interesting to note that the title of a society founded in England for the rescuing of drowning persons in 1774 was the Humane Society (*OED*, sub. Humane, 1c).

we determine how much sacrifice the rich countries should be prepared to make?

I shall begin my discussion by taking up and considering the argument put forward by Peter Singer in his article 'Famine, Affluence and Morality'.[2] Singer puts forward a simple, clear, and forceful case for a humanitarian obligation for those in rich countries to give economic aid to those in poor countries. The premises of his argument are as follows. The first is 'that suffering and death from lack of food, shelter, and medical care are bad'. The second is given in two alternative forms. One is that 'if it is in our power to prevent something bad from happening, without thereby sacrificing anything of comparable moral importance, we ought, morally, to do it'. The other, and weaker, form is that 'if it is in our power to prevent something very bad from happening, without sacrificing anything morally significant, we ought, morally, to do it'. He goes on to say that 'an application of this principle [i.e. the second version] would be as follows: if I am walking past a shallow pond and see a child drowning in it, I ought to wade in and pull the child out. This will mean getting my clothes muddy, but this is insignificant, while the death of the child would presumably be a very bad thing.' All that has to be added is that the application of the second premiss is unaffected by proximity or distance and 'makes no distinction between cases in which I am the only person who could possibly do anything and cases in which I am just one among millions in the same position'.[3] If we accept these premisses we are committed, Singer claims, to the conclusion that people in the rich countries have a moral obligation to help those in the poor countries.

For the purpose of this chapter, I am going to take it as common ground that one would indeed be doing wrong to walk past Peter Singer's drowning child and do nothing to save it. This of course entails that, at least in the most favourable cases, duties of humanity must exist. In the space available, it hardly makes sense to try to argue for a complete theory of morality from which this can be deduced, and in any case I myself am more sure of the conclusion than of any of the alternative premisses from which it would follow. Anyone who disagrees with the claim that there is an obligation to rescue the child in the case as stated will not find what follows persuasive, since I

---

[2] Peter Singer, 'Famine, Affluence and Morality', *Philosophy & Public Affairs*, 1 (1972), 229–43. See, for a briefer and more recent statement of the same basic case, Peter Singer, *Practical Ethics* (Cambridge: Cambridge University Press, 1979), ch. 8, pp. 158–81.

[3] All quotations in this paragraph from Singer, 'Famine, Affluence and Morality', p. 231.

certainly do not think that the case for international aid on humanitarian grounds is *stronger* than the case for rescuing the drowning child.

The extension of the drowning child case may be challenged along several lines. Here I can only state them and say briefly why I do not think that they undercut the claim that the case for an obligation to save the drowning child applies also to giving international aid. (The appearance of dogmatism here is purely a result of compression.)

The first argument is that the child may be supposed not to be responsible for his plight (or at any rate it may be on that supposition that the example gets to us) but that countries are responsible for their economic problems. My comments here are two. First, even if it were true that the death by disease and/or starvation of somebody in a poor country were to some degree the result of past acts or omissions by the entire population, that scarcely makes it morally decent to hold the individual responsible for his plight; nor, similarly, if his predicament could have been avoided had the policies of his government been different.

Let us move on to consider another way in which a challenge may be mounted to Singer's extension of the argument for a duty to aid from the case of the drowning child to that of famine relief. It may be recalled that Singer explicitly made the shift from one case to the other via the statement that neither proximity nor the one-to-one relation between the victim and the potential rescuer makes any moral difference. Clearly, if this claim is denied, we can again agree on the duty to rescue the drowning child but deny that this is an appropriate analogue to the putative duty of people in rich countries to aid those in poor ones. A number of philosophers have tried to drive a wedge between the cases in this way, but I have to say that I am not very impressed by their efforts. The argument for proximity as a relevant factor is that, if we posit a duty to rescue those near at hand, we keep the duty within narrow bounds and thus do not let it interfere with people's life plans; but, if we allow the duty to range over the whole of mankind, it becomes too demanding. Although some people see merit in this, it appears to me that it is invoked simply because it provides a way of arbitrarily truncating the application of the principle so as to arrive at a convenient answer. I shall go on later to agree that there are limits to what people can be required to sacrifice. But I see no ethically defensible reason for saying that, if we cannot (or cannot be required to) do anything we might, we should simply contract the geographical scope of the principle that we are obliged to relieve suffering. Perhaps we should channel our limited humanitarian efforts to where they are most needed, which, if we live in a relatively rich country, is likely to be outside its boundaries.

Singer also made it explicit that, if the case of the drowning child were to be extended to international aid, one would have to rule out the one-to-one relation between the rescuer and the potential rescuee as a morally relevant factor. Attempts have been made to do so, but they likewise seem to me to lack merit. If there are several people who could save the drowning child, it is sometimes said that none of them is particularly responsible for saving it. But if the child drowns because none of them saves it, they are all morally responsible for its death. Conversely, suppose that several people are drowning at some distance from one another, that there is only one person around to save them, and that he can save any one of them but no more than one. It has been argued that this person cannot do his duty, defined as saving all those whom he might save, since he could save any of them. It is then concluded that, since there can be no duty to do the impossible, no duty to rescue exists in such a case. The conclusion is, however, fallacious. For the terms of the duty have been misstated. There is indeed no duty to save all of the drowning people. But there is in the case as stated a duty to save one of them. That the duty does not have a determinate object is no objection to its standing. It does not pick out a particular person to save but it still insists that somebody should be saved.

Finally, it might be accepted that the case of the drowning child would extend to international aid if the aid would do any good, but then denied that it will. The main lines of this argument are two. The first is the one from waste and inefficiency: aid does not get to the right people; development projects are a disaster; and so on. But I would claim that even if waste is endemic in aid to poor (and probably ill-organized) countries, the difference it makes to health and nutrition is sufficient to make it worth giving even if only part of it gets to the people it is supposed to get to. And if, as is all too true, aid in the past has often been inappropriate, the answer is not to withhold aid but to make it more appropriate: no more massive dams, electricity-generating stations, or steel mills, but cheaper, less complex, and more decentralized technology.

The second line of argument is the neo-Malthusian: that the only effect of aid in the long run is to lead to population increase and thus to even more suffering. I agree that if this is the only effect of aid the humanitarian case for it falls to the ground. But it is clear that economic development combined with appropriate social policies and the widespread availability of contraception can acually reduce the rate of population growth. The implication is thus that aid should be given in large amounts where the social and political conditions are right, so as to get countries through the demographic transition from high birth-rate and high death-rate to low birth-rate and low death-rate as rapidly as possible.

Where ideological or religious dogmas result in pro-natalist government policies or rejection of contraception by the population, one might conclude that aid would be better withheld, since the only foreseeable effect of economic improvement will be to increase numbers. But can we really be so sure that attitudes will not change? The election of a relatively young and doctrinally reactionary Pope does not encourage hopes of any early change in official doctrine. But even without any change at that level, it is striking how, in the developed countries, the practices of Roman Catholics have altered dramatically in just a couple of decades. For example, in the Province of Quebec, which had for more than two centuries a birth-rate close to the physical maximum, with families of more than ten children being quite common, the birth-rate fell over the course of just a few years to one that is among the lowest in North America.

If we accept the conclusion that the rich have some obligation on humanitarian grounds to provide economic aid to the poor, the next question is, how much sacrifice is required? In my view, no simple and determinate criterion is available. This is a problem of the obligation of humanity in general, not a peculiarity of the international context. In the standard case of rescuing someone in danger of drowning, the usual guidance one gets from moral philosophers is that the obligation does not extend to risking one's life, though it does require that one suffer a fair amount of inconvenience. However, the decision in cases such as that of Singer's drowning child characteristically has clear and finite limits to its implications. But, given the failure of most people or governments in rich countries to give much aid, it would clearly be possible for individuals to give up a high proportion of their incomes without risking their lives and still leave millions of saveable lives in poor countries unsaved. Thus, the question of limits is pressing.

There is an answer that is, in principle, straightforward. It is the one embodied in Singer's claim that one is obliged to help up to the point at which one is sacrificing something of 'comparable moral importance'. This is, of course, a maximizing form of consequentialism. If you say that pains and pleasures are what is of moral importance, you get Benthamite utilitarianism (in the traditional interpretation, anyway);

if you say it is the enjoyment of beauty and personal relationships, you get G. E. Moore's ideal consequentialism; and so on. The trouble with this is, needless to say, that most of us do not see any reason for accepting an obligation to maximize the total amount of good in the universe. (See above, chapter XII.)

Singer's weaker principle is that we should give aid up to the point at which we are sacrificing anything of moral importance. But this seems to me useless: for a Benthamite utilitarian, for example, even getting one's trousers muddy would be in itself an evil—not one comparable to the death of a child, but an evil none the less. Even Singer's chosen case would therefore be eliminated on this criterion, let alone any more strenuous sacrifices.

I conclude, provisionally and in the absence of any plausible alternative, that there is no firm criterion for the amount of sacrifice required to relieve distress. This does not mean that nothing can be said. It is fairly clear that there is a greater obligation the more severe the distress, the better off the potential helper would still be after helping, and the higher the ratio of benefit to cost. What is indefinite is where the line is to be drawn. In the words of C. D. Broad, in what may be the best single article in philosophical ethics ever written, 'it is no objection to say that it is totally impossible to determine exactly where this point comes in any particular case. This is quite true, but it is too common a difficulty in ethics to worry us, and we know that we are lucky in ethical questions if we can state upper and lower limits that are not too ridiculously far apart.'[4]

What, in any case, are we talking about here as the range? We could perhaps wonder whether the level of aid from a country like the United States should be 3 per cent of GNP (the level of Marshall aid), or 10, or 25 per cent. But, unless we reject the idea of an obligation to aid those in distress altogether, we can hardly doubt that one quarter of one per cent is grotesquely too little.

II JUSTICE

'Are we not trying to pack too much into the concept of justice and the correlative concept of rights? The question of whether it is *wrong* to act in certain ways is not the same question as whether it is *unjust* so to act.'[5] I think the answer to John Passmore's rhetorical question is in the

---

[4] C. D. Broad, 'On the Function of False Hypotheses in Ethics', *International Journal of Ethics*, 26 (1916), 377–97, at 389–90.

[5] John Passmore, 'Civil Justice and Its Rivals', in Eugene Kamenka and Alice Erh-Soon Tay (eds.), *Justice* (London: Edward Arnold, 1979), 25–49, at 47 (italics in original).

affirmative. We should not expect to get out of 'justice' a blueprint for the good society—nor should we wish to, since that degree of specificity would inevitably limit potential applicability. Surely it ought to be possible for a just society to be rich or poor, cultivated or philistine, religious or secular, and (within some limits that are inherent in justice itself) to have more or less of liberty, equality, and fraternity.

Up to this point I have studiously avoided any reference to justice. I have been talking about the obligation to relieve suffering as a matter of humanity. The fact that the obligation is not derived from justice does not make it a matter of generosity, nor does it entail that it should be left to voluntary action to adhere to it. It is an obligation that it would be wrong not to carry out and that could quite properly be enforced upon rich countries if the world political system made this feasible. And the core of the discussion has been the claim that the obligation to help (and *a fortiori* the obligation not to harm) is not limited in its application to those who form a single political community.

It is of course open to anyone who wishes to do so to argue that, if the rich have a properly enforceable obligation to give, this is all we need in order to be able to say that the rich must give to the poor as a matter of justice. I have no way of proving that it is a mistake to use the term 'just' to mark out the line between, on the one hand, what is morally required and, on the other, what is praiseworthy to do but not wrong to omit doing. All I can say is that such a way of talking seems to me to result in the blunting of our moral vocabulary and therefore a loss of precision in our moral thinking. Justice, I wish to maintain, is not merely one end of a monochromatic scale that has at the other end sacrifice of self-interest for the good of others to a heroic or saintly degree. Rather, it points to a particular set of reasons why people (or societies) may have duties to one another and picks out particular features of institutions that make them morally condemnable.[6]

I shall return to the distinction between humanity and justice in section III, where I shall be able to refer to the results of my discussions of each of them. My plan is to analyse justice under two heads. The first is justice as reciprocity; the second, justice as equal rights. These are both familiar ideas, though I shall give the second a slightly unfamiliar twist. Justice as reciprocity I will discuss in three aspects: justice as fidelity, justice as requital, and justice as fair play. (The

---

[6] For a sustained argument along these lines, see T. D. Campbell, 'Humanity before Justice', *British Journal of Political Science*, 4 (1974), 1–16.

analysis of justice as reciprocity is carried out in a much extended form in chapter 17 below.)

The notion of justice as fidelity is that of keeping faith. In addition to covering contracts and promises, it extends, in a rather indefinite way, to meeting legitimate expectations not derived from explicit voluntary agreement. Clearly it is an essentially conservative principle and tends if anything to operate contrary to the interests of poor countries, in so far as they often find themselves in the position of seeking to renegotiate disadvantageous deals with transnational corporations within their territories.

Justice as requital is also a basically conservative principle but can, on occasion, have revisionist implications *vis-à-vis* justice as fidelity. No simple rule governs what happens when they conflict. Henry Sidgwick, with characteristic caution, said that we have two standards of justice, as the customary distribution and as the ideal distribution, and added that 'it is the reconciliation between these two views which is the problem of political justice'.[7] I shall not take up that large challenge here. I shall confine myself to an exploration of the possible implications of justice as requital for international distribution.

The idea of justice as requital is that of a fair return: a fair exchange, a fair share of benefits from common endeavour, and so on. The most obvious application in the relations between rich and poor countries is in prompting us to ask whether poor countries are getting fair prices for their exports and paying fair prices for their imports. This raises the obvious question of what the criterion of a 'fair price' is. Suppose, however, that we say, minimally, that it is the prevailing world price. Then it seems clear that, even on this criterion, many poor countries have legitimate complaints about the transfer pricing of transnational corporations. For example, when in the late 1960s the Andean Pact countries (Bolivia, Colombia, Ecuador, and Peru) started taking a serious interest in the pricing policies of transnational corporations operating within their territories, they found overpricing of imports to be the norm, sometimes by factors of hundreds of per cent, and, less spectacularly but still significantly, underpricing of the value of exports.[8] This enabled the companies to attain rates of return on capital of often more than 100 per cent while at the same time evading government limits on repatriation of profits. Since the Andean Pact countries have been politically independent for a century and a half

[7] Henry Sidgwick, *The Methods of Ethics* (London: Macmillan, 7th edn. 1907), 273.

[8] Constantine V. Vaitsos, *Intercountry Income Distribution and Transnational Enterprises* (Oxford: Clarendon Press, 1974), esp. ch. 4.

and have relatively sophisticated bureaucracies compared with those of most countries in the Third World, it is inconceivable that similar practices do not obtain in other, more vulnerable countries.

When we turn to the structure of world prices itself, the criterion of justice as requital becomes less helpful. The countries of the Third World, as part of their demands for a 'New International Economic Order', have demanded an 'Integrated Program' of commodity management that would be designed to push up the prices of raw materials in relation to manufactured products.

The success of the Organization of Petroleum Exporting Countries (OPEC) was unquestionably significant here in providing a dazzling example of the effectiveness of a producer cartel. Oil, however, seems to be unique in that it is so cheap to extract and worth so much to consumers. This means that it has always, since the days of the Pennsylvania oilfields, yielded enormous economic rents. The only question has been who captured them. And clearly, until 1973, the Middle Eastern oil producers were getting only a small proportion of the economic rent.

Other commodities are not like oil. It may indeed be possible to push up the prices by restricting supply, but substitution or recycling is likely to set in. From the long-run point of view of the world, this pressure towards conservation would be desirable, no doubt, but the point is that it does not spell a bonanza for the raw material producers.

Clearly, this is only scratching the surface, but I think that it is at any rate important to keep in mind that, even if commodity prices could be raised substantially across the board, this would not make most poor countries *appreciably* better off; and it would make some, including almost all of the world's most desperately poor countries, worse off. Whatever conclusion one wishes to draw, therefore, about the applicability to world prices of justice as requital, the implications are not going to be such as to solve the problem of poor countries that are also resource poor.

We still have to see if any redistributive implications flow from the third branch of justice as reciprocity: justice as fair play. The idea here is that, if one benefits (or stands to benefit) from some co-operative practice, one should not be a 'free rider' by taking the benefits (or being ready to take them if the occasion arises) while failing to do one's part in sustaining the practice when it is one's turn to do so. Thus, if others burn smokeless fuel in their fireplaces, take their litter home from the countryside, or clean up after their dogs, it is unfair for you to refuse to do the same.

The principle of fair play has a potentiality for underwriting a certain amount of redistribution from rich to poor in so far as one practice that might be regarded as prospectively beneficial to all concerned would be the practice of helping those in need. If such a practice existed, it would operate analogously to insurance, which is a contractual way of transferring money from those who have not suffered from certain specified calamities to those who have. The principle of fair play would then hold that it would be unfair to be a free rider on a scheme of helping those in need by refusing to do your part when called upon.

The invocation of this notion of what the sociobiologists call 'reciprocal altruism' may appear to provide a new way of distinguishing the drowning child case from that of international aid. Perhaps what motivates us in agreeing that there is an obligation to rescue the child is an unarticulated contextual assumption that the child belongs to our community (however widely we may conceive that 'community') and that there are norms within that community calling for low-cost rescue—norms from which we stand to gain if ever we find ourselves in need of rescue. Such feelings of obligation as we have in this case can therefore be adequately explained by supposing that they arise from the application of the principle of fair play. It was, thus, an error to have taken it for granted that an acknowledgement of an obligation to help in the drowning child case must show that we accepted a general principle of an obligation to aid those in distress.

I believe that the objection is formally valid. That is to say, it is possible by invoking the principle of fair play to underwrite the obligation to rescue the drowning child without committing oneself to a universal obligation to rescue. One could respond to this by arguing that the conclusions in section I of this chapter can be reinstated by deriving universal obligations from the existence of a world community. I shall consider this argument below. But before doing so, I should like to follow an alternative and more aggressive line.

The point to observe is that, although we may indeed be motivated to agree that we ought to rescue the drowning child by considerations of justice as reciprocity, it does not follow that we are motivated solely by those considerations. Suppose that you are briefly visiting a foreign country, with an entirely alien culture, and have no idea about the local norms of rescue. Would you, if you came across Singer's drowning child, have an obligation to wade in and rescue it? I think that most people would say yes in answer to that question. And, clearly, those who do so are acknowledging obligations of humanity as distinct from obligations of justice.

None of this, of course, is intended to suggest that the difficulties in moving from a general obligation of humanity to an obligation on the part of rich countries to give economic aid to poor ones is any less problematic than it appeared earlier. But it does fend off a possible challenge to the move from the drowning child case to the universal obligation to aid. The view I want to maintain is that the answer in the drowning child case is over-determined where the duty of fair play also underwrites rescue. The strength of the obligation depends upon the circumstances, but it never disappears. Both psychologically and morally, the obligation to aid would be strongest if there were an explicit and generally observed agreement among a group of parents to keep an eye on one another's children: humanity, fidelity, and fair play would then coincide and reinforce each other. The obligation would be perhaps a little less strong but still very strong in a small, stable, and close-knit community with a well-developed tradition of 'neighbourliness', since the obligation of fair play would here have maximum force. It would be less strong if the norm of rescue were more widely diffused over a whole society, and would of course vary according to the society. (New Zealand would rate much higher than the United States on the strength of the norm of helping strangers within the society, for example.) And, finally, in the absence of any established practice of aiding strangers that would give rise to obligations of fair play, there is still, I am suggesting, an obligation of humanity that does not in any way depend upon considerations of reciprocity. (See above, chapter 12 section II for an amplification of these ideas.)

I have been taking for granted that the existence of a practice of rescue does give rise to an obligation to play one's part. This can be questioned. Somebody might say: 'Why should I co-operate with the scheme if I'm willing to renounce any benefits that might be due to me under it?'[9] But the cogency of the objection depends upon the existence of stringent conditions of publicity: it must be possible to make this declaration known to all those in the scheme and everyone

---

[9] Adam Smith expressed this view: 'As a man doth, so it shall be done to him, and retaliation seems to be the great law which is dictated to us by nature. Beneficence and generosity we think due to the generous and beneficent. Those whose hearts never open to the feelings of humanity should, we think, be shut out in the same manner, from the affections of all their fellow-creatures, and be allowed to live in the midst of society, as in a great desert, where there is nobody to care for them, or to enquire after them.' Adam Smith, *The Theory of Moral Sentiments* (Indianapolis, Ind.: Liberty Classics, n.d.), 160.

must thereafter remember its having been made. (This is essential, since many transfers to those in need are going to be predominantly from the young and middle-aged to the old, so it would undermine the integrity of any such co-operative scheme if people could change their minds about its value as they got older.) Neither condition is generally met. Consider a practice of rescuing the victims of accidents—drowning swimmers are the case that is usually cited. If this practice exists in a whole society, it is not feasible for those who wish to opt out to notify everybody else in advance. And how many could be counted on to be strong-minded enough to wave away a would-be rescuer when they were in need of help themselves? Even if they could, in many cases the rescuer has to incur the trouble and risk in order to get there (as with rescuing a swimmer), or the victim may be unconscious and thus incapable of spurning help.

It is crucially important to notice, however, that the principle of fair play is conditional: that is to say, it stipulates that it is unfair to be a free rider on a co-operative practice that actually exists, and that it *would* be unfair to free ride on other mutually beneficial practices if they did exist. But it does not say that it is unfair for a practice not to exist that would be mutually beneficial if it existed.

As anyone familiar with Rawls's theory of justice will have been aware for some time, we are here on the edge of deep waters. For one strand of Rawls's theory is precisely the notion of justice as reciprocity that is embodied in the principle of fair play. According to Rawls, a society is a scheme of social co-operation, and from this fact we can generate, via the notion of fair play, principles of justice. But, clearly, any actual society simply generates whatever is generated by its actual co-operative practices. If it provides retirement pensions out of social security taxes, it is unfair to be a free rider on the scheme by dodging your share of the cost. And so on. But if I am right about the applicability of the principle of fair play, the most Rawls can say about a society that does not have such a scheme is that it suffers from collective irrationality in that it is passing up a chance to do itself some good. He cannot employ the principle as a step in an argument that such a society is unjust.

I make this point because Charles Beitz, in the last part of his admirable book, *Political Philosophy and International Relations*,[10] has argued, within a Rawlsian framework, for a global difference

---

[10] Charles Beitz, *Political Philosophy and International Relations* (Princeton, NJ: Princeton University Press, 1979). The part of the book in question was first published in substantially the same form as 'Justice and International Relations', *Philosophy & Public Affairs*, 4 (1975), 360–89.

principle. That is to say, income should be redistributed internationally so that the worst-off representative individual in the world
is as well off as possible. Beitz acknowledges that he is taking for
granted the general validity of Rawls's theory and is simply arguing
from within its basic premises for the dropping of Rawls's restriction
on the application of the two principles of justice to societies. I have
been suggesting that, even within a society, one cannot use the fact
that it is a co-operative scheme to argue that it is unfair not to have
more extensive co-operation, though not to do so may be collectively
irrational. But the international scene presents two further difficulties.
First, I think that Rawls is broadly right in (implicitly) denying that
the whole world constitutes a single co-operative partnership in the
required sense. Second, I do not think that international redistribution
can plausibly be said to be advantageous to rich as well as poor
countries. Rawls is therefore probably correct in deducing from his
system only non-aggression, diplomatic immunity, and the like as
mutually advantageous to countries and thus, on the principle of fair
play, just. If I am right, however, they are simply collectively rational
and give rise to duties of fair play only to the extent that they are
instantiated in actual practice.

Beitz's argument for extending the Rawlsian difference principle is
in essence that the network of international trade is sufficiently
extensive to draw all countries together in a single co-operative
scheme. But it seems to me that trade, however multilateral, does not
constitute a co-operative scheme of the relevant kind. Trade, if freely
undertaken, is (presumably) beneficial to the exchanging parties, but it
is not the kind of relationship that gives rise to duties of fair play. To
the extent that justice is involved it is justice as requital, that is, giving
a fair return. Justice as fair play arises not from simple exchange but
either from the provision of public goods that are collectively enjoyed
(parks, defence, a litter-free or unpolluted environment, and so on) or
from quasi-insurance schemes for mutual aid of the kind just discussed. Trade in pottery, ornamentation, and weapons can be traced
back to prehistoric times, but we would hardly feel inclined to think
of, say, the Beaker Folk as forming a single co-operative enterprise
with their trading partners on the Mediterranean. No more did the
spice trade unite East and West.

To the extent that we are inclined to think of the world as more of a
co-operative enterprise now, this is not because trade is more extensive or multilateral, but because there really are rudimentary organs of
international co-operation in the form of United Nations agencies and

such entities as the International Monetary Fund and the World Bank. But the resulting relationships clearly fall short of those of mutual dependence found within societies. And my second point comes in here to draw attention to the fact that the extent of increased co-operation that would really be mutually beneficial is probably quite limited. In particular, redistribution on the insurance principle seems to have little appeal to rich countries. In the foreseeable future, aid to the needy is going to flow from, say, the United States to Bangladesh rather than vice versa. The conditions for reciprocity—that all the parties stand prospectively to benefit from the scheme—simply do not exist. One could again retreat behind the 'veil of ignorance' and argue that, if people did not know to which society they belonged, they would surely choose something like a global difference principle—or at any rate a floor below which nobody should be allowed to fall. And this seems plausible enough. (I have argued it myself in an earlier work.[11]) But this move clearly points up even more sharply than in the case of a single society the degree to which inserting the 'veil of ignorance' takes us away from the sphere of the principle of fair play.

In his well-known article, 'Are There Any Natural Rights?',[12] H. L. A. Hart argued that special rights must presuppose general rights. Before people can act in ways that modify their rights and those of others (paradigmatically by promising) they must, as a matter of elementary logic, have rights that do not stem from such modifications. Putting this in terms of the present discussion, we can say that justice as reciprocity needs a prior assignment of rights before it can get off the ground.

Now we might try to solve the problem by sanctifying the status quo. We could, in other words, simply declare that we are going to push the principle of justice as the fulfilment of reasonable expectations to the limit, and say that whatever rights somebody now has are to be taken as the baseline in relation to which all future developments must satisfy the requirements of fidelity, requital, and fair play. If we note that the conservation of value is akin to the Pareto principle, we may observe that this would give us the Virginia school of political economy especially associated with James Buchanan.

I have criticized his approach elsewhere,[13] and I shall not repeat my criticisms here. But it is surely enough for the present purpose to point out that, on the principle of the unquestioned justice of the status quo,

[11] Brian Barry, *The Liberal Theory of Justice* (Oxford: Clarendon Press, 1973), ch. 12.
[12] H. L. A. Hart, 'Are There Any Natural Rights?', *Philosophical Review*, 64 (1955), 175–91.
[13] See my extended review of Buchanan's ideas in *Theory and Decision*, 12 (1980), 95–106.

the most grotesque features of the existing allocation of rights would be frozen in place forever unless those who suffered from them could find some quid pro quo that would make it worth the while of, say, a Shah of Iran or a General Somoza to accept change. But that would be, if it could be found, an improvement in efficiency arising from the reallocation of the existing rights. It would not face the real problem, which was of course the injustice of the initial allocation of rights.

Hart's answer to his own question is that the general right that is presupposed by any special rights is an equal right to liberty. He does not give any explicit argument, as far as I can see, for its being equal. But I take the point to be that, since a general right is something that is necessarily anterior to any act giving rise to a special right, there is simply no basis for discriminating among people in respect of general rights. In order to discriminate, one would either have to do so on the basis of some quality that is obviously irrelevant to the assignment of rights (e.g. skin colour), or on the basis of something the person has done (e.g. made a promise) that provides a reason for attributing different rights to him. But then we get back to the original point, namely that such a differentiation in rights entails that we have an idea of the proper distribution of rights without the special factor adduced. And that must, it seems, be an equal distribution.

In this chapter I want to take this idea and apply it to the case of natural resources. I shall suggest that they fit all the requirements for being the subjects of a general right and that therefore everyone has an equal right to enjoy their benefits.

As Hillel Steiner has remarked, 'Nozick rightly insists that our commonsense view of what is just—of what is owed to individuals by right—is inextricably bound up with what they *have done* . . . [but] unlike other objects, the objects of appropriative rights . . . are *not* the results of individuals' past actions. . . . Appropriative claims, and the rules governing them, can have nothing to do with desert.'[14] Consider, for example, Bruce Ackerman's fable of the spaceship and the manna. One of the claimants, 'Rusher', says: 'I say that the first person who grabs a piece of manna should be recognized as its true owner' and, when asked for a reason, says, 'Because people who grab first are better than people who grab second.'[15] That, I think, illustrates my

---

[14] Hillel Steiner, 'The Natural Right to the Means of Production', *The Philosophical Quarterly*, 27 (1977), 41–9 at 44–5 (italics in original). The reference to Robert Nozick is to *Anarchy, State, and Utopia* (New York: Basic Books, 1974), 154.

[15] Bruce A. Ackerman, *Social Justice in the Liberal State* (New Haven: Yale University Press, 1980), 38.

point. What exactly is supposed to be the virtue of getting there first, or in merely having some ancestor who got there first?

The position with regard to countries is parallel to that of individuals. Today the basis of state sovereignty over natural resources is convention reinforced by international declarations such as votes of the United Nations General Assembly in 1970, 1972, and 1974 to the effect that each country has 'permanent sovereignty over natural resources' within its territory.[16] It is easy enough to see the basis of the convention. It has a transcendent simplicity and definiteness that must recommend it in international relations. For, in the absence of a 'common power', stability depends heavily on conventions that leave the minimum amount of room for interpretation. Within a municipal legal system, by contrast, it is possible to introduce and enforce complex rules limiting the rights of individual appropriation (e.g. restricting the amount of water that can be drawn off from a river) and transferring a portion of the economic rent from the property owner to the state. Moreover, in the absence of a 'common power', it is a convention that is relatively easy to enforce—at any rate easier than any alternative. For a state may be presumed, other things being equal, to be in a better position to control the appropriation of the natural resources of its own territory than to control those of some other country.

In practice things are not always equal, and many Third World countries have found that controlling foreign companies that own their natural resources is no easy matter: an unholy alliance of multinational corporations and their patron governments (for most, this is the United States) stands ready to organize international boycotts, to manipulate institutions such as the World Bank and the IMF against them, and, if all else fails, go in for 'destabilization' on the Chilean model. The problem is exacerbated when a country seeks to gain control of the exploitation of its own natural resources by expropriating the foreign-based companies that have been there, often long before the country became independent. For the issue of compensation then arises, and this is likely to be contentious, not only because of the possibility of dispute about the current value of the investment, but also because the country may claim compensation for inadequate (or no) royalties paid on extraction in the past—a claim that (as we noted above) falls validly under the heading of justice as requital.

---

[16] Oscar Schachter, *Sharing the World's Resources* (New York: Columbia University Press, 1977), 124, references in n. 52, p. 159.

However, no substantial body of opinion in either the North or the South (or, perhaps more remarkably, in the East or the West) is adverse to the principle that each country is entitled to benefit exclusively from its own natural resources and to take decisions about their exploitation. In recent years, practice has increasingly come into line with the principle. The outstanding illustration is OPEC, but the same pattern of improved royalties and more control over how much and what is extracted obtains also in other countries and for other commodities.

It would hardly be surprising if, when the principle of national sovereignty over natural resources has been so recently and precariously established, Third World countries should be highly suspicious of any suggestion that natural resources should in future be treated as collective international property. They may well wonder whether this is anything more than a cover for the reintroduction of colonialism. I do not see how such doubts can be allayed by mere assertion. Clearly, everything would depend on the principle's being applied across the board rather than in a one-sided way that lets the industrialized countries act on the maxim 'What's yours is mine and what's mine is my own.' So far, that is precisely how it has been used, as in the proposals of American chauvinists such as Robert Tucker that the United States should be prepared to occupy the Saudi Arabian oilfields by military force in order to maintain the flow of oil at a 'reasonable' price, so that Americans can continue to use up a grossly disproportionate share of the world's oil. Since the United States, if it used only domestically produced oil, would still have one of the world's highest per capita levels of consumption, the effrontery of this proposal for the international control of other countries' oil would be hard to beat.

If the Third World countries were too weak to do anything more than hang on to the present position of national sovereignty over natural resources, we would have to regard that as the best outcome that could be obtained. It is clearly preferable to the earlier set-up, in which countries with the power to do so controlled the natural resources of others. For, although the distribution of natural resources is entirely arbitrary from a moral point of view, it has at any rate the kind of fairness displayed by a lottery. That is presumably better than a situation in which the weak are despoiled of their prizes by force and fraud.

In spite of these forebodings about the potential misuse of the principle that natural resources are the joint possession of the human race as a whole, I think it is worth pursuing. For it is scarcely possible to be satisfied with the present situation from any angle except that of extreme pessimism about the chances of changing it for the better rather than for the worse. The overwhelming fact about the existing system is that it makes the economic prospects of a country depend, to a significant degree, on something for which its inhabitants (present or past) can take absolutely no credit and to whose benefits they can lay no just claim, namely its natural resources—including in this soil, water, minerals, sunlight, and so on. The claims of collectivities to appropriate natural resources rest, as do those of individuals, on convention or on law (in this case, such quasi-law as the United Nations resolutions cited above). No doubt the point has been impressed on people in the West by examples such as Kuwait, the United Arab Emirates, or Saudi Arabia, and it may be that such small numbers of people have never before become so rich without any effort on their own part, simply as a result of sitting on top of rich deposits. But I see no coherent way of saying why there is anything grotesque about, say, the case of Kuwait, without acknowledging that the fault lies in the whole principle of national sovereignty over natural resources. If it were simply a matter of a few million people hitting the jackpot things would not be bad, but of course the obverse of that is the existence of countries that have poor land, or little land per head, and few mineral resources or other sources of energy such as hydroelectric power.

Obviously, some countries are richer than others for many reasons, and some, like Japan, are among the more affluent in spite of having to import almost all their oil and the greatest part of many other natural resources. What, then, about the other advantages that the people in the rich countries inherit—productive capital, good systems of communications, orderly administration, well-developed systems of education and training, and so on? If the point about special rights is that someone must have done something to acquire a special right, what have the fortunate inheritors of all these advantages done to give them an exclusive claim to the benefits flowing from them?

The answer that the defenders of property rights normally give at this point is that, although the inheritors have done nothing to establish any special rights, those who left it to them did do something (namely, help to create the advantages) and had a right to dispose of it to some rather than to others. The special rights of those in the present generation thus derive from the use made by those in the previous generation of *their* special rights.

I cannot, in this already long chapter, undertake here to ask how far this answer takes us. We would have to get into questions that seem to me very difficult, such as the extent to which the fact that people who are no longer alive wanted something to happen, and perhaps even made sacrifices in order to insure that it could happen, provides any basis in justice for determining what those now alive should do. (See chapter 6 *ad fin.* for a discussion of this question.) I shall simply say here that I regard any claims that those now alive can make to special advantages derived from the efforts of their ancestors as quite limited. First, the inheritance must itself have been justly acquired in the first place, and that cannot be said of any country that violated the equal claims of all on natural resources—which means almost all industrial countries. Second, the claims to inheritance seem to me to attenuate with time, so that, although the present generation might legitimately derive some special advantages from the efforts of the preceding one, and perhaps the one before that, the part of what they passed on that was in turn inherited from their predecessors should be regarded as by now forming part of the common heritage of mankind.

Obviously, making this case out would require elaboration beyond the space available. But I do want to emphasize that what follows constitutes, in my view, a minimalist strategy. That is to say, whatever obligations of justice follow from it represent the absolutely rock-bottom requirements of justice in international affairs. To the extent that other advantages can be brought within the net of the principle of equal rights, the obligations of rich countries go beyond what is argued for here.

It would be ridiculous to spend time here on a blueprint for a scheme to put into effect the principle that I have been advancing. Its implementation on a world-wide scale, if it happens at all, is going to occur over a period measured in decades and, indeed, centuries. It will depend both on fundamental changes in outlook and on the development of international organs capable of taking decisions and carrying them out with reasonable efficiency and honesty.

The history of domestic redistribution is very much to the point here in suggesting that there is a virtuous circle in which the existence of redistributive institutions and beliefs in the legitimacy of redistribution are mutually reinforcing and have a strong tendency to become more extensive together over time. When Hume discussed redistribution in the *Enquiry*, the only form of it that he considered was 'perfect equality of possessions'.[17] The notion of continuous redistribution of

[17] David Hume, *An Enquiry Concerning the Principles of Morals*, in *Enquiries*, L. A. Selby-Bigge (ed.), 3rd edn. by P. H. Niddich (Oxford: Clarendon Press, 1975), 193–4.

income through a system of progressive taxation does not seem to have occurred to him. The Poor Law did, of course, provide a minimum of relief to the indigent, but it was organized by parishes and it is doubtful that the amateurish and nepotistic central administration of the eighteenth century could have handled a national scheme. The introduction of unemployment and sickness benefits and old age pensions in one Western European country after another from the late nineteenth century onward was made possible by the development of competent national administrations.

At the same time, these programmes constituted a political response to the extension of the suffrage, or one might more precisely say a response to conditions that, among other things, made the extension of the suffrage necessary for the continued legitimacy of the state. A certain measure of redistribution was the price the privileged were prepared to pay for mass acceptance of their remaining advantages. Once in place, however, such programmes have shown a universal tendency to take on a life of their own and to grow incrementally as gaps in the original coverage are filled in and the whole level of benefits is gradually raised. Indeed, it has been found in cross-national studies that the best predictor of the relative size of a given programme (say, aid to the blind) within the whole welfare system is the amount of time the programme has been running compared with others. In the long run the programme seems to generate supporting sentiments, so that even Margaret Thatcher and Ronald Reagan propose only reductions of a few percentage points in programmes that only thirty years ago would have seemed quite ambitious.

I do not want to drive the comparison with the international arena into the ground, but I think that, if nothing else, reflecting on domestic experience ought to lead us to look at international transfers from an appropriate time perspective. The United Nations Organization obviously has a lot wrong with it, for example, but its administration is probably less corrupt, self-serving, and inefficient than that which served Sir Robert Walpole. If one takes a time span of thirty years, it is, I suggest, more remarkable that the network of international co-operation has developed as far as it has than that it has not gone further. And in the realm of ideas the notion that poor countries have claims of one sort or another to aid from rich ones has moved from being quite exotic to one that is widely accepted in principle. At any rate in public, the representatives of the rich countries on international bodies no longer deny such a responsibility. They merely seek to evade any binding commitment based on it. But in the long run what is professed in public makes a difference to what gets done because it sets the terms of the discussion.

It is not at all difficult to come up with proposals for a system by which revenues would be raised on a regular basis from the rich countries and transferred to the poor ones. If any such scheme ever gained enough momentum to be a serious international issue, economists and accountants would no doubt have a field day arguing about the details and there is no point in anticipating such arguments here. However, the small amount of space I shall devote to redistributive mechanisms does not mean that I do not regard them as being of crucial importance.

Now, broadly speaking, two alternative approaches are possible. One would be to take up each of the aspects of international justice that have been discussed—and whatever others might be raised—and to base a system of taxes and receipts upon each. This would be messy and endlessly contentious. The alternative, which is, I predict, the only way in which any systematic redistribution will ever take place, if it ever does, is to have one or two comprehensive taxes and to distribute the proceeds according to some relatively simple formula among the poor countries.

The most obvious, and in my view the best, would be a tax on the governments of rich countries, assessed as a proportion of gross national product that increases with per capita income, the proceeds to be distributed to poor countries on a parallel basis of negative income tax. Gross national product reflects, roughly, the use of irreplaceable natural resources, the burden on the ecosphere, and advantages derived from the efforts of past generations and past exploitation of other countries. Ideally, this tax would be supplemented by a severance tax on the extraction of mineral resources and a shadow tax on the value of land and similar resources. (States could be left to collect the money by any means they chose. But their aggregate liability would be assessed by valuing the taxable base and applying the set rate.) This would certainly be required to take care of some glaring inequities that would still otherwise remain. But the simple system of transfer based on gross national product would be such an advance over the status quo that it would be a mistake to miss any chance to implement it by pursuing further refinements.

I believe that any other kinds of general tax, that is to say, taxes not related specifically to some aspect of justice, should be rejected. For example, a tax on foreign trade or on foreign trade in fossil fuels has been proposed.[18] This is so obviously arbitrary that it is hard to see how anyone can have considered it worth mooting. It has the manifest effect of penalizing small countries and countries that export coal and oil—and those that import it as well, if one believes that the incidence of the tax would be shifted to the consumer. Conversely, it has an absurdly favourable effect on very large countries that import and export little in relation to the size of their GNP and are relatively self-sufficient in energy derived from fossil fuels. No doubt the US State Department loves it, but why anyone else should be imposed on is a mystery to me.

I have assumed without discussion that resources transferred to satisfy the requirements of justice should go straight to poor countries rather than being channelled through international agencies and dispensed in the form of aid for specific projects. I shall spell out the rationale for this in the next section. But I will simply remark here that nothing I have said about justice rules out additional humanitarian transfers. And these would appropriately be administered by international organizations. The basis for raising such revenues for humanitarian aid would very reasonably be a progressive international shadow income tax, since this would perfectly reflect ability to pay. We might thus envisage a dual system of international taxation—one part, corresponding to the requirements of justice, going directly to poor countries to be spent at their own discretion; the other going to the World Bank or some successor organization less dominated by the donor countries.

III   THE RELATIONS BETWEEN HUMANITY AND JUSTICE

I have been arguing that both humanity and justice require a substantial expansion in the scale of economic transfers from rich countries to poor ones. I should now like to show that, as the two rationales are very different, so are their practical implications. This point is worth emphasizing because those who pride themselves on the possession of sturdy Anglo-Saxon 'common sense' tend to conclude that, if we agree on the humanitarian obligation, we are wasting our breath in arguing about claims of injustice—claims for the rectification of alleged unrequited transfers from poor to rich countries in the past that are hard to assess and impossible to quantify, or involve more or less abstruse doctrines about the nature of justice in the contemporary

---

[18]   Eleanor B. Steinberg and Joseph Y. Yager (eds.), *New Means of Financing International Needs* (Washington, DC: The Brookings Institution, 1978), ch. 3.

world. If we recognize the case for action on simple and straightforward humanitarian grounds, the idea goes, should we not concentrate on putting into place the appropriate aid policies, rather than
allow ourselves to get sidetracked into fruitless wrangles about
justice? In this context it is often said that the demands made by the
countries of the South are 'symbolic' or 'ideological' and have the
effect only of making more difficult the real, practical task of negotiating actual concessions by the countries of the North. The question that
seems to me of more import is the following: if an obligation of
humanity is accepted, under whatever name, how much difference
does it make whether or not the kinds of claims I have been discussing
under the heading of 'justice' are also conceded?

The answer is I believe that it makes a great deal of difference.
Putting it in the most abstract terms, the obligations of humanity are
goal-based, whereas those of justice are rights-based.[19] I would once
have expressed the distinction between humanity and justice as one
between an aggregative principle and a distributive principle.[20] I now,
however, regard that distinction as less fundamental than the one I
wish to mark by talking of goal-based and rights-based obligations.
The point is that humanity and justice are not simply alternative
prescriptions with respect to the same thing. Rather, they have
different subject-matters.

Humanity, understood as a principle that directs us not to cause
suffering and to relieve it where it occurs, is a leading member of a
family of principles concerned with what happens to people (and other
sentient creatures)—with what I shall call their well-being, intending
to include in this such notions as welfare, happiness, self-fulfilment,
freedom from malnutrition and disease, and satisfaction of basic
needs. Justice, by contrast, is not directly concerned with such matters
at all. As well as principles that tell us what are good and bad states of
affairs and what responsibilities we have to foster the one and to avert
the other, we also have principles that tell us how control over
resources should be allocated. If we understand 'resources' in a very
wide sense, so that it includes all kinds of rights to act without
interference from others, to constrain the actions of others, and to
bring about changes in the non-human environment, then we can say
that the subject-matter of justice (at any rate in modern usage) is the

---

[19] For a distinction stated in these terms see Ronald Dworkin, 'The Original Position',
Chicago Law Review, 4 (1973), 500–33, repr. in Norman Daniels (ed.), *Reading Rawls* (Oxford:
Basil Blackwell, 1975), 16–53. The relevant discussion is on pp. 38–40 of this reprint.

[20] Brian Barry, *Political Argument* (London: Routledge and Kegan Paul, 1965), 43–4.

distribution of control over material resources. At this high level of generality, it is complemented by the principle of equal liberty, which is concerned with the control over non-material resources. To put it in a slogan, which has the advantages as well as the disadvantages of any slogan: humanity is a question of doing good whereas justice is a question of power.

When the contrast is stated in those terms, it might seem that bothering about justice is indeed a waste of time and that the bluff Anglo-Saxon advocates of common-sensical utilitarianism have the best of it after all. Why, it may naturally be asked, should we care about the distribution of *stuff* as against the distribution of *welfare*? Is this not simply commodity fetishism in a new guise?

The easy but inadequate answer is that the concept of justice is concerned not only with any old stuff but with the kind of stuff that has the capacity to provide those who use it with the material means of well-being: food, housing, clothing, medical care, and so on. This is correct as far as it goes and shows that being concerned with justice is not irrational. But it is inadequate because it leaves the supporter of justice open to an obvious flanking movement. His opponent may reply: 'You say that the only reason for concern about the distribution of the things whose proper allocation constitutes the subject-matter of justice is that they are the means to well-being. Very well. But are you not then in effect conceding that your "deep theory" is goal-based? For what you are saying is that we really are ultimately concerned with the distribution of well-being. We simply take an interest in the distribution of the means of well-being because they are what we can actually allocate. But this means that justice is a derivative principle.'

There are two lines of response open at this point. One is to concede that criteria for the distribution of resources are ultimately to be referred to the goal of well-being, but at the same time to deny that it follows from that concession that we can cut out the middleman and set out our principles for the allocation of resources with an eye directly on the well-being they are likely to produce. Or, more precisely, we may say that among the constituents of well-being is autonomy, and autonomy includes the power to choose frivolously or imprudently. Thus, on one (admittedly controversial) interpretation, John Stuart Mill's talk of justice in Book v of *Utilitarianism* and his presentation of the 'simple principle' of *On Liberty* in terms of rights is all consistent with an underlying utilitarian commitment if we allow for the importance to people of being able to plan their own lives and make their own decisions.

I think that this is by no means an unreasonable view and has more to be said for it than is, perhaps, fashionable to admit. Anyone who wishes at all costs to hold up a monistic ethical position is, I suspect, almost bound to finish up by trying to make some such argument as this. But I think that it is, nevertheless, in the last analysis a heroic attempt to fudge the issue by using the concept of autonomy to smuggle a basically foreign idea into the goal-based notion of advancing well-being.

The alternative is to deny that, in conceding that control over resources is important only because of the connection between resources and well-being, one is thereby committed to the view that principles for the distribution of resources are derivative. According to this view, there simply are two separate kinds of question. One concerns the deployment of resources to promote happiness and reduce misery. The other concerns the ethically defensible basis for allocating control over resources. Neither is reducible, even circuitously, to the other. When they conflict, we get hard questions, such as those involved in the whole issue of paternalism. But there is no overarching criterion within which such conflicts can be solved as is offered (at least in principle) by the idea that autonomy is an important, but not the only, ingredient in well-being.

As may be gathered, this is the position that I hold. In what follows, I want to show what difference it makes to employ an independent principle of justice in considering issues of international distribution. To make the discussion as clear as possible, I shall draw my contrast with a principle of humanity understood in the kind of pretty straightforward way exemplified in section I of this chapter. The contrast would be softened the more weight we were to give to autonomy as a component in well-being. Note, however, that even those who might wish to emphasize the importance of individual autonomy are likely to doubt the value to individual well-being of autonomy for states; yet it is precisely the question of autonomy for states that is going to turn out to be the main dividing line between humanity and justice at the international level.

The point is one of control. The rich countries already mostly concede, at least in verbal declarations, that they have a humanitarian obligation to assist the poor countries economically. The importance to the future of the world of their beginning to live up to those declarations can scarcely be overestimated. I trust that nothing in this chapter will be taken as disparaging humanitarian aid. To the extent that it does in fact relieve problems of poverty, disease, malnutrition, and population growth it is, obviously, of enormous value.

But to see its limitations, let us be really utopian about humanitarian aid. Let us imagine that it is collected on a regular and automatic basis from rich countries according to some formula that more or less reflects ability to pay; for example, a shadow tax on GNP graduated by the level of GNP per capita. And suppose that the proceeds were pooled and dispersed through agencies of the United Nations, according to general criteria for entitlement to assistance.

Now, undoubtedly, such a world would be an immense improvement on the present one, just as the modern welfare state has transformed, say, Henry Mayhew's London. But it would still leave us with a division between the donor countries, free to spend 'their' incomes as they pleased, and the recipient countries, which would have to spend their incomes 'responsibly'. No doubt, this would be less objectionable if the criteria for 'responsible' expenditures were drawn up in partnership between donor and recipient countries rather than, as now, being laid down by bodies such as the IMF and the World Bank in whose governing councils the rich countries have a preponderant voice. But funds earmarked and conditional upon approved use would still be basically different from income of the usual kind.

In contrast, transfers that were consequential upon considerations of justice would simply reduce the resources of one set of countries and augment those of another set. The distribution of control of resources would actually be shifted. It is therefore easy to see that the question of justice in the relations between rich and poor countries is by no means a purely 'symbolic' one. Real issues are at stake, and it is no self-delusion that leads the poor countries to press for a recognition of the claims of justice and the rich countries to resist these claims.

The conclusion we have reached, then, is that the crucial characteristic of justice is that the obligation to make the transfers required by it does not depend upon the use made of them by the recipient. At this point, I find that the following kinds of objection are usually made. What if the recipient country wastes the resources transferred to it? What if it is going to spend the money on armaments? What if it has a very unequal distribution of income and the additional income will be divided in the same unequal way? Such objections illustrate how difficult it is to get across the idea that, if some share of resources is justly owed to a country, then the money is (even before it has actually been transferred) as much that country's as the rest of its income.

The answer that I give is that there are extreme circumstances in which the international community or some particular donor country would be justified in withholding resources owed as a matter of justice to some country. But these are exactly the same extreme conditions under which it would also be justifiable to refuse to pay debts to it, to freeze its assets overseas, to subject it to economic sanctions, or perhaps to intervene with force to change its government.

One could envisage a world in which there were indeed an international authority that allowed countries to keep only that portion of the national income that was justly distributed internally and used in approved, non-wasteful ways. Such a world would not be at all like ours, since it would accept no principle of national autonomy. It would be one in which a global society (not now in existence) had inscribed on its banner: 'From each according to his ability, to each according to his needs.'

The alternative to that world, so different from ours, is one in which the general presumption is of national autonomy, with countries being treated as units capable of determining the use of those resources to which they were justly entitled. This is the world that we now have, and the only modification in the status quo I am arguing for is a redefinition of what justly belongs to a country. Inevitably, as the price of autonomy, it permits countries to use resources that are justly theirs in wasteful ways, and it does not insist that a country that allows some to live in luxury while others have basic needs unfulfilled should lose income to which it is entitled as a matter of justice.

My point here is that both of the models I have sketched are internally consistent. We could have a system in which there are no entitlements based on justice and in which, assuming that states are still the administrative intermediaries, funds are allocated for worthy purposes and cut off if they are misspent, just as in the United States the Federal government cuts off funds to state and local governments that do not comply with various guidelines. Or we could have a world in which, once the demands of just distribution between countries are satisfied, we say that we have justice at the world level, and the question of domestic distribution and national priorities then becomes one for each country to decide for itself.

What is not consistent is to have a world in which those countries that are required by international justice to be donors live under the easygoing second system while those that are recipients live under the stern dispensation of the first. If the idea is going to be that countries should have their entitlements reduced if they are wasteful and fail in internal equity, then the obvious place to start is not with some poor country in sub-Saharan Africa or South Asia but with, say, a country that burns one ninth of the world's daily oil consumption on its roads alone and that, in spite of having a quarter of the world's GNP, is unable to provide decent medical care for much of its population, while a substantial proportion live in material conditions of abject squalor that (except for being more dirty and dangerous) recall the cities of Germany and Britain in the aftermath of the Second World War.

None of this, let me emphasize, denies the independent significance of humanity as a criterion in international morality. But we cannot sensibly talk about humanity unless we have a baseline set by justice. To talk about what I ought, as a matter of humanity, to do with what is mine makes no sense until we have established what is mine in the first place. If I have stolen what is rightfully somebody else's property, or if I have borrowed from him and refuse to repay the debt when it is due and as a result he is destitute, it would be unbecoming on my part to dole out some part of the money that should belong to him, with various strings attached as to the way in which he should spend it, and then go around posing as a great humanitarian. That is an exact description of the position in which the rich countries have currently placed themselves.

The need for humanitarian aid would be reduced in a world that had a basically just international distribution. It would still be required to meet special problems caused by crop failure owing to drought, destruction owing to floods and earthquakes, and similar losses resulting from other natural disasters. It would also, unhappily, continue to be required to cope with the massive refugee problems that periodically arise from political upheavals.

Beyond that, humanitarian aid in the form of food, technical assistance, or plain money is no doubt always a good thing. How much the rich countries would have to give on the basis of an obligation of humanity depends first on the extent of redistribution we hold to be required by justice and, second, on the stringency that we assign to the obligation of humanity—how much sacrifice can be demanded to deal with what level of need.

As will be clear, this chapter is concerned only with a preliminary investigation of the principles relevant to an ethical appraisal of international distribution and redistribution. I must therefore leave any more precise statement of implications for future discussions —and not necessarily by me. Ultimately, if anything is to be done, it will require a widespread shift in ideas. Greater precision can be expected to develop *pari passu* with such a shift. I very much doubt the value of single-handed attempts to produce a blueprint in advance of that.

IO

JUSTICE AS RECIPROCITY

I INTRODUCTION

What, if anything, do rich nations owe to poor ones? What, if anything, does the present generation owe to those who are to come after it? In the last few years we have seen an enormous increase in the salience of these questions. The poor countries have a comfortable majority in the General Assembly of the United Nations and have established in UNCTAD a permanent international organization dedicated to furthering their interests. The spectacular success of OPEC has forcibly drawn attention to the extent to which the prices of raw materials are subject to economic power and thus brought commodity prices more explicitly into the political arena. The East-West theme of cold war confrontation that ran through the third quarter of the century is being replaced in the final quarter by the North-South theme of confrontation between rich and poor nations.[1] At the same time, a new understanding of the complex interrelations that make life possible on earth has made us more aware of the way in which quite minor alterations of the ecological balance may have catastrophic long-run consequences. The interests of our remote descendants have started to figure explicitly in debates on the disposal of nuclear waste and the proposal to ban fluorocarbon aerosol propellants. Moreover, the literature of 'limits to growth', 'spaceship earth', and so on has served to emphasize the fact that, however sanguine one might be about new discoveries of raw materials and substitutes, resources are finite and we cannot therefore avoid facing the fact that the more we use the less there will be left for our descendants.

Most of us have only the haziest ideas about what justice requires in these cases. Even worse, we feel that the framework within which we normally think about justice—the framework that serves us well enough for thinking about relations among contemporaries in the same society—fails to give us a grip on these problems of international and intergenerational justice. In this chapter I shall explore them by

[1] See, for an analysis of the changing character of international politics, Robert O. Keohane and Joseph S. Nye, *Power and Interdependence: World Politics In Transition* (Boston, Mass.: Little Brown, 1977).

setting out this framework of everyday thought, seeing exactly how international and intergenerational justice relate to it and then arguing that there is another conception of justice, also deeply rooted in our common ideas, that provides a key to the problems of justice between countries and between generations.

The framework within which we ordinarily discuss questions of justice among contemporaries who are members of the same society is, I suggest, that of justice as reciprocity. Every society of which I have read has some notion as to the rightness of meeting reasonable expectations that a favour will be returned, of pulling one's weight in co-operative enterprises, of keeping agreements that provide for mutual benefits, and so on.[2] Thus, Marcel Mauss, in his classic *The Gift*, 'stresses that there is a universally recognized obligation to reciprocate gifts which have been accepted', while A. R. Radcliffe-Brown 'assumed a principle of reciprocity which he called "the principle of equivalent return". This he held was expressed in the *lex talionis*, in the principle of indemnification for injury, and in the principle that those who give benefits should receive equivalent benefits.'[3]

Again, the most significant recent work of political philosophy, *A Theory of Justice* by John Rawls,[4] is built around the notion of justice as reciprocity. It has been said correctly that 'it is the contractualist conception of equality as reciprocity that is at the root of Rawls's interpretation of justice'.[5] The essence of justice as reciprocity for Rawls is what in his article 'Justice as Fairness' he called the duty of fair play: 'the obligation which participants who have knowingly accepted the benefits of their common practice owe to each other to act in accordance with it when their performance falls due'.[6] 'Fair play' in this sense is an important part of justice as reciprocity but we have many other usages involving the concepts of fairness which we employ to assess the extent to which reciprocity is being satisfied or violated. Thus, we speak of a fair exchange when the values of the

[2] See Alvin W. Gouldner, 'The Norm of Reciprocity', *American Sociological Review*, 25 (1960), 161–78 and 'Reciprocity and Autonomy in Functional Theory', in N. J. Demerath III and Richard A. Peterson (eds.), *System, Change, and Conflict* (New York: Free Press, 1967), 141–69.

[3] Quotations from Gouldner, 'Reciprocity and Autonomy', p. 150 nn. 17 and 18. The first refers to Marcel Mauss, *The Gift* (Glencoe, Ill.: Free Press, 1954), the second to a Chicago University seminar of 1937, 'The Nature of a Theoretical Science of Society'.

[4] John Rawls, *A Theory of Justice* (Cambridge, Mass.: Harvard University Press, 1971).

[5] John W. Chapman, *Nomos*, 6, Carl J. Friedrich and John W. Chapman (eds.) (New York: Atherton Press, 1963), 147–69, at 149.

[6] John Rawls, 'Justice as Fairness', repr. in P. Laslett and W. G. Runciman (eds.), *Philosophy, Politics and Society*, 2nd ser. (Oxford: Basil Blackwell, 1962), 132–57, at 146.

things exchanged are equivalent, and of a fair offer as a proposal for a fair exchange. We speak of fair compensation when the value of the compensation matches the loss sustained. And we speak of fairness not only in relation to the way in which the burdens of a common enterprise are distributed but also in relation to the way in which the benefits are distributed. Other things being equal, if one person puts more into an activity yielding a common benefit, it is considered fair that he should get more out.[7]

The first half of this chapter will be devoted to the further analysis of justice as reciprocity. I shall look at justice as reciprocity under three heads. The first is justice as requital, that is to say, making a fair return for benefits received (section II). The second is justice as fidelity, that is to say, carrying out one's side of a bargain voluntarily entered into (section III). The third is justice as mutual aid, that is to say, playing one's part in a practice of helping those in need (section IV).

The second half of the chapter will be concerned with the limitations of justice as reciprocity, even when its bounds are drawn quite widely as in my discussion. After pointing out these limitations in relation to justice between countries (section V) and justice between generations (section VI), I shall put forward another conception of justice—justice as equal opportunity (section VII). In conclusion (section VIII) I shall sketch in the implications of this conception for justice between nations and justice between generations.

II JUSTICE AS REQUITAL

I intend under this heading to include a mixed bag, united only by the general idea of *quid pro quo*. Thus, I include fair dealing in explicit trading situations and the more diffuse notion of making an adequate return contained in the notion that 'one good turn deserves another'. The converse of this, for bad turns, is that anyone who harms another should provide compensation or suffer punishment. I include Rawls's duty of fair play, which calls on those who have enjoyed, or stand to enjoy, a public good to be willing to contribute to the cost of

---

[7] See George Caspar Homans, *Social Behavior: Its Elementary Forms* (London: Routledge and Kegan Paul, 1961), ch. 12, for an exposition of the view that 'men are alike in holding the notion of proportionality between investment and profit that lies at the heart of distributive justice' (p. 246). Homans explicitly equates distributive justice and fair exchange: 'Fair exchange, or distributive justice in the relations among men, is realized when the profit, or reward less cost, of each man is directly proportional to his investments' (p. 264). See Elaine Walster and G. William Walster, 'Equity and Social Justice', *Journal of Social Issues*, 31 (1975), 21–43 for a review of the small-group literature subsequent to *Social Behavior*.

providing it. (In 'Justice as Fairness' Rawls gave the examples of taxes for the provision of government services and of trade union dues.[8]) The converse of the 'anti-free rider' principle is that anyone who contributes especially effectively to the provision of a collective benefit is in fairness entitled to be rewarded more highly by the (other) recipients of the benefit. Clearly, justice as requital could be analysed in much more detail and the types of justice as requital roughly distinguished here could be further developed. But for my present purpose it is enough if I have pointed in an unambiguous way to a conception of justice that is at least in some forms non-controversial and universal.[9]

III   JUSTICE AS FIDELITY

This is the aspect of justice that was for Hobbes the whole of it: 'that men perform their covenants made'. The connection between fidelity and reciprocity is obvious, so much so that it is not surprising to find the part taken for the whole and all of justice as reciprocity reduced to contractual relations. Thus, Hobbes takes up two aspects of what I have been calling justice as requital: commutative justice as 'equality of value of the things contracted for' and distributive justice as 'the distribution of equal benefit, to men of equal merit'. And he disposes of them as criteria of justice by arguing, against the first, that 'the just value, is that which [the contractors] be contented to give', and, against the second, that 'Merit . . . is not due by Justice; but is rewarded of Grace only'.[10] This, however, simply presupposes the definition of 'justice' that Hobbes has already given, in terms of keeping covenant.

Charles Fried has expressed the Hobbesian position on the first as follows:

The plausibility of [mutual promising] as showing the kind of practice which must be considered just depends on this—that the sacrifices which are made

---

[8] Rawls, 'Justice as Fairness', p. 146. The inadequacy of voluntary contributions as a way of supporting the cost of public goods is argued in Mancur Olson, Jr., *The Logic of Collective Action* (Cambridge, Mass.: Harvard University Press, 1965). For a sophisticated formal analysis which explores the question of under what circumstances co-operative behaviour can be maintained without coercion, see Michael Taylor, *Anarchy and Cooperation* (Chichester: Wiley, 1967) revised as *The Possibility of Cooperation* (Cambridge: University of Cambridge Press, 1987).

[9] For a discussion of some of the ramifications of justice as requital and the difficulties that arise in applying it, see Robert E. Goodin, *The Politics of Rational Man* (Chichester: Wiley, 1976), chs. 6 and 7.

[10] Thomas Hobbes, *Leviathan*, C. B. Macpherson (ed.) (Harmondsworth: Penguin, 1968), ch. 15, p. 208.

by each individual are by hypothesis less than the gain to that individual. Furthermore, we need not determine whether any individual has in fact received full value, and more, for his sacrifice, since as the practice is defined, it is the individual himself who approves the exchange.[11]

Consider a case such as one reads of now and then, of somebody who digs out a picture or a stamp collection that has been gathering dust in the attic and sells it to a dealer at a fraction of its market value. The dealer has not used force or fraud and was under no legal obligation to supply information as to the true value of the object purchased. And the object was clearly less valuable to the seller at the time of the sale than the money he was offered for it, otherwise he would not have chosen to sell. Yet there is surely a perfectly clear sense in which this deal is unfair: the profit from the transaction is too unequally divided between the parties. Notice that we may say that a morally scrupulous dealer would not have taken unfair advantage of the seller's inexperience in this way without committing ourselves to the view that the law should void the contract or even to the view that the dealer had violated a duty. Yet the basis of our judgement that the dealer would have been more admirable if he had behaved differently is surely not that he would have shown himself generous or benevolent but that he would have shown sensitivity to the requirements of fairness.

Thus we can, and do, say intelligibly that a contract is unfair between the parties because the value of the things exchanged is unequal, although it is still a contract. And we do, quite rightly, say that it is unfair if 'men of equal merit' are treated differently, even if the giving of a reward is a matter of grace. The parable of the labourer in the vineyard (Matthew 20: 1–16) illustrates the point. That the lord of the vineyard gave more than the customary rate to those who had worked less than a full stint was a matter of 'grace' in Hobbes's terminology, and the lord's reply to one who had 'borne the burden and heat of the day'—'Friend, I do thee no wrong; didst not thou agree with me for a penny?'—is undeniably to the point. But there is surely also a genuine issue of fairness embodied in the complaint, 'these last have wrought but one hour, and thou hast made them equal to us'. Indeed, unless it is assumed that there is a natural sentiment of fairness—equal pay for equal work—that is being flouted, the parable loses its force which is, I take it, to emphasize the difference between the grace of God and human justice.

Hobbes had an ulterior political motive in denying that there were

---

[11] Charles Fried, 'Justice and Liberty', *Nomos*, 6, pp. 126–46, at 133.

alternative criteria of justice: he did not want to provide any excuses for non-performance of covenants since that might weaken the absolute claims of the sovereign. But it is quite consistent to say that a contract you entered into is unfair in that it does not exchange equal values or give a greater return for a greater contribution but that it would be unfair not to carry out your side of a bargain freely agreed to.

A quite different ulterior political motive has led Robert Nozick, in *Anarchy, State, and Utopia*, to deprecate the Rawlsian duty of 'fair play'. Nozick's fear is that it will license any group of people to create a duty to contribute to some common enterprise simply by providing unasked-for benefits. 'One cannot, whatever one's purposes, just act so as to give people benefits and then demand (or seize) payment. Nor can a group of people do this.'[12] He therefore wants to insist that there must be actual consent before it is legitimate to coerce people to contribute to a common good. Once again, the implication is that justice as reciprocity is reduced to contractual relations.

Characteristically, Nozick does not bother to offer any arguments, and rests the burden of his case on an eccentric example involving a public address system and 'some of the people in your neighbourhood' who put down everybody's name on a list to broadcast over it for a day.[13] It is indeed doubtful whether the case as stated gives rise to a duty to broadcast, still less that it gives the others a right to coerce you to do so (though I do think that as a matter of decency you should give advance notice of your intention not to perform). However, it is far from clear that the case as stated falls under Rawls's principle of fair play. For Rawls defined the duty of fair play by saying that 'a person is required to do his part as defined by the rules of an institution when two conditions are met: first the institution is just (or fair) . . . and second, one has voluntarily accepted the benefits of the arrangement or taken advantage of the opportunities it offers to further one's interests'.[14] Nozick's case may be defective as a counter-example on all three possible counts: it does not constitute an example of an 'institution' for the purpose of the principle; it is not just for 'some people' in the neighbourhood to arrogate to themselves the right to direct the use others make of their time; and listening to the public address system is scarcely voluntary.

If we turn to the real-life analogue of Nozick's example, it seems

[12]	Robert Nozick, *Anarchy, State, and Utopia* (New York: Basic Books, 1974), 95.

[13]	Ibid. 93–5.

[14]	Rawls, *A Theory of Justice*, pp. 111–12. I am indebted to the comments on Nozick's example in Thomas Scanlon, 'Nozick on Rights, Liberty, and Property', *Philosophy & Public Affairs*, 6 (1976), 3–25, at 15–17.

clear to me that the American public television stations have a good case for appealing (as they do) to the sense of fairness of those 'free riders' who choose to watch but do not contribute to the expenses of running the service. And I would add that considerations of fairness legitimate (if they do not require) that public television should be supported by a compulsory levy on the owners of television sets, as it is in many countries. It may be argued, of course, that this is unfair because some will be forced to contribute who do not watch public television or (in a country where there is no commercial television) would prefer having commercial television to paying for a licence. But to anyone except a fanatic the issue presents itself as a choice between the unfairness of permitting 'free riders' and the unfairness of collecting from non-beneficiaries, and there is no reason why the judgement should always go the same way. Let us leave aside the question of enforcement, however. The crucial point for present purposes is the simple one that the public television stations do have a legitimate claim in terms of fairness against those who benefit from the programmes but fail to contribute—a claim that Nozick's thesis would render unintelligible.[15]

The Rawlsian duty of fair play, as I noted above, requires that the benefits should have been accepted voluntarily. However, the general anti-free-rider principle is not limited in this way. It is unfair to enjoy the benefits of a practice without doing your part, even if you could not avoid enjoying these benefits. For example, if you live in an area where only smokeless fuel is permitted to be burned, you cannot help breathing cleaner air, having to wash curtains less often, and so on, but that does not in any way diminish your obligation to play your part and burn only smokeless fuel. Similarly, if other visitors to some remote beauty spot obey the rule that they should take their litter away with them, you cannot help enjoying the absence of litter, but again that would not make it any less unfair for you to leave yours behind.

Nozick's nightmare of people arbitrarily being able to impose obligations of fairness on you by doing you favours fails to take account of the fact that it takes more to create a practice (or in Rawls's terms an institution) than a few people getting together and starting to provide benefits for others. One of the main purposes of law is to define practices and thus create well-defined duties of fairness. The

[15] For an analysis of the implications for the provision of public goods of a morality favouring each person who benefits giving his 'fair share' of the costs, see Russell Hardin, *Collective Action* (Baltimore: The Johns Hopkins University Press for Resources for the Future, 1982), ch. 6. Hardin notes the importance of setting a standard 'membership fee' to create a 'uniquely prominent, relatively fair solution for cost-sharing'.

threat of criminal penalties is not very important as a motive for compliance with rules against domestic air pollution or littering. The law is, however, significant as a co-ordinating device, defining a standard of conduct that it would be fair for all to adhere to provided that others do so too. Nozick's idea, that if a random collection of self-appointed do-gooders cannot create obligations of fairness then neither can a public authority, entirely misses the point.

'The law', Paul Freund has said, 'is addicted to the device of finding "implied" contracts as a way out of novel problems, and of assimilating relations—such as public utility and customer—to a contractual mold'.[16] No doubt there are good technical reasons for this device, but in general the argument against trying to cram all cases of reciprocity into contract is an extension of that deployed by David Hume against the use of a fictitious 'original contract' to underwrite political obligation. If the real point is that of reciprocal advantage, nothing is gained by going through an extra loop and saying that the obligation derives from the fact that it would have been worth contracting had the occasion arisen.[17]

I have criticized the reduction of requital to fidelity. Rawls, in *A Theory of Justice*, goes in the other direction. He says that 'the principle of fidelity is but a special case of the principle of fairness applied to the social practice of promising' and that 'the obligation to keep a promise is a consequence of the principle of fairness'.[18] If he meant simply that the principle of fidelity and the principle of fair play both derive from justice as reciprocity this would be unexceptionable. But to assimilate them, as Rawls does, results in slighting the significance of voluntary agreement.

In the case of practices where participation is not optional, Rawls says (reasonably enough) that the duty of fair play comes into operation to require performance only when the practice is itself just in the way in which it distributes benefits and burdens. He tries to extend this to promising by saying that the principle of fairness makes the carrying out of promises obligatory only where the practice of

---

[16] Paul A. Freund, 'Social Justice and the Law', in *On Law and Justice* (Cambridge, Mass.: Harvard University Press, 1968), 82–107, at 84.

[17] Freund's remarks on the history of Roman and English contract law seem to me to suggest that the notion of justice as fidelity was a development out of that of justice as requital. According to Freund, the generalized notion of a contract arose in Roman law from 'either a delivery of a thing in expectation of a performance . . . or . . . the performance of an act in expectation of counterperformance' (p. 84), while in English law 'the elements of both *quid pro quo* and reliance entered into its inheritance' (p. 85). It is worth noting that these are precisely the bases of an enforceable duty of fair play ridiculed by Nozick.

[18] Rawls, *A Theory of Justice*, pp. 344, 346.

promising is itself just. An example of an unjust practice of promising would be one in which people were 'bound by words uttered while asleep, or extorted by force'.[19] This is of course right but it does not establish what Rawls wants. For the analogy of a particular non-voluntary practice is not the general practice of promising but 'a particular pattern of transactions' established by a set of mutual promises.[20] And the point is that justice as fidelity requires performance even if the 'small-scale scheme of cooperation' established by this set of mutual promises violates justice as requital in the way in which it distributes benefits and burdens among the participants. This is simply to reiterate that justice as requital and justice as fidelity are independent derivations from the generic notion of justice as reciprocity, and may on occasion conflict.

IV JUSTICE AS MUTUAL AID

Consider, to begin with, an ordinary case of voluntary insurance—against fire, theft, or accident, for example. If we look at the operation of the scheme within a certain slice of time, and overlook the contractual basis of the arrangements, we see a large number of fortunate citizens who have not had fires (and so on) in the period each paying in money which is dispensed to the small number who have been unfortunate. Simply observing the pattern of transfers we could not distinguish the insurance company from a charitable institution appealing to the generosity of the fortunate to give succour to the unfortunate. What makes the difference is reciprocity. Even the most coldly calculating egoist will, if he is rational and risk-averse, willingly pay insurance premiums because only by doing so can he establish a claim to compensation for unlikely but potentially devastating contingencies.

Private insurance is, as I have said, based on contractual relationships. Inasfar as it exhibits reciprocity, it is the kind dealt with in my remarks on justice as fidelity. The exchange is simply of a regular premium for a right to be paid in some contingency. The reason for beginning my discussion of justice as mutual aid with it is that it illustrates how, even in a society made up of devotees of Ayn Rand, there would be continuous redistribution from the fortunate to the unfortunate—on a purely voluntary basis. In what follows I shall argue that the insurance model can be extended to (*a*) a non-

[19] Ibid. 345.   [20] Ibid. 346.

contractual practice of mutual aid; and (*b*) a non-voluntary system of redistribution.

Imagine a small community a hundred miles from the nearest town. Each family possesses a car, but cars are, of course, liable to break down. To meet this contingency a two-part practice has developed: anyone who is going into town anyway should be prepared to give a ride to a person whose car is not in use, even at some minor inconvenience of scheduling, picking up, setting down, and so on; and in case of genuine emergency anyone for whom it is not unduly inconvenient should be prepared to make a special trip into town. This practice would, I suggest, generate a duty of mutual aid derived from the general notion of justice as reciprocity.

It is interesting to speculate how the practice of mutual aid might extend to those without a car at all. Suppose that, because of either loss of earnings or increasing infirmity, some of the old people in the community are no longer able to run a car. It might seem that, since they can no longer pay the 'premium'—the liability to give lifts to others—the insurance model should entail that they be excluded from the benefits. Any help they receive would then have to be put down to charity rather than reciprocity. But those who have cause to fear that they may some day themselves be reduced to the same circumstances will favour extending the benefits of the practice as an insurance measure.

This is still reciprocity but in a more complex form. Those who contribute benefits in a given period do not necessarily have any expectation of being able to claim them in future from the present beneficiaries. But they expect to be able to make claims themselves in the future on others, as defined by the practice. At any given time, the young could get a short-run gain by reneging on the extension of mutual aid to the old. But a social practice defined by informal norms and underwritten by informal sanctions (the exclusion from benefits of those who violate 'fair play' by failing to perform when required to) cannot simply be stopped and then started up again later. The age cohort that is thinking of reneging on its obligations to the old cannot, therefore, reasonably expect to be able to impose the same obligation later on its juniors.

The young have reason, derived from the insurance motive, for maintaining the extended practice in order to be in a position to benefit from it later themselves if they need to. This, it should be conceded, presupposes that those who make the sacrifices now will actually be around when they will stand to benefit from the operation of the same practice. We should therefore anticipate that reciprocity of this intertemporal kind will be weakened by mobility, and this does indeed seem to accord with experience. If the community were known to be due to be dissolved in a few years' time (suppose, for example, that its economy is entirely based on the exploitation of a non-renewable natural resource and that when that comes to an end its members will scatter), then we have to say that giving lifts to those without cars would switch from reciprocity to charity.

It should be observed that waiving the 'premium' for some does not entail waiving it for all. Anyone who, relying on the practice to get him out of trouble, chose to save the expense of having a car or ran one that was notoriously unreliable would be condemned as a free (or cheap) rider. If he has no less reason for paying the premium than anyone else, it is unfair of him not to. He would therefore be excluded or—given that there is a humanitarian duty in life-and-death emergencies to help, which is not dependent on reciprocity—subject to condemnation. (We could extend the story to more generalized reciprocity, so that someone who relied on others for transport provided some other service to members of the community, but there is no need to get into such further extensions here.)

I now have to say a little about the way in which justice as mutual aid underwrites compulsory redistribution. This theme has in recent years been taken up by economists under the label 'Pareto-optimal redistribution'.[21] Saying that a redistribution is Pareto optimal is to say that everybody prefers the distribution after redistribution has been carried out to the one before. The apparent paradox involved in saying that all might gain from redistribution is resolved by recalling that those who did not have a fire in a certain year have had their premiums redistributed to those that did; yet at the start of the year they thought they were better off with the insurance than without it, otherwise they presumably would not have chosen to buy it. I shall not discuss other things that economists include under 'Pareto-optimal redistribution', such as redistribution required by altruism (feeling better if others are happy) or malice (feeling better if others are unhappy), since these do not have any relevance to justice. Some economists even include relief from individual or collective violence

---

[21] See Geoffrey Brennan, 'Pareto-Desirable Redistribution: the Non-Altruistic Dimension', *Public Choice*, 14 (1973), 43–67; and three essays in Harold H. Hochman and George E. Peterson (eds.), *Redistribution through Public Choice* (New York: Columbia University Press, 1974): James D. Rodgers, 'Explaining Income Redistribution' (pp. 165–205); Richard Zeckhauser, 'Risk Spreading and Distribution' (pp. 206–28); and A. Mitchell Polinsky, 'Imperfect Capital Markets, Intertemporal Redistribution and Progressive Taxation' (pp. 229–58).

from the poor as a motive for 'Pareto-optimal redistribution', but this makes sense only if we count handing over one's wallet to a mugger as a Pareto-optimal redistribution. I shall divide the case for redistribution deriving from reciprocity into three elements: first, insurance for categorical contingencies; second, insurance for non-categorical contingencies; and, third, redistribution through time.

First, then, by 'categorical contingencies' I mean specifiable misfortunes: being sick, going blind, being thrown out of work by a general recession or a sudden fall in the market for one's skills (for example the redundancies of engineers and draughtsmen attendant upon the cut-back of the US aerospace industry). The state can accept risks (like that of compensation for long-term unemployment) that a private insurance company cannot. Suppose, for example, that a company were to offer a medical insurance policy to all in good health at age 21, with a guarantee that it would never cancel it and that premiums would not reflect subsequent individual experience or health prospects. Rational risk-averse people would welcome such a policy; but, if they are free to opt out at any time, then those whose health is still good twenty or thirty years later would have an incentive to join a scheme that offered lower rates than those it accepted after a medical examination. The original scheme would thus be undermined, since only those in poor health would be left in it and would in effect form a pool of bad risks. This is a sort of prisoner's dilemma situation: at age 21 everyone would prefer the scheme with everyone staying in, but those who remain healthy have an incentive to defect. The solution is for the state to collect the premiums from everyone through ordinary taxes or a special social security levy.

Over and above this, it would be rational to insure against 'bad luck', and this is what I mean by the second head of insurance against non-categorical contingencies. Looking at his prospects at the age of 21, say, a person with normal tastes would be willing to buy insurance, if it could be purchased, that would take some of his income if he is lucky enough to make a lot and give him some if he is unsuccessful. The state can achieve this by positive and negative taxation and, again, unless the state is going to enforce insurance agreements that do not allow for withdrawal on either side any time during the life of the insured person, only the state can bring about this kind of redistribution.

There are two obvious constraints on the amount of redistribution that would be generated by the state providing 'luck insurance' in the amount that would be purchased voluntarily. First, the redistribution package offered to each person would have to be related to his expected income: redistribution from those with good prospects at age 21 to those with poor prospects at age 21 falls outside the present rationale.[22] And second, since the 'bad luck' to be insured against is simply imputed from an income that falls below the average for one with such prospects at age 21, the problem of 'moral hazard' —the bane of all insurers—rears its ugly head. The perfect insurance (considered aside from moral hazard) makes the client indifferent between escaping the contingency insured against and suffering the contingency plus getting the compensation. But that means there is no incentive to avoid the contingency—to lock doors, check wiring, avoid health risks, and so on. Where the probability of the contingency's occurring can be affected by choices, therefore, insurance must be less than perfect to avoid skyrocketing premiums or the bankruptcy of the insurance scheme. If each person were offered a guaranteed income equal to the average for those with his prospects (that is, 100 per cent tax on income above and 100 per cent supplementation of income below), bad luck would be seriously contaminated by lack of exertion and the scheme would be in danger of going broke because of actual average incomes falling below those projected.

Finally, we should consider redistribution through time. If the normal human career is to have no earned income in the early years of one's life and again after retirement, then a lot of what looks like interpersonal redistribution when viewed at a single point in time, may be thought of alternatively as intertemporal redistribution within each person's lifetime income. Economists have been particularly concerned with the state's role in distributing income backward. Babies and children cannot (legally) borrow to get themselves a good education, medical and dental care, a nutritious diet, and so on; yet someone might see clearly, on reaching the age of majority, that it would have been worth paying money out in the future to have had those things earlier on. Even when the legal bar to borrowing falls at the age of majority, it is difficult to borrow much on future earnings. The problems set by making loans to be repaid out of future income over a long period are illustrated by the high rate of default in the USA on loans to college students. The state can overcome these problems by providing benefits, in the form of education, free milk, subsidized

---

[22] If we assume that the best the insurer could do in setting rates was to use educational level, achievement test scores, socio-economic background, race, and so on as evidence, the risk to be insured against would be 'luck' as defined by Christopher Jencks in *Inequality: A Reassessment of the Effect of Family and Schooling in America* (London: Allen Lane, 1973)—that variation in lifetime earnings not explained by such factors.

school meals, medical services, child allowances, and so on, and then collecting the cost later in taxes.

Redistribution forward is easier to the extent that saving is easier than borrowing. But in an uncertain world, where in many countries no form of investment yields a positive (inflation-discounted) return, it is highly rational to want to have any private superannuation scheme or savings programme underpinned by a scheme of state pensions that is, when it comes down to it (whatever its insurance trimmings may be), a scheme for transferring from those who are earning to those who are retired. It may be noted that such a (non-actuarial) scheme corresponds to the extended practice of mutual aid in my example of the isolated community.

V   RECIPROCITY AND RELATIONS BETWEEN COUNTRIES

From the viewpoint of justice as reciprocity, we must say that even the meagre redistribution that takes place now (in the form of aid, soft loans, and commodity contracts at above world prices) has to be counted as charity rather than justice. Justice as fidelity does not help: poor countries tend to break contracts (whether excusably or not need not be asked here) more often than rich countries. Justice as requital is a complicated matter. Obviously, in the imperialist period raw materials were extracted and labour employed without adequate return, and there is now a case for reparations. It may be said that the descendants of the exploiters have no obligation to atone for the injustice of their ancestors; but surely they do if they are themselves richer as a result of that injustice and the descendants of the exploited are poorer.[23]

It is a good deal harder to show that current transactions fail to meet the standard of justice as requital. To my knowledge, the most elaborate and sustained attempt to argue that international trade between rich and poor countries is a process by which the rich exploit the poor is Arghiri Emmanuel's book *Unequal Exchange*.[24] According to Emmanuel, 'as far as the underdeveloped countries are concerned . . . international aid has ceased to be regarded as a one-sided and gratuitous act on the part of the rich countries and is seen as an obligation that corresponds to a certain right of compensation'.

[23] For an analysis of some of the problems arising from group reparations for misdeeds of earlier generations, see Boris I. Bittker, *The Case for Black Reparations* (New York: Random House, 1973).

[24] Arghiri Emmanuel, *Unequal Exchange: A Study of the Imperialism of Trade* (New York: Monthly Review Press, 1972).

He goes on: 'Compensation for what? That is indeed the question, and this is what I have tried to answer'.[25] As I understand it, the essence of his answer is that the large difference in wages paid in different countries for the same number of hours of qualitatively similar work (measured in terms of skill, physical exertion, and so on) shows that the system of international exchange is unequal. Thus, he says:

While one may be able to find reasons, whether good or bad, to explain the difference between the wages of an American metal worker who controls a power press worth a million dollars and those of a worker on a Brazilian coffee plantation who uses only a simple machete, it is much harder to explain why a building worker who puts up a bungalow in the suburbs of New York has to be paid thirty times as much as his counterpart in the Lebanon, though both of them use the same tools and perform exactly the same movements as their Assyrian fellow worker of four thousand years ago.[26]

Surely it would be harder to explain how it would be possible to find building workers in New York at Lebanese (or Assyrian) rates of pay. Assuming the existence of some kind of labour market, any work in rich countries will be better paid across the board than the same kind of work in poor countries—hence the rule of thumb that the quickest way of judging the standard of living of a country is to see what a haircut costs, because a haircut is a standardized service almost all of whose price is made up of labour costs.

On Emmanuel's theory, the scale of unequal exchange in international trade today is truly enormous: it can be measured by asking what the terms of trade would be if wage rates were the same in all countries, and comparing that hypothetical state of affairs with the status quo.

If we assume that wages account for fifty per cent of the cost of [Third World] exports, and that the relevant rate of wages is one-twentieth of that prevailing in the advanced countries, a simple calculation will show us that the difference between the present value and the equivalence value is . . . a difference . . . in hundreds of thousands of millions. If fifty sacks of coffee are at present exchanged for one automobile, whereas, in order to pay coffee plantation workers at the same rate as workers in the automobile industry, fifty sacks would have to be exchanged for ten automobiles, the loss suffered by the coffee producers and the gain made by the other party in this transaction are not *less than* the value of fifty sacks, but *nine times as much*.[27]

[25] Ibid. 264.   [26] Ibid. 263–4.

[27] Ibid. 368 (italics in original). Notice that this passage shows a shift in ground from the earlier one quoted, in that the standard is now taken to be one in which the pay of the machete-wielding coffee worker and the power press operative in the car plant is equalized.

Now I think it is a perfectly intelligible view of the requirements of international justice that being born into one country rather than another should not determine one's fate to the extent that it does now, so that a person born into a poor society is condemned to almost certain disease, malnutrition, and poverty, while another, who has the good fortune to be born into a rich society, has an excellent chance of living a healthy and comfortable life. Later in the chapter (see below, section VI), I shall examine the conception of justice—justice as equal opportunity—from which such a view might be derived. But it seems to me simply perverse to try to derive any such notion from justice as requital, that is from the criterion of fair exchange.

To say, for example, that the poor countries actually lose from trading with the rich ones immediately raises the question of why they should choose to trade at all in that case. Unless trade benefits both parties (compared with the absence of trade), the general presumption is that it does not take place. Doubtless, Brazilians would prefer obtaining ten automobiles in exchange for fifty sacks of coffee to obtaining one automobile; but, if we are asking whether or not Brazilians actually *lose* from exchange, the relevant question is whether or not they would be better off keeping the coffee themselves. Emmanuel nowhere suggests that they would be, and I see no reason to believe they would.

In this context, we must, however, be careful not to abstract from the possibility of conflicts of interest within the poorer countries. 'Brazilians' do not, for example, collectively decide how much coffee to exchange for so many automobiles. One strand in the critique of the contemporary international economic order is that in many countries there is an alliance between foreign corporations and a small stratum of indigenous beneficiaries (importers, franchise-holders, and so on) at the expense of the rest of the population. A poor country may therefore engage in uncoerced exchanges that are actually worse for the bulk of the population than no exchange at all. But we should not regard any one pattern as universal. What is in fact striking is the very wide range of ways in which poor countries handle their trading relations with the developed world.[28] I am inclined to doubt that a great deal of trade is literally worse for the Third World country concerned than no trade at all. In any case, it seems clear that the elimination of all such trade would do very little to narrow the gap that now exists between rich and poor countries.

---

[28] See Michael Moran, 'Review Article: The Politics of International Business', *British Journal of Political Science*, 8 (1978), 217–36.

Justice as requital in exchanges is not, indeed, to be identified with a condition in which all that can be said is that both parties gain something from trade. As I suggested earlier (in section III), the criterion is that both sides gain equally from an exchange. Some economists would say that this is a hopelessly metaphysical notion. At any rate in simple cases, however, its application seems fairly straightforward. Suppose someone is selling a house and there is one interested buyer. The seller would rather keep the house than accept less than £100,000, while the buyer would rather keep his money than pay more than £120,000 for the house. If the price is close to £100,000 the buyer realizes almost all the gain from the exchange; and if the price is close to £120,000 the seller realizes almost all the gain. Surely the gain is shared equally if the price is roughly half way between the two figures. Where variable amounts may be traded between the parties, the analysis is more complicated than where the only question is what price something like a house sells at. But the idea of an equal gain from the whole transaction (with the amount traded being whatever the parties agree on at the price set) still seems to me to make sense, at least in that gross departures may be detected.

We may now introduce another strand in the critique of contemporary international economics, which is popular in UNCTAD. This is that there is an asymmetry between the way in which goods typically exported by rich countries are priced and the way in which those typically exported by poor countries are priced. A car manufacturer sets his price and sells however many cars he can sell at that price, whereas the raw materials and agricultural products that form the bulk of exports of most poor countries are much more likely to be sold on a competitive world market in which sellers will unload their goods at any price that leaves them better off selling than not selling. There is thus, it is argued, a built-in advantage for the industrial nations in international trade, because they can control production so as to obtain the profit margins they aim for.

As it stands, this claim is clearly overstated, since it is apparent that there is a good deal of competition in world markets between, say, the car manufacturers of different countries. A firm which arbitrarily decrees a certain profit margin and refuses to sell at any price that does not yield that margin is liable to find itself out of business. Suppose, however, that it were accepted that the industrial nations do gain differentially from the present set-up. How different would the distribution of income over the world look if the poor countries were to succeed in controlling the prices of their exports through some system of collective action? The answer is, as far as I can tell, that it would not look greatly different from the way it is now.

This may appear perverse when one considers the dramatic improvement in the economic circumstances of the oil-producing states that was brought about by OPEC. But oil has two remarkable characteristics. First, the cost of extracting the oil from the largest deposits (in Saudi Arabia and the Persian Gulf) is a matter of a few cents per barrel: in Kuwait it does not even need to be pumped out, and all that has to be done is fill the tankers.[29] Second, for some uses there is no feasible substitute for oil, and these include the important ones of fuelling the internal combustion engine and providing raw materials for the petrochemical industry; and for the rest (especially heating and electricity generation) the substitutes available in most places are much more expensive, like coal or atomic power. Oil thus generates a lot of economic rent, and the appropriation of a much larger share of this economic rent by the countries with the oil naturally makes a noticeable difference.

At the opposite end of the spectrum from oil are commodities such as sisal and jute whose maximum price is set by the point at which it is cheaper for users to switch to other fibres (including synthetics). Even ironclad controls over price could do little in these cases to redistribute income towards the producers. Justice as requital is satisfied even at a low price because, although the seller is not gaining much (compared with the next best use of the land or doing nothing at all with it), the buyer is also not gaining much (compared with the next most expensive alternative purchase). Equal exchange, it must be emphasized, has no inherent tendency to equalize the overall position of the parties. It is concerned purely with the distribution of the gains from the transaction between them.

Obviously, the crucial question is whether most of the commodities exported by Third World countries are more like oil or more like sisal and jute, and the answer is apparently that, although they form a spectrum, they lie mostly towards the sisal and jute end. It may be possible, for many products, to raise the price without too serious a drop in sales in the short run, but in the long run it will pay users to adapt to the higher prices by substituting other materials, using less, recycling, and so on. It may be recalled, incidentally, that Emmanuel, in calculating the 'loss' from exchange to the poorer countries, took the amount they would get if they were able to sell the *present* amount

[29] Anthony Sampson, *The Seven Sisters: The Great Oil Companies and The World they Shaped* (New York: The Viking Press, 1975), 94.

of exports at a price *ten times higher*. But this figure has no significance because the sales at ten times the price would be far smaller. Perhaps in the long run tea will go the same way as handmade lace—too labour-intensive to be affordable. Perhaps it should. But it does not seem to me very sensible to say that tea is 'really' worth ten times what it costs now, and that tea pickers are being exploited by tea drinkers, if the effect of increasing the price of tea ten times would be simply to throw the tea pickers out of work.

Even leaving aside the tendency over a period of a few years for users to find substitutes, the introduction of an international cartel in commodities other than oil (the 'Integrated Programme') has only limited prospects. David McNicol has calculated, using short-run elasticities of demand, that a doubling of the prices of fourteen commodities would increase the incomes of the LDCs ('less developed countries') by $20. 5 billion per year.[30] This is an amount less than twice the present sum of international economic assistance and is to be compared with the $80 billion by which the OPEC countries increased their oil revenues in *each* of 1974, 1975, and 1976.[31]

Even more serious than the relatively limited overall impact of these increases is their distribution among countries.

The principal *gainers* would be the major producers of cocoa, coffee, cotton, copper and sugar. . . . The *losers* would be nations who export relatively low-value commodities and who import substantial quantities of other commodities—especially cotton, copper, sugar and wool. . . . India, the nations just below the Sahara, and many of the nations in northern Africa and southeast Asia export relatively low-value crops; and there is some indication that they tend to be importers of agricultural products. These nations, which are a majority of the poorest of the LDCs, would probably be net losers under a system of restrictive commodity agreements.[32]

Thus, the final result would actually be a widening of the existing gap between rich and poor countries.

I have been assuming that the Integrated Programme would operate on the basis of price-fixing and production quotas, with the redistribution from rich countries to poor countries proceeding from the higher revenues generated by the increased prices. It would, of course, be

[30] David L. McNicol, *Commodity Agreements and the New Economic Order* (California Institute of Technology Social Science Working Paper, 1976). The fourteen commodities are cocoa, coffee, tea, wool, cotton, sugar, bananas, jute, sisal, beef, copper, tin, and iron. Wheat and rice are imported heavily by Third World countries and McNicol assumes that they would be excluded from price-raising efforts.
[31] Ibid. 133.
[32] Ibid. 132–3.

possible in principle (though hardly politically realistic in the foreseeable future) for the rich countries to go further and offer to pay for more of the controlled commodities than could be cleared on the market. In the short run, the surplus could be stored. But eventually only two solutions would be open. One would be to subsidize sales so as to increase demand either on a regular basis (British agricultural policy until the 1970s) or in order to dump a particular 'mountain' that has accumulated (as the EEC has done). The other would be to restrict supply by paying for non-production on the lines of the US 'acreage retirement' schemes. Subsidization would reduce the objectionable distributive effects of the straight production-quota scheme, whereas paying for non-production would do nothing about them. But both would be enormously expensive, and would constitute an irrational, inefficient, and inequitable way of transferring income from rich countries to poor ones. The lessons of British and American policies towards farming would be equally applicable to global analogues: 'In the United States, as in Britain, farm subsidies have been both economically inefficient and socially indefensible, distributing benefits preponderantly to the wealthiest minority of farmers.'[33]

We still have to ask whether any case for international redistribution from rich countries to poor ones could be established under the third heading of justice as reciprocity—justice as mutual aid. The answer is negative. And it is negative precisely because the minimal similarity of circumstances required to underwrite obligations of mutual aid is lacking here. Justice as reciprocity, we must again emphasize, has no comfort to offer to those who are chronically bad risks. Just as banks prefer to lend to the rich rather than the poor, mutual aid extends only to those who are sufficiently well off to have a reasonable prospect of being able to reciprocate any aid they may receive when the occasion to do so arises.

Such endeavours as the organized efforts in international development aid, or the objectives of the European Development Fund, and the proposed Southeast Asian Development Fund cannot be adequately understood in terms of reciprocity. . . . [The law governing diplomatic immunity] is strictly conditioned upon reciprocal interest and reciprocal enforcement. . . . In any meaningful sense, however, there is no reciprocity between the interest of the United States or Britain or France in assisting, bilaterally and through multilateral institutions, the development of Tanzania or India or Colombia and the interest of these countries in receiving such assistance.[34]

[33] Graham K. Wilson, *Special Interests and Policymaking: Agricultural Policies and Politics in Britain and the United States of America, 1956–70* (London: John Wiley and Sons, 1977), 73.

[34] Wolfgang Friedmann, 'The Relevance of International Law to the Processes of Economic

To illustrate the point, even if the USA were hit in one year by a major earthquake, a serious drought and several disastrous hurricanes, it could still pull through economically by borrowing or realizing foreign assets. The probability, in the lifetime of anyone now alive, that the USA will be asking Bangladesh for aid is so low as to mean that aid from the USA simply cannot be construed as mutual aid.

VI RECIPROCITY AND RELATIONS BETWEEN GENERATIONS

On the face of it, there is no room for justice as reciprocity to operate between people who are not alive at the same time. The man who asked what posterity has ever done for us got to the heart of the problem.[35] Since, in the nature of the case, posterity cannot do anything for us, there can be no obligation arising from justice as reciprocity to do anything for posterity. However, there are two possible escape routes, and they are worth some examination.

The first line of escape has a powerful intuitive appeal to many people, for I have found that whenever I press the conclusion that justice as reciprocity does not have application to future generations somebody proposes it. I have not found it worked out in print, though Edmund Burke's *Reflections on the Revolution in France* contains some ideas in the general area. There is his famous vision of society as 'a partnership between those who are living, those who are dead, and those who are to be born'.[36] And there is the panegyric on the 'idea of inheritance': 'People will not look forward to their posterity, who never look backward to their ancestors. . . . The institutions of policy, the goods of fortune, the gifts of providence, are handed down to us, and from us, in the same course and order'.[37]

The line of argument is, I take it, as follows: since we have received benefits from our predecessors, some notion of equity requires us to provide benefits for our successors. The notion of equity involved is, it would appear, somehow related to reciprocity. In my discussion of justice as mutual aid (above, section IV), I considered a case in which the young provide transport for the old in the expectation that when

and Social Development', in Richard A. Falk and Cyril E. Black (eds.), *The Future of the International Legal Order* ii: *Wealth and Resources* (Princeton, NJ: Princeton University Press, 1970), 3–35, at 12 and 13.

[35] '"We are always doing", says he, "something for Posterity, but I would fain see Posterity do something for us."' Joseph Addison, *The Spectator*, No. 583.

[36] Edmund Burke, *Reflections on the Revolution in France*, in A. J. Grieve (ed.), *Reflections on the French Revolution and Other Essays* (London: J. M. Dent, 1910), 93.

[37] Ibid. 31.

they themselves are old the young will do the same for them. I emphasized there the advantage to all (taking a long time span) of maintaining the practice. We can add that, even if the young could somehow get away with neglecting the old now and reintroducing the practice in time to benefit when they are old themselves, it would be unfair—a violation of justice as reciprocity—for them to do so. The extended reciprocity here runs in the opposite direction: having received benefits, we have an obligation of justice to pass on comparable benefits. The analogy lies in the fact that in both instances there is an ongoing practice from which we stand to benefit and which therefore creates a duty of 'fair play' to do our part in it.

I do not think that it is possible to sustain a completely general principle to the effect that the receipt of a benefit creates a prima facie obligation to pass on a similar benefit to others. R. M. Hare put forward such a principle in a context somewhat analogous to the present one in that it involves the question of bringing people into existence as against providing for them. Hare argued that, if we are glad we were born, this entails that we ought (in the absence of countervailing reasons) to maximize the number of people born. And he derives this from what he calls a 'logical extension' of the Golden Rule, which he takes to mean that 'we should do to others as we wish them to do to us'. The extension is 'to say that we should do to others what *we are glad was* done to us'.[38]

There are two arguments against this extended Golden Rule. First, the result it reaches for issues of population is ridiculous. This, however, may be circumvented if it can be shown that the extended Golden Rule does not have these implications.[39] The more serious argument is simply that the extended Golden Rule is silly in quite straightforward cases not involving the difficulties imported by worrying about the claims of potential people. If someone offers me a toffee apple, out of the blue, and I accept it, does my enjoyment of the toffee apple create even the tiniest obligation to distribute toffee apples to others? I do not see that it does. If it would spread happiness to give away toffee apples, *that* is no doubt a reason for doing so (though hardly one amounting to an obligation). But the reason thus generated does not seem to be in any way affected by whether or not I happen to have myself been the lucky recipient of a toffee apple. As a matter of moral psychology, it may be that receiving a toffee apple is what it

[38] R. M. Hare, 'Abortion and the Golden Rule', *Philosophy & Public Affairs*, 6 (1977), 185–90, at 208 (italics in original).

[39] For an argument, which seems to me plausible, to that effect, see George Sher, 'Hare, Abortion, and the Golden Rule', *Philosophy & Public Affairs*, 6 (1977), 185–90.

takes to get my sluggish benevolent tendencies going, in bringing to my attention how much others might enjoy one. But that is another matter.

In my view, the so-called extended Golden Rule is plausible only in the context of a practice, when it becomes synonymous with justice as reciprocity (see above, section III). If there is a practice of handing round toffee apples and I have taken and enjoyed those given out by others it is unfair not to hand round some myself, just as someone who ducks out when it gets to his turn to buy a round of drinks is behaving unfairly.

If we could establish the existence of a practice of looking after the interests of later generations, there would seem to be some sort of case, based on justice as reciprocity, for saying we should play our part in the practice and take account of the interests of our successors. The obligation would not fit very well into the threefold classification I developed earlier, but I suppose it would best be regarded as a sort of extension of justice as requital.

The question then is, does such a practice exist, of which we are the beneficiaries? I am not sure exactly what kind of evidence is relevant to this question, but I would take it that the kind of thing we should look for is (*a*) evidence that our ancestors had a norm to the effect that the interests of future generations should be given serious weight in decisionmaking; and (*b*) evidence that such a norm, if it was generally professed, was acted on. I cannot hope here to enter in any systematic way into such an enquiry. But it does not appear to me that the interests of later generations have ever played a very important role in public deliberations, still less in actual decisions. Let us take up the central issue—the degrading of the environment and the exhaustion of non-replaceable natural resources. My impression is that the only reason why our ancestors did not do more damage is that they lacked the technology to do so. I can see little evidence that they held back from anything that was technologically feasible and immediately profitable from any consideration about the costs they were imposing on their descendants. I do not therefore think that we would be under much of an obligation to our own descendants if we were constrained by nothing more stringent than the ecological morality of our ancestors. I am inclined, therefore, to suggest that the only implication of justice as reciprocity in this extended form is to give us an extra reason for adopting a more responsible attitude towards our successors. If we have some reason to do so anyway (which still remains to be shown), there is a bonus from justice as reciprocity in that we may be in on the foundation of a practice that will make it more likely that our successors will do likewise.

I now come to the second argument against the conclusion that we have no obligation to our successors derived from justice as reciprocity. This also appeals to the duty of fair play, but this time it is fair play among contemporaries rather than fair play over the generations. The argument is that, although we do not have obligations *to* future generations, we may have obligations *with respect to* future generations. The idea here is that, to the extent that the welfare of future generations is something nearly all of us as a matter of fact care about, it can be treated as a public good; and justice as requital (it will be recalled) requires us to play a fair part in contributing to a public good from which we benefit. That the 'benefit' is, as it were, a sentimental one directed at the future, rather than a personal one here and now, does not affect the logic.[40]

The obvious limitation to this argument is that the obligation with respect to future generations is entirely parasitic upon our actual sentiments about them. If we care about their welfare (or more specifically if enough of us care about their welfare to make it qualify as a public good), we can generate a derivative obligation among ourselves. But there is nothing in the argument that says we should care for their welfare. Since in practice it does not appear that many people have a time-horizon for public policy extending much beyond thirty years, this does not get us very far.

Discussions by experts of threatened crises in raw materials, energy, pollution, food shortages, and so on generally appear to be founded on the belief that they have shown fears to be alarmist if they can produce evidence that we can probably get through the next thirty years without catastrophe. The notion that we should be thinking how to arrange things so that the human race has even a fighting chance of getting through the next ten thousand or hundred thousand years would, I am sure, be regarded by these experts as bizarre. The question of justice between generations is precisely the question of whether we *should* care about the welfare of our successors, and what sacrifices we ought to be prepared to make now in their interests. I am not impressed by the bland assurance that all we have to do is feed in our own prejudices and they will come out as obligations of justice.[41]

---

[40] See D. Clayton Hubin, 'Justice and Future Generations', *Philosophy & Public Affairs*, 6 (1976), 70–83, and Thomas Schwartz, 'Obligations to Posterity', in R. I. Sikora and Brian Barry (eds.), *Obligations to Future Generations* (Philadelphia: Temple University Press, 1978).

[41] For a more extended discussion of this point see my paper 'The Circumstances of Justice and Future Generations', in Sikora and Barry (eds.), *Obligations to Future Generations*.

VII ANOTHER PRINCIPLE OF JUSTICE

My primary aim in this chapter has been to analyse the principle of justice as reciprocity and to show how limited it is in its application to problems of justice between nations and justice between generations. I have also tried to show that the attempt to derive more acceptable conclusions from justice as reciprocity than those that appear at first sight to follow (and I share the views of those who find those conclusions unacceptable) are pursuing an unprofitable enterprise. Their efforts are a tribute to the power and appeal of the paradigm of justice as reciprocity. But I am convinced that the way forward is not to devote further efforts to trying to square the circle, that is to say, trying to get non-outrageous conclusions from justice as reciprocity. The solution is rather, I suggest, to see if there is not some principle of justice complementary to justice as reciprocity that comes into its own when we move outside the special case of justice among contemporaries who are members of the same society.

I emphasize that it must be complementary because I believe that justice as reciprocity is here to stay. It is (as I suggested earlier in section I) a cultural universal, and anyway it makes a lot of sense. Any theory of justice that tried to eliminate justice as reciprocity would be doomed from the start. We must therefore seek to show how justice as reciprocity needs to be supplemented, not displaced.

I believe that this can be done without great difficulty. The glaring limitation of justice as reciprocity is that it can say nothing about the initial control over natural resources. Once ownership rights are assigned, justice as reciprocity can tell us about fair trading. But it is silent on the crucial first stage. Theorists who wish to place fair exchange at the centre of their conceptions of justice, from John Locke to James Buchanan and Robert Nozick, have always recognized that some other kind of theory has to be brought in to get things started or that one must simply be agnostic about the initial distribution of resources.

We could, of course, take the heroic path of saying that justice as reciprocity is the only sort of justice and that, however we may characterize the initial distribution of resources, 'just' and 'unjust' are not appropriate words. But that seems rather preposterous, since we surely want to have some distributive concept to evaluate distributions. If we can't have 'just' (or 'fair') we will have to invent some other; but we will surely want some distributive criterion.

Consider a 'state of nature' story. A number of people occupy a certain territory and live by hunting. It has been found by experience that bands of six are the most efficient for hunting, and on the principle of requital it is just for members of each band to be rewarded in accordance with their contribution to its success. Justice as mutual aid requires that a band experiencing a run of bad luck in hunting should be saved from starvation by others. But this does not entail systematic transfer from a more skilful band to a less skilful one.

So far so good. But now consider a development in this story. Suppose that in one half of the territory the terrain is more favourable so that game is more easy to catch. Specifically, let us assume that for any band (whatever its level of skill) exactly half as much effort is required in the more favoured half of the territory to catch any given amount of game. Now suppose that one half of the people in the area declare that access to the more favoured half of the territory is henceforth to be controlled by them. And suppose also that they somehow succeed in enforcing this against the others. (Call them the 'dominant group' and the others the 'subordinate group'.) The dominant group now has a choice. The members can hunt for themselves, catching an adequate supply of game with half the effort that the subordinate group has to exert to make the same catch. Or they can permit the members of the subordinate group to hunt in the favoured territory on condition that they hand over a share of whatever they catch.

According to a common view, it makes a big difference to the analysis of the situation which of these paths is taken. If the dominant group offer a deal to the subordinate group and it is accepted, the members of the dominant group are living off the labour of the others; whereas if they simply exclude the others and hunt for themselves they are not. But this seems to me a misguided way of looking at the position. The advantage lies in controlling access to the favoured part of the territory, and the question of what use that advantage is put to is secondary. *Given* that the advantage is going to be maintained, the subordinate group would rationally prefer to have the option of hunting in the more favoured territory in return for giving up a share of the catch. So it would seem strange if the dominant group were to be judged more severely for providing the option to the subordinate group than otherwise.

What has justice as reciprocity to say about all this? If the dominant group excludes the subordinate group, it has nothing to say. If the dominant group permits the subordinate group to hunt in return for a share of the proceeds, justice as requital says that there should be a fair exchange. But since an hour spent hunting in the more favoured terrain is twice as productive as an hour spent outside it, it is obviously a fair exchange that the privilege should cost a share of the catch. On the question of whether it is just for the dominant group to control access, justice as reciprocity is silent. If we want to make a judgement about the justice of that, it looks as if we must go to some sense of justice not derivable from justice as reciprocity. Tentatively, let me suggest that the principle is one of justice as equal access to natural resources.

To reinforce but at the same time refine this idea, let us turn to a society that is, by almost universal agreement, exceedingly unjust —South Africa. I believe that, although some countries may be more violent and others more repressive, South Africa is *the* most unjust society in the world, but nothing I have to say turns on the acceptance of that view, which would require for its support much more about the distinction between injustice and other evils.

Let us now ask what it is that makes South Africa *economically* unjust. I suggest that there are at least these three features:

1. Non-Whites are not allowed to unionize, and are paid less than the value they contribute to the economy.
2. Non-Whites are provided with poor opportunities for acquiring education, and are prevented by the job reservation system from filling the better-paid jobs, even if they are qualified.
3. Under apartheid, non-Whites are prohibited from owning land in any of the more productive areas of the country. The so-called 'tribal homelands' are carefully chosen to be barren and devoid of mineral resources.[42]

The first of these points falls squarely within the scope of justice as reciprocity: non-Whites are not allowed a fair bargaining position and are not receiving fair exchange for the value of their work. But the other two points cannot be related to justice as reciprocity. Suppose that non-Whites *were* paid the full value of their product: the other two points would still be valid. Justice demands not only that people should be paid the value they contribute but that they should have a fair opportunity to increase the value they contribute. Justice as reciprocity has nothing to say about this.

It might perhaps be suggested that justice as requital can be employed to argue that non-Whites are not getting their fair share of

[42] See Pierre van den Berghe, *South Africa: A Study in Conflict* (Berkeley and Los Angeles: University of California Press, 1967), 196–8.

school expenditures, in that per capita educational costs of White children are many times those of non-White children. But it must be recalled that justice as requital demands only that benefits received should be matched to taxes paid. Apologists of the South African regime can say quite truthfully that since Whites pay most of the taxes it is just, in this sense, for Whites to receive most of the benefits. This illustrates the way in which, given a fundamental pattern of injustice, justice as reciprocity operates merely so as to maintain it in equilibrium.

I think that this discussion of South Africa, sketchy as it is, can form the basis for a second shot at the principle we are looking for. It is, I suggest, none other than equality of opportunity, understood in a very broad sense that goes way beyond equal chances to get ahead in a meritocratic rat-race. The minimal claim of equal opportunity is an equal claim on the earth's natural resources. The maximum claim is that the same abilities and efforts should reap the same rewards. This, it may be noticed, is the driving force behind Emmanuel's criticism of the present international economic order. His error was, I believe, not in saying that there is something unjust about one person getting a huge multiple of the other's pay for performing the identical task, but rather in attempting to fit this idea in to the framework of justice as reciprocity.

VIII   SOME IMPLICATIONS OF THE PRINCIPLE

I realize that there are many difficulties in clarifying the conception of equal opportunity and also in thinking through its implications. In this closing section, I shall therefore tackle a more modest (but still formidable) task. I shall take up the narrow conception and ask what implications it has for international and intergenerational justice. This discussion is offered as a sketch of what might be said; I hope elsewhere to expand and refine it. (See below, chapter 19.)

The main implication is that the claim of each country to control access to the natural resources of its territory cannot be accepted as absolute, nor can the claim of any given generation to use the earth's resources as it sees fit. It is wrong (to quote Burke again) for 'the temporary possessors and life-renters in [the commonwealth . . . to] act as if they were the entire masters . . . [to] cut off the entail, or commit waste on the inheritance'.[43] The planet is the common

---

[43] Burke, *Reflections on the Revolution in France*, p. 137.

heritage of all men at all times and any appropriation of its resources must be subject to appraisal from the point of view of justice.

It has to be said that recent moves in international forums do not suggest an easy road for the principle that the world's resources are a common possession of all human beings. The United Nations General Assembly has declared the 'permanent sovereignty over natural resources' of the country in which the natural resources occur.[44] The International Law of the Sea convention is apparently going to move away from the ocean as a 'common' by extending national territorial claims over the sea-bed and marine life rather than by internationalizing the sea's resources. And the emphasis that the Third World countries are putting (through UNCTAD) on the raising of commodity prices as the favoured means of international redistribution is also inauspicious. As we have seen (section V), it has the same effect as the other two moves: it is good for those countries with resources but is if anything on balance disadvantageous for countries whose problem is that they are resource-poor. However, if it is assumed (not implausibly) that the only realistic alternative at present to national sovereignty is letting the rich countries have a free hand in using up the world's natural resources and that the citizens of rich countries will accept higher prices but not higher taxes, these moves can be understood as defining a politically feasible second-best.[45]

It is important to see that, if it is a matter of justice to give countries more equal access to the world's resources, the duty to make transfers to a resource-poor country does not depend on the use made of the additional income by that country.[46] This is how justice differs from charity. If a man approaches me and asks for money to feed his wife and children, I can quite properly ask myself if there is reason to believe that he will spend anything I give him on buying alcohol. But an employer may not legitimately refuse to pay his employee what he owes him on the ground that he disapproves of the way it is going to get spent. This is not to say that there should not be some requirement that the employee support his wife and children; but there are two separate issues which should be kept distinct.

[44] Charles R. Beitz, 'Justice and International Relations', *Philosophy & Public Affairs*, 4 (1975), 360–89, at 371 n. 9.

[45] For a useful introduction to these questions see Oscar Schachter, *Sharing the World's Resources* (New York: Columbia University Press, 1977).

[46] Conservatives (or, if they are a distinguishable category, those who are reluctant to give up what they have got) naturally fasten on to the argument that the obligation to redistribute is voided by the nature of the regime. See, for a string of similar arguments against redistribution, Robert W. Tucker, *The Inequality of Nations* (New York: Basic Books, 1977).

The application of this example in international affairs is as follows:

1. Where aid is given as charity to relieve suffering, it is legitimate for the donor country to insist that the aid be disbursed to the needy within the recipient country.
2. In as far as redistribution is required by the demands of justice, the criterion of justice is that countries, as collectivities, should have their fair share of the world's resources.
3. Failure of a country to have a just internal distribution does not relieve donor countries of the obligations of international justice.
4. International pressure, economic sanctions, or even military intervention may sometimes be legitimate as a way of improving the internal justice of a society.
5. The right of other countries to apply such pressure is not increased if the country in question is a beneficiary of international transfers based on justice. Nor is the right decreased if the country in question is a net contributor. (Of course, it is politically *easier* to bring pressure on poor countries, but that is a separate question.)

One final point. We might agree that the employer could, without committing injustice, withhold the pay he owes the employee if he knows that the employee is going to use it to buy an armoury and terrorize the neighbourhood or to destroy his family. But in an extreme case like that the employer (or anybody else) would also be justified in taking away money the employee already has. The international analogy is that a transfer to a country whose government plans to buy weapons for external aggression or internal repression may legitimately be cancelled; but in any situation where that would be legitimate it would also be legitimate to withhold any other payments that were due. (The UK government's freezing of all financial obligations to Rhodesia after the latter's Unilateral Declaration of Independence would be a case in point.)

What about intergenerational relations? I believe that the notion of fair access to resources can be deployed to deal with them. In my 'state of nature' example it would surely be unfair (in a sense which has nothing to do with reciprocity) for one generation of hunters to hunt the game to extinction and leave their successors to starve. Access to the earth's resources can be unfairly distributed over time as well as over space.

What justice requires is that the range of opportunities open to successor generations should not be narrowed. If some openings are closed off by depletion or other irreversible damage to the environment, others should be created (if necessary at the cost of some sacrifice) to make up. (See chapter 19 below.)

This conception of intergenerational justice has several attractive features. First, it is a global extension of a principle that families with possessions to pass on have traditionally espoused: 'Keep the capital intact!' Second, it underwrites the asymmetry that many people (including myself) feel between making successors better off, which is a nice thing to do but not required by justice, and not making them worse off, which *is* required by justice. And third, it does not make the demands of justice to our successors depend on our knowing their tastes—still less on our approving of them.[47] (The notion that our obligations depend on our empathy with future generations is discussed further in chapter 18 below.)

[47] See M. P. Golding, 'Obligations to Future Generations', *Monist*, 56 (1972), 85–99.

JUSTICE BETWEEN GENERATIONS

> Suppose that, as a result of using up all the world's resources, human life did come to an end. So what? What is so desirable about an indefinite continuation of the human species, religious convictions apart?
>
> Wilfred Beckerman, 'The Myth of "Finite" Resources'

My object in this chapter is to ask what if anything those alive at any given time owe their descendants, whether in the form of positive efforts (e.g. investment in capital goods) or in the form of forbearance from possible actions (e.g. those causing irreversible damage to the natural environment). We scan the 'classics' in vain for guidance on this question, and for understandable reasons. Among human beings, unlike (say) mayflies, generations do not succeed one another in the sense that one is off the scene before the next comes into existence. 'Generations' are an abstraction from a continuous process of population replacement. Prudent provision for the welfare of all those currently alive therefore entails some considerable regard for the future. The way we get into problems that cannot be handled in this way is that there may be 'sleepers' (actions taken at one time that have much more significant effects in the long run than in the short run) or actions that are on balance beneficial in the short run and harmful in the long run (or vice versa).

More precisely, the problem arises (as a problem requiring decision) not when actions actually have long-run effects that are different in scale or direction from their short-run effects but when they are *believed* to do so. The increased salience of the problem for us comes about not just because we are more likely to have the opportunity, thanks to technology, of doing things with long-run consequences not mediated by similar short-run consequences but also because there is more chance of our knowing about it. A useful new technology that we have no reason to believe has adverse long-term effects does not present any problem of decisionmaking for us, even if, unknown to us, it actually has the most deleterious long-run consequences. Conversely, new knowledge may suggest that things we have been doing for some time have harmful long-term effects. Even if people have been doing something with adverse long-term effects for hundreds or thousands of years, so that we are currently experiencing the ill effects in the form of, say, higher disease rates or lower crop yields than we should otherwise be enjoying, it may still require some breakthrough in scientific understanding to show that the current situation has been brought about by certain human practices.

In recent years we have all been made aware by the 'ecological' movement how delicately balanced are the processes that support life on the earth's surface and how easily some disequilibrium may ramify through a variety of processes with cumulative effects. The stage is set for some potentially very awkward decisions by this increased awareness that apparently insignificant impacts on the environment may, by the time they have fully worked themselves through, have serious consequences for human life. We may, any day, be confronted with convincing evidence for believing that something on which we rely heavily—the internal-combustion engine, say—is doing irreversible damage to the ecosystem, even if the effects of our current actions will not build up to a catastrophic deterioration for many years (perhaps centuries) to come.

If we ask what makes our relations with our successors in hundreds of years' time so different from our relations with our contemporaries as to challenge the ordinary moral notions that we use in everyday affairs, there are two candidates that come to mind, one concerned with power and one with knowledge. I shall consider these in turn.

A truistic but fundamental difference between our relations with our successors and our relations with our contemporaries, then, is the absolute difference in power. The present inhabitants of Britain may believe that, although they have some discretion in the amount of aid they give to the people of Bangladesh, they have little to hope or fear from the present inhabitants of Bangladesh in return. But they cannot be sure that later geopolitical events may not change this in their own lifetime. We can be quite certain, however, that people alive in several centuries' time will not be able to do anything that will make us better off or worse off now, although we can to some degree make them better off or worse off.

Admittedly, our successors have absolute control of something in the future that we may care about now: our reputations. It is up to them to decide what they think of us—or indeed whether they think about us at all. And presumably what, or whether, they think of us is going to be in some way affected by the way that we act towards them. I must confess, however, to doubting that this does much to level up the asymmetry of power between us and our successors, for two reasons. First, although they control a resource which may matter to us, we have no way of negotiating an agreement with them to the effect that they will treat our reputations in a certain way if we behave now in a certain way. We therefore have to guess how they will react to the way we behave, and in the nature of the case such guesses are bound to be inexact. Second, and more important, although individuals are undoubtedly moved by thoughts of posthumous fame for their artistic achievements or political records, it does not seem plausible to suppose that the same motivation would operate collectively so as to lead a mass electorate to support, say, measures of energy conservation. Altogether, therefore, I do not think that the fact of later generations determining our reputations deserves to be given much weight as an offset to the otherwise completely unilateral power that we have over our successors.

How important is this asymmetry of power between us and our successors—the fact that we can help or hurt them but they cannot help or hurt us? It is tempting to say at once that this cannot possibly in itself make any moral difference. Yet it is perhaps surprising to realize that a variety of commonly held views about the basis of morality seem to entail that the absence of reciprocal power relations eliminates the possibility of our having moral obligations (or at any rate obligations of justice) to our successors.

There is a tradition of thought running from Hobbes and Hume to Hart and Warnock according to which the point of morality is that it offers (in Hobbes's terms) 'convenient articles of peace': human beings are sufficiently equal in their capacity to hurt one another, and in their dependence on one another's co-operation to live well, that it is mutually advantageous to all of them to support an institution designed to give people artificial motives for respecting the interests of others.

It seems plain that such a view cannot generate the conclusion that we have moral obligations to those who will not be alive until long after we are dead. Thus, G. J. Warnock, in *The Object of Morality*, offers two reasons for saying that moral principles should have universal application rather than being confined to particular groups. 'First, everyone presumably will be a non-member of some group, and cannot in general have any absolute guarantee that he will encounter no members of groups that are not his own; thus if principles are group-bound, he remains, so to speak, at risk. . . .

Second . . . if conduct is to be seen as regulated only *within* groups, we still have the possibility of unrestricted hostility and conflict *between* groups. . . . '[1] Obviously, neither of these reasons carries weight in relation to our successors, since we do precisely have an absolute guarantee that we shall never encounter them and cannot conceivably suffer from their hostility to us. It should be added in fairness to Warnock that he himself suggests that morality requires us to take account of the interests of future generations and also of animals. But my point is that I do not see how this squares with his premises.

It is, indeed, possible to get some distance by invoking the fact with which I began this chapter, that the notion of 'successive generations' is an artificial one since there is a continuous process of replacement in human populations. Once we have universalized our moral principles to apply to everyone alive now, there are because of this continuity severe practical problems in drawing a neat cut-off point in the future. In the absence of a definite cut-off point, it may seem natural to say that our moral principles hold without temporal limit. But could what is in effect no stronger force than inertia be sufficient to lead us to make big sacrifices for remote generations if these seemed to be called for by atemporal morality? Surely, if morality is at base no more than mutual self-defence, we would (whether or not we made it explicit) agree to ignore the interests of those coming hundreds of years after us.

There is an alternative line of argument about the basis of moral obligations, also involving reciprocity, from which the denial of obligations to future generations follows directly. This view is seldom put forward systematically though it crops up often enough in conversation. This is the idea that by living in a society one gets caught up in a network of interdependencies and from these somehow arise obligations. A recent statement of this view may be found in Burton Zwiebach, who says that 'the basis of our obligation is the common life'.[2] The same idea—that obligations to others arise from actual relations with them—underlies Michael Walzer's *Obligations*.[3] Obviously, this more parochial view, which makes obligations depend on actual rather than potential reciprocal relationships, rules out any obligations to subsequent generations, since there is no reciprocity with them.

As T. D. Weldon recognized when he put forward a similar view in

---

[1] G. J. Warnock, *The Object of Morality* (London: Methuen, 1967), 150.
[2] Burton Zwiebach, *Civility and Disobedience* (London: Cambridge University Press, 1975), 75.
[3] Michael Walzer, *Obligations* (Cambridge, Mass.: Harvard University Press, 1970).

the last chapter of *States and Morals*,[4] it is very close to basing obligations on sentiments. This further move is made in one of the very few papers addressed explicitly to the present topic[5] and permits some consideration to be given to future generations—but in a way that I personally find more morally offensive than a blunt disregard of all future interests. According to Martin Golding, obligations rest on a sense of 'moral community'. Whether or not we have any obligations to future generations depends on whether we expect them to live in ways that would lead us to regard them as part of our 'moral community'. If we think they will develop in ways we disapprove of, we have no obligations to them. This view is obviously a diachronic version of the common American attitude that famine need only be relieved in countries with the right attitude to capitalism.

A third view which appears to leave little room for obligations to future generations is the kind of Lockean philosophy recently revived by Robert Nozick in *Anarchy, State, and Utopia*.[6] Indeed, it is scarcely accidental that the uniquely short-sighted destruction of trees, animals, and soil in the United States should have been perpetrated by believers in a natural right to property. According to Nozick, any attempt to use the state to redistribute resources among contemporaries in order to bring about some 'end state' is illegitimate, so presumably by the same token any deliberate collective action aimed at distributing resources over time would fall under the same ban. Provided an individual has come by a good justly, he may justly dispose of it in any way he likes—by giving it away or bequeathing it, trading it for something else, consuming it, or destroying it. No question of justice arises in all this so long as he does not injure the rights to property and security from physical harm of anyone else. Since we have a right to dispose of our property as we wish, subsequent generations could not charge us with injustice if we were to consume whatever we could in our own lifetimes and direct that what was left should be destroyed at our deaths. (Having one's property destroyed at death has been popular at various times and places and could presumably become so again.) It would clearly be, on Nozick's view, unjust for the survivors to fail to carry out such directions.

Once again we can see that the problem is the lack of bargaining power in the hands of later generations. Those without bargaining

---

[4] T. D. Weldon, *States and Morals* (London: John Murray, 1946).

[5] M. P. Golding, 'Obligations to Future Generations', *Monist*, 56 (1972), 85–99.

[6] Robert Nozick, *Anarchy, State, and Utopia* (New York: Basic Books, 1974).

power may appeal to the generous sentiments of others but they cannot make legitimate moral demands, as Nozick's examples of the men on their desert islands vividly illustrates. He asks us to imagine a number of men washed up on desert islands, with the possibility of sending goods to each other and transmitting messages by radio transmitter, but with no means of travelling themselves. Sternly resisting the temptation to comment further on the outlook of a man for whom the paradigm of human relations is a number of adult males on desert islands, let us ask what moral obligations they have to each other. Nozick's answer is simple: none. Even if one has the good fortune to have landed on an island flowing with milk and honey while his neighbour is gradually starving on a barren waste, there is no obligation on one to supply the other's needs. Where could such an obligation possibly come from? To get a parallel with the relations between generations all we have to do is imagine that the islands are situated along an ocean current. Goods can be dispatched in one direction only, down the current. Even if those further down the line could call for help (as later generations in fact cannot) they could make no moral claims on those higher up.

I have so far concentrated on one potentially relevant fact about our relations with our successors: the asymmetry of power. The second one, which is invariably mentioned in this context, is the fact that we have less and less knowledge about the future the more remote the time ahead we are thinking about. Whether or not this is (like the asymmetry of power relations) an absolutely necessary truth derivable from the very concept of the future is a question any attempt to answer which would involve opening the can of worms labelled 'Determinism'. I shall therefore simply accept the basic assertion as true—since it is surely true for us now, anyway—and ask what its implications are.

The answer seems to be fairly clear. As far as I can see, no theory that survives the first consideration and still holds that we have some sort of obligation to take account of the interests of remote future generations would have its conclusions upset by our unavoidable ignorance about the future. It may, of course, be held that we have *no* knowledge of the way in which our present actions will affect the interests of those who come after us in more than k years' time—either because we don't know what effects our actions will have on the state of the universe then or because we can have no idea what their interests will be. In that case, it obviously follows that our accepting an obligation to concern ourselves with their interests does not entail our behaving any differently from the way we would behave if we did not accept such an obligation. We can decide what to do without having to bother about any effects it may have beyond *k* years' time. But the obligation still remains latent in the sense that, if at some future date we do come to believe that we have relevant information about the effects of our actions on people living in more than *k* years' time, we should take account of it in determining our actions. The obligation would have been activated.

Ignorance of the future may be invoked to deny that obligations to remote descendants have any practical implications so that we can ignore them with a good conscience in deciding what to do. Thus, John Passmore, in his book *Man's Responsibility for Nature*,[7] canvasses among other possibilities the rigorous atemporal utilitarianism put forward by Sidgwick, according to which 'the time at which a man exists cannot affect the value of his happiness from a universal point of view'.[8] But he says that, because of the existence of uncertainty, even Sidgwick's approach would lead us to the conclusion that 'our obligations are to *immediate* posterity, we ought to try to improve the world so that we shall be able to hand it over to our immediate successors in a better condition, and that is all'.[9]

I think this all too convenient conclusion ought to be treated with great mistrust. It is true that we do not know what the precise tastes of our remote descendants will be, but they are unlikely to include a desire for skin cancer, soil erosion, or the inundation of all low-lying areas as a result of the melting of the ice-caps. And, other things being equal, the interests of future generations cannot be harmed by our leaving them more choices rather than fewer.

Even more dubious, it seems to me, is the habit (especially common among economists for some reason) of drawing blank cheques on the future to cover our own deficiencies. The shortages, pollution, over-population, etc. that we leave behind will be no problem for our successors because, it is said, they will invent ways of dealing with them. This Micawberish attitude of expecting something to turn up would be rightly considered imprudent in an individual and I do not see how it is any less so when extended to our successors.

My own view is that, especially in the context of universalistic utilitarianism, the appeal to ignorance normally functions as a smoke-screen, to conceal the fact that we are simply not willing to act in the kind of saintly way that a serious application of the doctrine must

---

[7] John Passmore, *Man's Responsibility for Nature* (London: Duckworth, 1974).
[8] Henry Sidgwick, *The Methods of Ethics* (London: Macmillan, 7th edn., 1907), 414.
[9] Passmore, *Man's Responsibility for Nature*, p. 91 (itals. in original).

entail. Passmore writes (claiming to paraphrase Rawls) that 'the utilitarian principle of impartiality, taken literally, demands too much of us; we cannot reasonably be expected to share our resources with the whole of posterity'.[10] He is more to the point here than when introducing ignorance as a 'fudge factor' to make the answer come out where in any case he feels it should be.

I entirely share the reluctance I have attributed to others to accept the full rigours of universal utilitarianism. Admittedly reluctance to accept a theory about our obligations is hardly enough to disqualify it. After all, the whole idea of talking about obligations is presumably to put to us a motive for doing things that we would (at least sometimes) not be inclined to do otherwise. But the demands of universal utilitarianism—that I should always act in such a way as to maximize the sum of happiness over the future course of human (or maybe sentient) history—are so extreme that I cannot bring myself to believe that there is any such obligation.

At the same time, I find it impossible to believe that it can be right to disregard totally the interests of even remotely future generations, to the extent that we have some idea of the way in which our current actions will affect those interests. If I am correct in saying that it is an implication of the three theories of morality considered earlier that there are no obligations to distant future generations, they too have to be rejected.

But if we dump mutual self-protection, entitlement, and community (with which we may roughly identify the holy trinity of political theory, first identified by T. H. Green and still faithfully worshipped by the Oxford Modern Greats degree—Hobbes, Locke, and Rousseau) what are we left with? Unless we are prepared to fall back on an appeal to intuitions (and it may come to that), the only general approach remaining is as far as I can see some sort of ideal contractarian construction: what is required by justice is that we should be prepared to do what we would demand of others if we didn't know the details of our situation or theirs.

The name of Rawls naturally, and rightly, springs to mind here. But it should be recognized that the ideal contractarian formula is open-ended and does not have to be identified with Rawls's use of it. Nevertheless, Rawls's *A Theory of Justice*[11] is the obvious place to start and I shall therefore now set out and criticize Rawls's contribution to the problem of justice between generations. The first point to notice is

[10] Ibid. 86.
[11] John Rawls, *A Theory of Justice* (Cambridge, Mass.: Harvard University Press, 1971).

that Rawls discusses the problem only in the context of the 'just savings rate' and this imposes two limitations on the generality of his conclusions. The obvious one is that if we concentrate on the question of how much we are obliged to make our successors better off, we miss the whole question of whether there may not be an obligation to avoid harm to people that is stronger than any obligation to make them better off. This is after all a common view about relations among contemporaries.

The second, and ultimately perhaps more serious, limitation is that investment has a characteristic that enables discussion of it to dodge the most awkward difficulties. The only way in which we can leave people in *n* years (where *n* is a large number) more productive capital than they would otherwise have had is to create the additional capital now and hope that the intervening generations will pass it on; or, more precisely, to create it now and hope our immediate descendants and their successors will each pass on a larger total to *their* successors than they would have done had we left them less ourselves. If they do, then thanks to our efforts members of remote future generations will indeed be better off than they would otherwise have been. But there is no way in which we can be confident that our efforts will have any net effect, because everything depends on the behaviour of the intervening generations, whom we have no way of binding.

Although it does not strictly follow from all this, it is easy to reach the conclusion if we concentrate on the 'just savings rate' that the problem of relations between generations can be reduced to the question of the relations between one generation and its immediate successors. There is no way of making remoter generations better off by making savings now that does not involve making nearer generations better off; conversely, if we make our immediate successors better off by making savings now we at any rate make it possible for them to make *their* successors better off than they would otherwise have been.

Obviously, it might still be held that if we take account of remoter generations this should lay on us a greater obligation to build up capital now than would arise if we knew that our immediate successors would be the last generation ever. But since we have no way of ensuring that our immediate successors will not go on a binge and run down the capital we leave them this must surely weaken the case for our having to make extra efforts to save merely so as to make it *possible* for our immediate successors to pass on more than they would otherwise have done.

When, by contrast, we look at the bads rather than the goods that we have the opportunity of passing on to our successors, we can see that the same convenient assumption is not generally applicable. True, resource depletion has something of the same characteristic. The only way in which we can leave more to our remote successors is to leave more to our immediate successors; and if we make extra efforts to conserve resources so as to give our immediate successors more scope to pass on resources in their turn, we take the risk that they will simply blue the lot anyway. (See further on this chapter 19 below.)

But this is not necessarily the case with other bads that we might pass on. There could in principle be some ecological sleeper-effect that we set off now with no ill effects for some hundreds of years and then catastrophic effects. And there are in any case real examples (such as the use of fluorocarbon sprays) of things that we do now that may well have continuous and irreversible ill effects during the rest of the period during which there is life on the planet and that can either not be counteracted at all or only counteracted at great cost or inconvenience.

Our successors may indeed make things even worse for remotely future generations, adding further ecological damage to that done by us. And if we refrain from causing some kind of ecological damage, there can be no guarantee that our successors will not cause it themselves. But this does not suffice to destroy the distinction between investment, which has the property that our successors can choose whether or not to pass on the benefits we leave them, and ecological damage, which has its own adverse effects on remote future generations whether or not our successors add to it. I suspect that it is because of the reduction of the problem that follows from taking investment as the paradigm of relations between generations that Rawls is satisfied with a solution that would otherwise be manifestly inadequate.

He postulates throughout *A Theory of Justice* (without ever adequately explaining why) that the people in the 'original position' (whose choices from behind the 'veil of ignorance' are to constitute principles of justice) know that they are all contemporaries, although they do not know to which generation they belong. The obvious problem that this raises is a sort of n-generation prisoner's dilemma. Generation k, who happen to be behind the veil of ignorance, may be willing to save on condition that their predecessors have saved. But there is no way in which they can take a conditional decision of this kind because there is no way of reaching a binding agreement (or indeed any agreement) with their predecessors. All *they* can do is to

decide themselves whether to save or not. As Rawls says, setting out
the problem: 'Either previous generations have saved or they have
not; there is nothing the parties [in the original position] can do to
affect it.'[12] How can we escape this difficulty?

It might appear that the obvious way out of the difficulty is to drop
the postulate that the people in the 'original position' are contemporaries, and this is I believe the path that Rawls should have taken
to be true to his own theory. But he does not take it. Instead, the tack
that he takes is, he says, to 'make a motivational assumption'. The
'goodwill' of the parties in the original position 'stretches over at least
two generations'. We may, though we need not, 'think of the parties
as heads of families, and therefore as having a desire to further the
welfare of their nearest descendants'. He concludes as follows:

What is essential is that each person in the original position should care about
the well-being of some of those in the next generation, it being presumed that
their concern is for different individuals in each case. Moreover for anyone in
the next generation, there is someone who cares for him in the present
generation. Thus the interests of all are looked after and, given the 'veil of
ignorance', the whole strand is tied together.[13]

One slightly technical objection that must be made to this is that the
conditions stated by Rawls as necessary for the interests of all to be
looked after are unnecessarily strong. Given the veil of ignorance, it is
not necessary for each party to be certain that there is someone in the
next generation he cares about. He will have a motive to support
principles giving weight to the welfare of the next generation provided he knows that he will probably care about somebody in the next
generation. Similarly, there is no need for everybody in the next
generation to have someone who cares for him in this one so long as
the uncared-for cannot be identified as a category and thus made the
object of discriminatory principle-choosing from behind the veil of
ignorance. And as far as I can see they are pretty safe from that risk.

This, however, is just a skirmish. There are two powerful objections to the use Rawls makes of his 'motivational assumption'. The
first, which I have already foreshadowed, is that even if it does
everything Rawls wants it to do, that is still not enough. The really
nasty problems (to some extent actual but even more potential)
involve obligations to remote descendants rather than immediate
descendants and on these Rawls has nothing to say. It has been
suggested that we might boost the extension of concern into the future

---

[12] Ibid. 292.   [13] Ibid., all quotes in this paragraph from pp. 128–9.

derivable from sentiment (which is what Rawls's derivation amounts to) by pointing to the fact that if we care about our grandchildren and they care about their grandchildren we should care about our grandchildren's grandchildren, and so on *ad infinitum*. But those who base themselves on sentiment must follow where it leads, and if primary concern is as short-winded as Rawls suggests, it is scarcely plausible that secondary concern will alter the picture much. Certainly, by a few centuries' time it would be asymptotically approaching zero.

The second objection, which seems to me decisive, is that the derivation of obligations to future generations from the 'motivational assumption' is a pretty thin performance. The only justification offered for the 'motivational assumption' is that it enables Rawls to derive obligations to future generations. But surely this is a little too easy, like a conjurer putting a rabbit in a hat, taking it out again and expecting a round of applause. What it comes to is that we impute to the people in the original position a desire for the welfare of their descendants; on the basis of this we 'deduce' that they will choose principles requiring some action in pursuit of that welfare; and on the basis of the general theory that what would be chosen in the original position constitutes principles of justice we say that the principle governing savings that they would choose is the 'just savings principle'. But if it is acceptable to introduce desires for the welfare of immediate descendants into the original position simply in order to get them out again as obligations, what grounds can there be for refusing to put into the original position a desire for the welfare of at least some contemporaries?

For the whole idea—and the intellectual fascination—of 'justice as fairness' is that it takes self-interested agents, and, by the alchemy of the 'original position', forces them to choose principles of universal scope. In relation to subsequent generations, the postulate of self-interest is relaxed to allow concern for successors, but this naturally limited sympathy is not forced by the logic of the 'original position' to be extended any further than it extends naturally. Our limited sympathies towards our successors are fed into the sausage-machine of 'justice as fairness' and returned to us duly certified as obligations. We come seeking moral guidance and simply get our existing prejudices underwritten—hardly what one would expect from a rationalist philosopher.

The alternative route out of Rawls's difficulties is to pursue the logic of his own analysis more rigorously. This entails scrapping the part of the construction specifying that all the people in the 'original position' are contemporaries and know that they are. We should now have to imagine that there is a meeting to decide on intergenerational relationships at which all generations are represented. Clearly, the 'veil of ignorance' would be required to conceal from them which generation each of them belonged to. Otherwise, an earlier generation would always have the whip-hand over a later one in the negotiations.

There are, obviously, formidable difficulties involved in the very notion of a meeting of all generations. But those difficulties are equally inherent in the bare notion of an individual choosing criteria for relations between generations either without knowing to which he belongs (Rawlsian individual choice) or on the basis that whatever criteria he chooses will apply to all generations (Kantian individual choice). It might therefore be offered as a point in favour of the 'general meeting' construction that it brings out the difficulties graphically.

If the whole notion of collecting representatives from all generations is difficult in itself, there is a special problem introduced by the fact that actions taken at one time may affect the number of subsequent generations by making the tenure of human life on the planet longer or shorter than it would otherwise have been. (In the extreme case, the actions of one generation may be such as to make it the last.) If every generation that *might* exist is represented at the meeting, everybody knows that the criteria chosen may turn out to make his or her generation non-existent.

This is an awkward problem and it is understandable that David Richards, who differs from Rawls in saying that 'the class of members of the original position includes, in a hypothetical sense, *all* persons, who have lived, live now, or will live'[14], suggests that the rational contractors would adopt a principle limiting population so as to make those who do live as well off as possible (I omit the details). He adds that 'the egoistic desire to exist of the contractors does not influence their consideration of this problem, for *ex hypothesi* the contractors know they exist in some point of time, and are thus only concerned to ensure that their existence be as satisfying as possible'.[15]

There are two objections to this way of disposing of the problem. First, although we may in the end want to say that people who do not get born do not count, this should surely be the conclusion rather than the premiss built in by virtue of the construction. Second, we must ask if there is not something incoherent in putting together (*a*) the idea that

[14] David A. J. Richards, *A Theory of Reasons for Action* (Oxford: Clarendon Press, 1971), 81 and 134 (itals. in original).   [15] Ibid. 134.

people in the original position are choosing among policies that will produce different total numbers of people and (*b*) the idea that they know at the outset that they are all the people who ever have existed or ever will exist. It is surely a curious sort of choice if the results of it are already instantiated in the composition of the group of people doing the choosing!

We cannot therefore avoid having to ask whether the interests of potential people in being born should be taken into account or whether each possible decision-rule should be evaluated simply by estimating how those who would actually be born under it would fare, and ignoring those who might have been born under some other decision-rule.

I confess that this is an area in which the light is, for me, fitful. One point, however, seems to me clear, though it is admittedly only a negative one. This is that we should not call one situation better than another simply because it contains some extra people whose lives are worth living. The attraction of such a view derives from two things, I suspect. One is an illegitimate extension of the Pareto principle. This says that one situation is better than another if everything else is the same but at least one person prefers the first to the second. The principle is hard to deny in general (see chapter 13 above) but its plausibility extends only to cases where there are the same people in the two situations.[16] To say that a hypothetical person is made better off by being actualized is an abuse of language.

The second cause of misplaced sentiment about the unborn is a tendency to think of them inhabiting 'never never land' while waiting anxiously for the chance to be born. The unborn have no regrets about not being born because they do not exist. It is essential, as Doctor Johnson said, to 'clear the mind of cant', and in particular of Victorian whimsy. In this context I may remark that it is a serious drawback to the idea of a convention of all possible generations (or all possible people) that it makes it almost impossible to escape from such a way of thinking. Not to be born after you have already attended a meeting of representatives takes on too much of the aspect of dying extremely prematurely. Admittedly, David Hume remarked on his death-bed that there is no more to being dead than to not having been born, but there is the crucial difference between them that one can have a conscious prospect of being dead but not one of not being born.

---

[16] As Ian Little pointed out in *A Critique of Welfare Economics* (Oxford: Clarendon Press, 1950, 2nd edn., 1957), if someone dies we cannot compare his welfare before and after (p. 49), and the same is true if someone is not born in one situation and is born in another.

However, if we can somehow exclude this artefact of the construction, I do not see how coming into existence can itself be regarded as a good from the point of view of the potential person, since potential people do not have points of view. And yet I must admit to feeling uneasy with the alternative conclusion that we should take into account only the conscious states of those who get born.

I find no difficulty in accepting this with regard to the numbers of people alive at any one time. In asking whether the world will be better off in the year 2000 with seven billion inhabitants than it is with four billion now, I do not feel any temptation to say that the extra numbers are themselves, other things being equal, an improvement —even if most of the enlarged population do not regret having been born. But in asking whether it would matter for human beings (or life on earth in general) to come to an end in five hundred years' time rather than 500,000, I do not find irrelevant the fact that in the first case many generations that might have come into existence will not have the opportunity of doing so.

It may, of course, be argued that good reasons can be given in terms of the interests of actual human beings for not choosing to do something that brings about a substantial risk of ending human life in five hundred years' time. The people in the original position would not care to risk the distress at the prospect or the suffering entailed in the process. But human life will presumably come to an end eventually anyway and in a congress at which all potential generations are represented, the risk of being the last generation that actually exists is the same whether that occurs early or late, and the risk of being non-existent (we are saying) is not to count. In any case, I feel fairly sure that my conviction that it would be monstrous to take risks with the existence of future generations in order to secure advantages or avoid hardships for those who will live during the shortened time span left does not rest on such calculations.

The Hobbesian, Lockean, and Rousseauan theories give only the most tenuous and contingent security to the interests of future generations. It now appears that no theory confining its attention to the states of actual human beings will do. If we say that those who do not get born do not count in the choice of an 'ideal contract', the relatively early end of the human race may be preferred to a longer history at a somewhat lower level. The solution chosen would not be exactly equivalent to average utilitarianism (maximizing the average happiness of those who actually live) if we accept Rawls's arguments that people choosing in the 'original position' would be more concerned to avoid very bad outcomes than to obtain very good ones. But we can certainly say that 'average utilitarianism' where only those who get born count in the denominator runs into the same problem as an 'ideal contract' where only those who get born have a vote. The highest average for those who live may entail not merely a relatively small population at any given time (which seems to me a quite unexceptionable conclusion) but a relatively short time span for the human race, as those who are alive splurge all the earth's resources with an attitude of *après nous le déluge*.

The 'total utility' view (that the sum total of happiness should be maximized) in effect enfranchises potential people.[17] However, the unpalatibility of this form of utilitarianism, which I have already remarked upon, seems to me greatly increased when we realize that it would call upon us to make sacrifices merely so that there could be more people, so long as each extra person adds any positive amount to the notional sum total of happiness. It may also be noted that, although the total utility doctrine is biased towards actualizing a lot of potential people, it is not biased towards spreading them over a long time span. It is consistent with total utilitarianism that we should have a massive population for another two centuries and then nothing. Perhaps it is unlikely that this is the way to maximize total happiness, but the point is that at any rate as far as I am concerned the continuation of human life into the future is something to be sought (or at least not sabotaged) even if it does not make for the maximum total happiness.

Certainly, if I try to analyse the source of my own strong conviction that we would be wrong to take risks with the continuation of human life, I find that it does not lie in any sense of injury to the interests of people who will not get born but rather in a sense of its cosmic impertinence—that we should be grossly abusing our position by taking it upon ourselves to put a term on human life and its possibilities. I must confess to feeling great intellectual discomfort in moving outside a framework in which ethical principles are related to human interests, but if I am right then these are the terms in which we have to start thinking. In contrast to Passmore, I conclude that those who say we need a 'new ethic' are in fact right. It need not entail the kind of

---

[17] It does not, however, follow that an 'ideal contract' chosen by all potential people—if we can make sense of that notion—would be for maximizing total happiness. If they were, in Rawlsian fashion, much more concerned to avoid very bad outcomes than to obtain very good ones, it would seem prudent to vote for not bringing the human race into existence. All this would require would be that there should be *some* people of whom Sophocles' 'highest of all is not to be born' would apply.

half-baked ideas that Passmore criticizes, but should surely as a minimum include the notion that those alive at any time are custodians rather than owners of the planet, and ought to pass it on in at least no worse shape than they found it in.

THE ETHICS OF RESOURCE DEPLETION

Why does the exploitation of non-renewable natural resources raise a special problem in intergenerational equity? The reason is, simply, that any resources we use will not be available in the future. It is true that most minerals can be recycled, and scrap metal is, indeed, an important constituent in goods manufactured today. But we are still digging out ore at a great rate. And it should be borne in mind that non-renewable energy resources—fossil fuels—cannot be recycled. Once they have been burned, they have gone forever, as far as any use to human beings is concerned.

It is true that there are estimated to be enormous quantities of minerals in the top mile of the earth's crust. However, much of the supply is inconveniently located in relation to demand and presents great difficulties in extracting it. (A great deal of it is under the deep seabed and Antarctica.) Future generations therefore face progressively greater costs in getting access to non-renewable resources.

It might appear at first blush that the only equitable solution is to ensure that future generations face the same stock of resources as we do. This, however, would obviously imply that no non-renewable resources should ever be used. The logic would be on a par with that of the (possibly apocryphal) town council which passed an ordinance to the effect that there should always be at least one taxi waiting at the station to ensure that taxis would be available for arriving passengers. We must come up with a criterion that allows for some exploitation of non-renewable resources even when that is going to mean that, other things being equal, future generations will inherit a diminished stock.

The solution that I propose is intended as a practical application of the intuition that underlay the solution that I have just rejected. That intuition was that we should not make the position of future generations worse than ours by our depletion of non-renewable resources. We can, I suggest, capture the spirit of this by stipulating that future generations are owed compensation in other ways for our reducing their access to easily extracted and conveniently located natural resources. In practice, this entails that the combination of improved technology and increased capital investment should be such as to offset the effects of depletion.

What, precisely, constitutes 'offsetting'? There are two possible interpretations. The one that would naturally occur to economists —and not only to economists—would be to define offsetting in terms of utility: we should do whatever is necessary to provide future generations with the same level of utility as they would have had if we had not depleted the natural resources. There are all kinds of difficulties in drawing practical implications from this idea, but the objection that I shall put is pitched at a level of principle and would still be relevant even if all the practical problems could be swept away.

The alternative that I wish to defend is that what constitutes offsetting the depletion of natural resources is the replacement of the productive opportunities we have destroyed by the creation of alternative ones. In other words, when we say that resource depletion makes future generations worse off than we are, this should be taken to mean that they will be worse off in terms of productive potential; and it is that loss of productive potential for which justice requires us to compensate. (The notion of productive potential will be explained below.) Questions immediately arise. What is an acceptable alternative, and what happens if future people have different tastes from ours (as seems a priori very likely)? I shall discuss these and other problems in due course.

First, I want to offer a general argument for defining the criterion in terms of opportunities rather than utilities. My answer is that this is true of justice in all contexts, so that intergenerational justice is simply an application of the general idea. We therefore need a discussion of the broad thesis rather than one confined to future generations, for the conclusion will surely be stronger for the rather strange case of future generations if it can be shown to be plausible in more familiar cases. To this end, let me return to the alternative interpretation of the criterion of compensation for resource depletion, that it should be defined in terms of utility. This idea stems from a general conception of what should be the subject-matter of moral assessment: that, although we perforce distribute rights, opportunities, or material goods rather than utility, the ultimate standard of judgement should be the utility to people that arises from those resources.

Utilitarianism, understood as the theory that the aggregate amount of utility should be maximized, is the best-known example of a theory that takes utility as the only thing that matters, in the last analysis.

Thus, as Sidgwick put it, utilitarianism is concerned with 'the distribution of *Happiness*, not the means of happiness'.[1] Ted Honderich advanced a 'Principle of Equality' defined not in terms of equal treatment but in terms of 'the qualities of the experience of individuals'. The principle was then 'that things should be so arranged that we approach as close as we can, which may not be all that close, to equality in satisfaction and distress'.[2] Again, Amartya Sen began an article by saying: 'Usual measures of economic inequality concentrate on income, but frequently one's interest may lie in the inequality of welfare rather than of income as such.' And he went on to say that this raises problems not only of 'interpersonal comparisons of welfare, but also those arising from differences in non-income circumstances, e.g. age, the state of one's health, the pattern of love, friendship, concern and hatred surrounding a person'.[3]

It is generally agreed that there are, in practice, severe limits to the extent to which distribution can be individuated so as to take account of the way in which different people either get different amounts of happiness from some baseline amount of the means of happiness, or gain unequal amounts of happiness from the same increments in the means of happiness. Thus, the relevant information is difficult to come by—some would say that the problem is not even well defined. Collecting the information would in any case intrude on personal privacy. The policy would place a premium on dissimulation, as people would try to give the appearance of having a utility function of a kind that would provide them with a large allocation of income or other means of happiness. And the implementation of a programme of adapting distribution to individual psychological characteristics would obviously place vast powers in the hands of those doing the allocating—powers to make decisions on a largely discretionary basis, because of the lack of precisely defined objective criteria for establishing the susceptibility of different people to external advantages or disadvantages.

For all these reasons it might be admitted that in practice idiosyncratic differences in the way people convert the means of happiness into happiness itself should be disregarded for purposes of public policy. And it might plausibly be added that the case for disregarding idiosyncrasies becomes overwhelming when we know nothing

---

[1] Henry Sidgwick, *The Methods of Ethics* (London: Macmillan and Co., 7th edn., 1907), 47 n. 1.
[2] Ted Honderich, *Three Essays on Political Violence* (Oxford: Basil Blackwell, 1976), 41.
[3] Amartya Sen, 'Welfare Inequalities and Rawlsian Axiomatics', *Theory and Decision*, 7 (1976), 243–62, at 243.

definite about the people concerned—as must be the case with people as yet unborn. We *could* therefore, by invoking ignorance, get from the premiss that the ultimate object of distribution is utility to the conclusion that justice between generations should be defined in terms of resources: in the absence of the appropriate information we must fall back on distributing resources without looking beyond resources to utilities. Instead, however, I want to suggest that the whole idea of treating utility as the object of distribution is wrong.

To strip away the practical complications, imagine that by some incredible advance in psychometric technology it became possible to fit people with tiny, tamper-proof 'black boxes' implanted under the skin, and that these 'black boxes' measured (and somehow could be shown to measure to the satisfaction of anyone with enough training in neurophysiology and electronics) the amount of utility received by the recipient within, say, a period of a year. I do not think that the availability of this kind of publicly verifiable information would eliminate the case against allocating the means of happiness so as to achieve a certain distribution of happiness. For my view is that such information is in principle irrelevant when it comes to determining a just distribution.

Suppose we believe that two people should be paid the same amount: they do the same work equally well, have equal seniority in the same firm, and so on. What this means is that they have an equal claim on the resources of society to do what they like with that chunk of resources. (Taking account of market distortions, we can say that prices do roughly correspond to the real claim on resources at the margin represented by alternative purchases.) Justice consists in their getting an equal crack at society's resources, without any mention of comparative utility. If we discover that one of them gets more fun out of spending his income than does the other, this is no reason for transferring income from the one who derives more utility to the one who derives less. Similarly, if the price of something one of them enjoys goes up (e.g. because of an increased demand for it), this is no reason for increasing his income in compensation. For he had no special claim on the amount of utility he was getting before. All he had a claim on was a fair share of resources.

The argument as applied to future generations is, then, that we should not hold ourselves responsible for the satisfaction they derive from their opportunities. What is important from the point of view of justice is the range of choice open to them, rather than what they get out of it. But choice of what? The range of choice I have so far discussed has been the range of consumption choices. Broadly speaking, I have been making the case for defining justice in terms of income rather than utility.

But this is not the whole story. For we obviously cannot literally provide people not yet born with income, any more than we can provide them with utility. The question is, in either case, whether we need to predict how much they will actually get if we do one thing rather than another. Even if this were feasible (which it is not), it would still be beside the point.

The important thing is that we should compensate for the reduction in opportunities to produce that are brought about by our depleting the supply of natural resources, and that compensation should be defined in terms of productive potential. If we could somehow predict that there would be a general decline in working hours or in the amount of effort people put into work, this would be no reason for saying that we must hand over additional productive resources to future generations. This notion of productive potential will be analysed below. For the present, all we need to grasp is that productive potential is equal in two situations if the same effort would produce the same output.

Two questions follow from this. First, why should future generations be left not worse off (in opportunity terms) than they would have been in the absence of our having depleted the resources? And second, if we say that our depletion of resources should not leave future generations with a smaller range of opportunities than they would otherwise have had, this requires us to have some standard on the basis of which we can establish what opportunities they would otherwise have had. What is the appropriate standard?

Let me begin with the first point. The basic argument for an equal claim on natural resources is that none of the usual justifications for an unequal claim—special relationships arising in virtue of past services, promises, etc.—applies here. From an atemporal perspective, no one generation has a better or worse claim than any other to enjoy the earth's resources. In the absence of any powerful argument to the contrary, there would seem to be a strong presumption in favour of arranging things so that, as far as possible, each generation faces the same range of opportunities with respect to natural resources. I must confess that I can see no further positive argument to be made at this point. All I can do is counter what may be arguments on the other side. Is there any way in which the present generation can claim that it is entitled to a larger share of the goods supplied by nature than its successors? If not, then equal shares is the only solution compatible with justice.

The only theory of distributive justice that might appear to have implications inconsistent with the equality of generations is the Lockean one of a 'natural right' to appropriate by 'mixing one's labour' with natural resources. This might be taken to imply that there is no criterion by which the collective exploitation of natural resources by a generation can be judged, as long as the individualistic requirements of the Lockean theory are met. However, even taking that theory seriously for a moment, we should bear in mind that Locke said that legitimate appropriation was limited by the proviso that 'enough and as good' should be left for others. If we interpret 'others' to include later generations as well as contemporaries, we get the notion of equality between generations. And Locke's attempt to fudge the application of the proviso once people have 'consented to the use of money', which is a fraud anyway, cannot even get a foothold in the intergenerational case, since future generations are obviously in no position to consent to our exploitation of natural resources in a way that fails to leave 'as good' for them.

Clearly, if each generation has an equal right to enjoy the productive opportunities provided by natural resources, it does not necessarily follow that compensation for violating that right is acceptable. We will all agree that doing harm is in general not cancelled out by doing good, and conversely that doing some good does not license one to do harm provided it does not exceed the amount of good. For example, if you paid for the realignment of a dangerous highway intersection and saved an average of two lives a year, that would not mean that you could shoot one motorist per year and simply reckon on coming out ahead.

That example, however, involves gratuitous infliction of harm. In the case of resources and future generations, the crucial feature is that we cannot possibly avoid harming them by using up some non-renewable resources, given the existing population level and the technology that has developed to sustain that level. So the choice is not between reducing the resource base for future generations and keeping it intact, but between depletion with compensation and depletion without compensation. The analogy is therefore with the traveller caught in a blizzard who, in order to survive, breaks into somebody's empty weekend cottage, builds a fire, and helps himself to food. Even the most obtuse defender of property rights would scarcely deny that this is a legitimate use of another's property without his permission. It will be generally agreed, also, that while the unauthorized taking of another's property was entirely justifiable in the circumstances, the traveller is not absolved from making restitution for whatever he damaged or consumed.

The second problem arises in this way. Suppose we say that justice requires us to compensate future generations for depleted resources, so that they have as much productive potential as they would have inherited had the resources not been depleted. To give this criterion any operational significance, we must obviously give some definite content to the notion of the amount of productive potential that future generations would have enjoyed in the absence of resource depletion. Otherwise we have no means of deciding what is required by justice in the way of compensation.

We cannot say that 'the productive potential that future generations would otherwise have enjoyed' is to be settled by *predicting*. Perhaps, in the absence of resource depletion, we would in fact be inclined to leave future generations with far less productive potential than, as a matter of justice, we ought to leave them with. If we were to leave them an inadequate amount plus an amount calculated to compensate for resource depletion, we would then be behaving unjustly. Conversely, in the absence of resource depletion, maybe we would leave future generations with far more productive potential than is required by justice—whatever that is. In that case, even when resource depletion is taken into account, the same amount would still more than satisfy the requirements of justice.

It is apparent, therefore, that 'the productive potential that future generations would otherwise have enjoyed' must be defined in terms of justice. We must understand it to mean the following: what future generations would justly have enjoyed in the absence of resource depletion. But how much is that? The answer is critical in determining the whole outcome of our enquiry. To make the most extreme case, suppose we said that the only things we owe to future generations are whatever natural resources we inherited plus due compensation (measured in terms of productive capacity) for what we depleted. If we left anything more than a few picks and shovels they would be ahead, since they would then be in a better position to exploit natural resources than if they had to use their bare hands. Anything more than that would go beyond the demands of justice. But human generations do not succeed one another with one generation marching off the stage as another marches on, so self-interest on the part of the living will in any case ensure that far more than that is handed on. However selfishly those alive at any given time behave, they can scarcely avoid passing on to their successors a pretty large capital stock that embodies thousands of years of technological development. Hence, the principle of compensation for the depletion of natural resources could be accepted without the slightest implication that more should be done to protect the interests of future generations than would inevitably be done as a by-product of the pursuit of self-interest by the current generation.

I imagine that few would really want to say that we would be beyond criticism on grounds of justice if we ran down capital and used up natural resources in whatever way best suited us, as long as we left our successors somewhat better equipped than people were in the Stone Age. But it is hard to come up with a clear-cut principle to say exactly how far the bounds of justice extend. I believe, however, that there are some leading ideas which can guide us.

Most of our technology and the capital stock embodying it are not by any stretch of the imagination the sole creation of the present generation; we cannot therefore claim exclusive credit for it. The whole process of capital formation presupposes an inheritance of capital and technology. To a considerable extent, then, we can say that, from the standpoint of the current generation, natural resources are not really as sharply distinguished from capital and technology as might at first appear. Both are originally inherited, and thus fall outside any special claims based on the present generation's having done something to deserve them. We can therefore make no special claim on *our* side. But can others (those who did create them) claim that they can endow us with exclusive control over what we inherit? This raises complicated issues.

It seems to me that inherited capital can be looked at from two standpoints, that of the creators and that of the receivers, and that the trick is to give weight to both perspectives. From the side of the recipients, inherited capital is exactly like inherited natural resources —the present generation can claim credit for neither. From the side of the earlier generations, on the other hand, accumulated capital and natural resources that are handed on have different statuses, in that capital is created and natural resources are not. Yet no generation creates from scratch all the capital it hands on. It seems reasonable to suggest that it should get credit at the most only for the capital it adds.

This gives us a rough basis for proceeding. Let us say that, as a reasonable reconciliation of the two perspectives, each generation's sacrifices (if any) to increase the capital stock it passes on give it a claim to some consideration by the following generation of its objectives in making these sacrifices. Beyond one generation, its specific wishes for the disposition of the increment become progressively less significant as constituting claims on the decisions of the living.

We can now venture a statement of what is required by justice towards future generations. As far as natural resources are concerned, depletion should be compensated for in the sense that later generations should be left no worse off (in terms of productive capacity) than they would have been without the depletion. And how well off they would have been is to be determined by applying the principles that have been worked out above. As a starting-point, we may say that the capital stock inherited should be passed on without diminution, but this can be modified somewhat to accommodate the claims of past generations. If we suppose, for example, that the previous generation made sacrifices to permit the present generation a higher standard of living without any expectation that this generation would pass it on, it would seem legitimate for the present generation to pass on slightly less. On the other hand, if one believes that successive past generations made sacrifices in the (no doubt vague) expectation that each generation would pass on more than it inherited, this would constitute a prima facie case for saying that the present generation has a certain obligation to continue with this process. The whole notion of obligations to continue the undertakings of past generations, however, raises difficulties that need further work. (See above, chapter 6.) I do not think we should go far wrong here if we set it aside and simply say that compensation should be reckoned as what is required to maintain productive potential.

Three practical problems arise in any attempt to apply the conclusions of this abstract discussion. The first is whether the compensation criterion can be given a workable significance. The second is where issues of intragenerational distribution fit in. And the third is how to deal with the difficulty that alternative policies have results in the future that are associated with varying degrees of uncertainty.

On the feasibility of the compensation criterion, the apparent problem is this: oil is oil is oil. How do we decide what is adequate compensation for running down the world's reserves of oil? In the most favourable case, it may be possible to compensate in a quite direct way. If we run down the oil by 10 per cent but develop technology that makes it possible to extract 10 per cent more oil from any given deposit, we have in effect left future generations with as much (exploitable) oil as we found. Or if we develop internal combustion engines that produce more power per gallon of petrol used, we have made the remaining stock of oil go further, measured in output terms—which is what counts—than it would otherwise have done. And so on.

I do not want to suggest that this will solve all the problems of implementation; where it is not applicable, we have to fall back on the more general idea of maintaining productive capacity. Within limits, which over a long time period may be very wide, it is always possible to substitute capital for raw materials by recycling, cutting down waste, and making things get results by being complicated and well engineered rather than big and heavy. Energy may appear unamenable to this treatment. But it can still be economized by a greater expenditure of capital, and the performance of Western economies in the period since 1973 has illustrated the way in which, with the right incentives, capital expenditure will be substituted for energy.

The second practical problem is this: what happens when the principles for justice between generations are combined with moral principles governing distribution among people who are contemporaries, whether they live now or in the future? One reason for confronting the question of intragenerational distribution is that there are some who profess impatience with a concern for the interests of unborn generations when there are so many existing people now starving or suffering from preventable malnutrition and disease. I must admit to some sympathy with this impatience. I have a possibly prejudiced idea that one could run in Marin County[4] more successfully on a platform of doing good things for future generations than of transferring money to poor people now, either domestically or internationally. Being in favour of future generations is somehow more antiseptically apolitical than being in favour of one's contemporaries, and also, in an odd way, gives an impression of being more high-minded.

If it were really necessary to make a choice between intragenerational and intergenerational justice, it would be a tough one. But in my view there is no such dilemma, because I do not believe that there will turn out to be any inconsistency between the requirements of each. In the absence of a full theory of both, I cannot show this. But I

---

[4] See Cyra McFadden, *The Serial: A Year in the Life of Marin County* (New York: Alfred A. Knopf, 1977). Of a typical couple in this affluent area north of San Francisco it is remarked that they 'belonged to the ACLU and the Sierra Club and went to the Mozart Festival at Stolte Grove every year with the picnic of the month from *Sunset* in a Cost Plus hamper. . . .' (p. 8).

predict that whatever redistribution among contemporaries is required by justice will also be able to observe the constraints that the interests of future generations be protected.

Of course, if citizens and governments in the rich countries are willing to make only token sacrifices to meet the demands of either intragenerational or intergenerational justice, a choice will have to be made. But we ought then to be clear that the necessity for choice arises not from any real incompatibility, but simply from the not unusual phenomenon that people are not prepared to behave justly when it is contrary to their immediate interests, unless they are somehow coerced into doing so. And while poor countries have a certain amount of ability to cause trouble to rich ones, future generations obviously have no way of enforcing a fair deal on the present generation. (See above, chapter 18.)

It will be apparent that the principles already enunciated for justice among generations may be applied equally well to relations among contemporaries. (See above, chapter 16.) Thus, the argument that there is no act by which the value of natural resources may be regarded as earned or deserved by whoever happens to find them suggests an equal claim of all contemporaries on that value. Similarly, the idea that inherited capital and technology gradually merge into the 'common heritage of mankind' clearly implies a just claim by poor countries on rich ones.

Intragenerational justice would best be met by a combination of a self-balancing, shadow (positive and negative) income tax on countries and a severance tax on the exploitation of natural resources, the proceeds being transferred to resource-poor countries such as India, Bangladesh, or some Central African countries. This would, in an admittedly rough and ready way (but no other is to be expected), make tax liability depend on both the special advantages arising from possession of rich natural resources and the more general advantages that make for high per capita income. Intergenerational justice requires, as we have seen, maintenance of capital (with certain modest exceptions) plus the creation of additional technology and capital to compensate for resource depletion. Yet this has an intragenerational aspect too. To say that 'the present generation' should pass on certain productive capabilities to 'future generations' leaves open the question of how the burdens and the benefits should be distributed among contemporaries, now and in the future. What can be said about this?

It is legitimate for those who form the current generation in a country to make special efforts to provide extra benefits for their own descendants if they choose to do so, since this is more than is called for by justice anyway. This is in effect an intergenerational gift of resources whose disposition the people in that country have a just claim to control. But the mere passing along of the amount of capital inherited draws no credit. And, as I have suggested, the wishes of those who originally made the sacrifices to accumulate it should be regarded as fading out over the course of a few generations. This implies that some of the capital stock should be diffused as claims to special benefits run out, in the same way as patents and copyrights expire with time.

The problem of resource depletion by those living in some country can be divided into two parts: who should provide the compensation, and who should receive it? I suggest that those countries which consume the largest quantities of non-renewable natural resources should be responsible for the bulk of the effort to provide the technology and capital formation to substitute for them.

On the other hand, I wish to argue that it would be extremely inequitable if the compensatory technology and capital were passed on for the exclusive benefit of the successors of those in the countries who depleted the natural resources. Since running down any natural resources deprives all future inhabitants of the world of the production from any given combination of capital and labour, the compensation is owed not to descendants of the current heavy users only, but to all in the future who are disadvantaged by that use—in fact, everybody.

The redistributive case is even stronger than this. For industrial countries have achieved their present prosperity by first using their own natural resources and then, when these began to get scarce, by using those of the rest of the world at relatively low cost to themselves—in the case of oil, for example, for a few cents per gallon through the 1950s and 1960s. In effect, this bonanza has been turned into accumulated capital that is regarded by these countries as their private property to do with as they choose. But it is obviously harder for countries that missed out on this era of cheap resources to undertake a similar course of economic development in the future. (The effect of oil price increases on Indian economic planning is a dramatic illustration, and many others could be offered.) The poor countries, therefore, have been especially disadvantaged because, unlike the rich countries, they have nothing to show for the past depletion of world resources except perhaps in free access to some unpatented technology that was part and parcel of Western development.

The upshot of this discussion is that, generally speaking, the countries with the highest per capita production and the highest use of non-renewable natural resources (the two are highly correlated) should be making transfers to the poor countries to meet the requirements of intergenerational justice. This clearly overlaps with the requirements of purely intragenerational justice that were outlined earlier. An across-the-board international income tax (levied on countries, to be raised through their own domestic tax systems), whether or not supplemented by a severance tax on the extraction of mineral resources, would meet all the requirements, as long as part of the proceeds of the tax were devoted to the building up of technology and capital in the recipient countries, and as long as those in the rich countries did not treat payment of the tax as an alternative to accumulating capital domestically to enable their own descendants to offset the effects of resource depletion.

The final problem is that of uncertainty. It cannot be avoided because, in deciding what technologies we ought to develop to compensate future generations for the depletion of resources, we must somehow deal with the fact that the risks and benefits are, to some degree, speculative. Suppose most competent authorities agree that there is a possibility (i.e. it cannot be excluded on the basis of existing scientific knowledge) that some action taken now (e.g. burying nuclear wastes deep underground, releasing fluorocarbons into the atmosphere, or carrying out experiments on recombinant DNA) will have serious and irreversible (or only doubtfully/expensively/gradually reversible) adverse consequences in the long term; and suppose further that either there is disagreement on the likelihood of these adverse consequences coming to pass or agreement on the impossibility, in the present state of knowledge, of quantifying the risk (or some mixture of the two). The question, then, is how we should react to this state of affairs. Should we say that the profound uncertainty makes it unreasonable (or 'premature', if one is optimistic about the prospects for finding out more in the future) to decide against taking the action? Or should we say that, in the absence of better information, the possibility of disastrous consequences is a decisive reason for not acting? *Ex hypothesi*, methods of decisionmaking that discount alternative outcomes by their probabilities of occurrence are not available here.

The simplest argument for giving the second answer rather than the first is a two-part one: (*a*) in the case of an individual making a choice that affects only himself, we should regard anyone who acted on the basis of the first alternative as crazy; and (*b*) when we change the case to one that involves millions of people and extends over many centuries, the same reasoning applies with increased force.

The best way to establish (*a*) is by means of an example. Imagine that your dentist were to say: 'The only way of saving this tooth is by means of a new procedure. There is every reason to believe that the procedure will succeed in saving the tooth, but it's conceivable that it will kill you. It may be that, however many times it were done, nobody would ever be killed by it. But it can't be ruled out on the basis of anything we currently know about physiology that it's highly lethal. It's not impossible that it has one chance in a hundred of killing you. Since we have no idea of the magnitude of the risks involved, I draw two conclusions: more research is needed, and in the meantime you should undergo the procedure.' I predict that not only would you decline his suggestion, but you would also think he should have his licence withdrawn for professional incompetence.

As far as (*b*) is concerned, I need only say that there is no prima facie reason for supposing that changing the case so that the numbers involved are larger and extend over a longer time is going to make the choice associated with an uncertain potential for catastrophe more palatable rather than less. If anything, the argument is even strengthened. Let me conclude by offering three considerations.

First, we might ask whether genocide is universally abhorred for no other reason than that it entails killing a large number of individual human beings. Or is it worse to wipe out an entire people than to kill an equal number of individuals scattered throughout the world? One answer might be that genocide is worse because it is the expression of an evil theory—that of racial superiority and inferiority. But genocidal attempts antedated the Nazis (e.g. the 'Armenian massacres' and the hunting to extinction of the native populations of Tasmania and California in the nineteenth century), yet those cases were no less terrible.

We can approach what I consider the critical point by discussing what has been called 'cultural genocide'—the practice of systematically exterminating the intelligentsia—the professionals, writers, journalists, students, and anyone with an above-average level of education. Those with greater knowledge of history than I can no doubt cite examples going back thousands of years, but well-attested examples from recent decades are Pakistan (the early stages of the civil war that led to the creation of Bangladesh) and Burundi. These examples of 'cultural genocide' seem to me less terrible than the destruction of the entire Bengali or Hutu populations would have been—numbers obviously do make a difference. At the same time they are, in my view, worse than random killing of the same numbers of the same populations.

My point is that the destruction of cultures is a bad over and above the physical destruction of its bearers. This, then, gives us a reason for holding that destroying a large population is more serious than killing the same number of random individuals. And this in turn is another reason why remote possibilities of catastrophic accidents (e.g. in nuclear reactors) should be treated as especially grave threats, and not simply balanced against the number of deaths from bronchitis or lung cancer that can be associated with the use of fossil fuel as an alternative. One chance in a million per annum of wiping out New York simply is not the same as having ten more people die each year.

Risk may be acceptable if it is accepted voluntarily in the pursuit of something that seems valuable to the person who chooses it. If somebody wishes to risk his or her life gratuitously by rock climbing or white-water canoeing, one might say that there is no case for preventing or discouraging these freely chosen activities. But the risks of, say, nuclear power generation are not at all plausibly construed on that model. The risk cannot be confined to the beneficiaries. We have a public good and a public bad; people who use the electricity get the good, and those who live near the plant get the bad, irrespective of whether they would prefer to do without both. If we were to respond that in the nature of the case consent cannot be obtained from everyone affected before any piece of collective action is undertaken, I would of course agree. But then the question of distributive equity arises. The canoeist gets the risk *and* the benefit. But with larger-scale projects, it is unlikely that the risks and the benefits will be distributed to each person in the same proportions. If nuclear plants are located in the country and mainly supply the cities, the rural people get a disproportionate share of the risks, while the city people benefit.

These problems are exacerbated across generations. First, cultural impoverishment is irreversible and continues to impoverish all successive generations. Second, if we do things now that impose risks on future people, there is clearly no way of getting their consent. And, finally, with some examples such as nuclear power plants, the benefits and risks are asymmetrically distributed across time: the benefits disproportionately occur while the plant is producing electricity, and the risks continue in some form for thousands of years, until the radioactivity of the waste decays to a safe level.

13

THE CONTINUING RELEVANCE OF SOCIALISM

I

A century ago Sir William Harcourt proclaimed 'We're all socialists now.' Today we have a Prime Minister whose declared purpose is to wipe socialism off the political map, and a Leader of the Labour Party who rarely uses the word except among gatherings of the faithful. I am therefore swimming against the current in arguing, as I propose to do here, that socialism is a doctrine that speaks to contemporary conditions in societies such as ours. But I believe that the case can be made. I make my claim only, of course, for socialism as I shall define it. But I wish to maintain that my definition captures the common core of socialism that united such disparate figures as Marx and the Fabians, and thus has good historical support.

Sir William Harcourt was, no doubt, exaggerating. But the element of truth in what he said is that, from the 1880s onwards, a broad agreement developed about the responsibilities of the state. Among the propositions that would have found general support, I shall pick out two: one is that taxes on wealth and income should be seen not only as a way of raising revenue but also as a way of bringing about a fairer distribution of wealth and income; the other is that the state should define a level of material well-being below which none of its citizens should fall, and then provide the resources necessary to ensure that nobody does fall below that level. The significance of Mrs Thatcher's term of office as Prime Minister is that we can no longer take it for granted that the government is committed to propositions such as the two I have just listed. Although she and her ministers may not have explicitly repudiated them, their actions have been such as to lead us to the conclusion that they have in fact abandoned them as guides to policy.

The easing of death duties, the abolition of the long-standing tax relief for earned income, and the reduction of the highest rate of income tax to 40 per cent all suggest a shift away from the notion that taxes should contribute to overall equity. And it is surely relevant in this context that the last of these measures was defended primarily as a 'simplification' of the tax system. On the face of it, there is something bizarre about treating a change that makes a well-off minority far better off as if its distributive implications were merely a by-product of administrative convenience. But it makes sense if we assume that the overall distribution of income is simply not seen as raising any moral issue.

The evidence for the government's repudiation of the second proposition is more direct. Under the reform of the welfare system inaugurated in April 1988, the arrangements under which payments were made to cover special expenses such as clothing or household necessities have been abolished, and replaced by a so-called Social Fund. The particular feature of this that is relevant here is that it has pre-set cash limits, which means that each local office has only a certain amount of money to give out, however many people may qualify for payments. (A further turn of the screw is that if someone is unlucky enough to apply for money when the local office has run out of the month's quota, that person cannot apply again until six months have elapsed, whatever the merits of the claim.[1]) Thus, for the first time in over fifty years—and perhaps for the first time since the Elizabethan Poor Law was enacted in 1601—the government has formally abandoned the undertaking to meet all the claims that are valid according to its own criteria, introducing instead a scheme under which it is predictable that many eligible claimants will be refused benefits simply on the grounds that the funds provided are inadequate.

As a political philosopher, if not as a citizen, I can only welcome the advent of Mrs Thatcher. By opening up to debate issues that had for a long time been regarded as closed she has extended our scope. Although she does not appear to be a very reflective person, I think that she should be given credit for having a coherent social vision, and one that is profoundly antithetical to socialism. In what follows I shall try to identify its roots in a certain kind of individualism, and argue that individualism so understood is a fatally flawed doctrine. I define socialism as the denial of the claims of individualism. If I succeed, therefore, in showing the limitations of individualism, I shall also have made out my case for the continuing relevance of socialism.

---

[1] Christian Wolmer, 'The New Poor Law', *Observer* (10 Apr. 1988), 15.

II

What is socialism? In proposing a definition, I want to steer between two common notions. One is that 'socialism' is simply a word to be applied nowadays to relatively egalitarian liberals. The other is that socialism is a kind of religion, which hopes for a transformation of human nature and rests on a series of predictions about historical events. Such a view is supported, for example, by *Pears' Cyclopaedia* (1967) where, in the 'Ideas and Beliefs' section, 'Socialism' is followed by Southcottism—the belief in the predictions of Joanna Southcott —and Spiritualism. The conception of socialism that I intend to put forward does not depend in any way on beliefs about the course of history and does not require a transformation of human nature. I can best approach it by asking what socialism is contrasted with. The two pairings that immediately come to mind are 'socialism versus capitalism' and 'socialism versus individualism'.

What can we learn from the opposition of socialism to capitalism and individualism? I think that both contrasts fit together with the following definition of socialism: A socialist society is one in which the citizens of that society are able, by acting together, to control the major features of the society and, in particular, to overcome the undesirable consequences of individual actions. Thus conceived, socialism is above all a theory of citizenship: it is concerned with empowering citizens to act collectively in pursuit of the interests and ideals that they share with one another and that can be realized only by collective action. Gaetano Mosca was, on this analysis, quite right to see Rousseau as the progenitor of the socialist idea.

Let me briefly follow through the relations between socialism as I have just defined it and the two contrasting terms, capitalism and individualism. The most prominent contemporary defenders of capitalism, Milton Friedman and F. A. Hayek, constantly claim that its primary virtue is its automatism. Thus, Friedman, in his well-known essay, 'Capitalism and Freedom', argued that in a capitalist society nobody exercises any power—even the managers of massive corporations—because all actors are so tightly constrained by the discipline of the market that on any given occasion only one course is open to them. Those who do anything different disappear from the system as a result of bankruptcy.[2] And, in his book *The Mirage of Social Justice*, Hayek argues that, precisely because the distribution of income

---

[2] Milton Friedman, *Capitalism and Freedom* (Chicago: Chicago University Press, 1963).

does not arise from any central decisionmaking process but from millions of independent decisions, the concept of social justice is inapplicable to market outcomes.[3]

Whether we look for our historical antecedents to Marxism or to Fabianism, I believe we are safe in saying that the core of socialism has always been the rejection of claims such as those of Friedman and Hayek. Where Friedman sees the market as a realm of freedom because nobody has any power, the socialist sees it as a realm of necessity, for precisely the same reason. The transformation from a society ruled by the tyranny of the market to one of freedom requires collective control over the economy. Similarly, the socialist turns Hayek's argument on its head. It is precisely because the market is incompatible with the introduction of considerations of distributive justice that it cannot be accepted as the arbiter of income distribution.

As I am presenting it, the core of socialism in its economic aspect is the constraint and modification of the market to accommodate the interests of people as workers, consumers, and citizens. The citizens of any society are quite naturally and rightly concerned with large accumulations of power in private hands, and it is a consequence of such a concern that socialism is opposed to private ownership of the means of production. It must, however, be emphasized that no reorganization of ownership (including ownership by the workers in a firm) can overcome the inadequacies of the market that I shall sketch in a moment. If so-called 'market socialism' denies this, then it is in my view a contradiction in terms.

I have been talking up to now about socialism versus capitalism. What about socialism versus individualism? Individualism is best seen, both historically and analytically, as the generalization of the case for capitalism to non-economic matters. It is no accident, I suggest, that the notion of the hidden hand originated in the heyday of deism. According to the deistic picture of the universe, God, having arranged things to operate according to universal laws, did not intervene any further in his creation. What appeared to be imperfections were merely the unavoidable by-products of the best possible set of general laws. The parallel with the standard rationale of the market could scarcely be clearer. Hayek particularly, who has often said that he finds himself most at home intellectually in the late eighteenth century, is identified strongly with the ideologically loaded concept of the 'rule of law'. According to this, states must operate by general

[3] Friedrich A. Hayek, *Law, Legislation, and Liberty*, vol. ii, *The Mirage of Social Justice* (Chicago: Chicago University Press, 1976).

laws only, and not intervene in the workings of the economy in order to bring about specific outcomes. And, like Leibniz, Hayek assures us that, even if the results in individual cases sometimes appear unfortunate, all is for the best in the best of all possible worlds so long as we have the best set of general laws.

Individualism, I suggest, is simply what you get if you take the optimistic analysis of the market and extend it beyond economics to the whole of social life. The market paradigm says that, given the right framework of general rules (enforcement of property rights and contracts, maintenance of competition, etc.), pursuit of individual self-interest is transmuted into social good. Individualism—epitomized, for example, in Mill's *On Liberty*—takes this structure of thought and makes it the basis for a whole theory of society.[4] So-called libertarianism, represented by, for example, Ayn Rand, Murray Rothbard, and their disciple Robert Nozick, is simply individualism that has run amok. Indeed, libertarianism has been well defined as the form taken by liberalism as common sense asymptotically approaches zero.

What marks liberal individualists of all kinds is a distaste, amounting in some cases to detestation, for politics. The wheeling and dealing, the messy compromises that are inseparable from politics, are anathema to them. To such people, the worst thing you can say about some area—education, say, or public transport—is that it has become 'politicized'. It might be naïvely supposed that, in what is supposed to be a democracy, subjecting important areas of public policy to political scrutiny and control would be thought of as a good thing. But no: according to the tenets of individualism, once the general rules have been laid down, people are free to act individually, but not collectively.

Some observers claim to have found something paradoxical in the fact that the Thatcher regime combines liberal individualist rhetoric with authoritarian action. But there is no paradox at all. The two are in fact simply opposite sides of the same coin. Even under the most repressive conditions—in Soweto or the Gaza Strip and the West Bank, say—people seek to act collectively in order to improve things for themselves, and it requires an enormous exercise of brutal coercion in order to fragment these efforts at organization and force people to pursue their interests individually. Things are no different here: left to themselves, people will inevitably tend to pursue their interests

---

[4] John Stuart Mill, *On Liberty*, in *Essays on Politics and Society*, ed. J. M. Robson (Toronto: Toronto University Press, 1977), i. pp. 213–310.

through collective action—in trade unions, tenants' associations, community organizations, and local government, for example. Only the pretty ruthless exercise of central power can defeat these tendencies: hence the common association between individualism and authoritarianism, well exemplified in the fact that the countries held up as models by the free-marketeers are, without exception, authoritarian regimes.

It was at one time fashionable to suggest that socialism should be defined as the pursuit of equality. There is, however, nothing distinctively socialist about equality: there can be (and are) egalitarian anarchists and egalitarian liberals as well as egalitarian socialists. Socialism thus has no monopoly on egalitarianism; but more than that, there is nothing in socialism itself that commits one to equality. The central demand of socialism is that outcomes—and this obviously includes the distribution of income—should fall under collective control. But this leaves open what the distribution of income ought to be. Some socialists believe that those who contribute more to the society through their work should get more; others believe that the ability to contribute more arises from good fortune and does not constitute a valid claim to finish up with more. I am inclined to think that the ultimate resolution of this issue depends on a satisfactory solution to the problem of free will, and I do not think this can be expected soon. (It is significant that the fallen angels in *Paradise Lost* pitched on this as a topic good for a few million years of debate.) Anyway, pending the cracking of the problem of free will, socialists can, I suggest, legitimately disagree about equality.

III

The idea has been put about that socialism is bound to be unattractive to most people because it demands too much in the way of sacrifice. In fact the paradigm of socialism is the prisoner's dilemma, where what is most in the interest of each prisoner individually—to confess—is contrary to the interests of both of them together.[5] Examples abound in real life: if we all try to drive our cars at once, the roads become so congested that none of us can get anywhere; if we all have garden bonfires whenever we wish, none of us can hang out the washing or sit outside in comfort; and so on. The remarkable ideological success of

[5] For an exposition and a discussion of the significance of the prisoner's dilemma see Brian Barry and Russell Hardin (eds.), *Rational Man and Irrational Society? An Introduction and Sourcebook* (Beverly Hills, Calif.: Sage, 1982), Pt. I.

Thatcherism is to identify the selfish, antisocial choice with self-interest. Obviously, if socialism is to succeed, this ideological obfuscation has to be removed; but it is important to recognize that the task is one of education rather than one of mass conversion to altruism. What is called for is not self-sacrifice but simply playing one's part in a collectively beneficial practice.

To any socialist, the operations of the market provide an unending source of illustrations for the thesis that the aggregate results of the pursuit of private interest may well be collectively damaging. The pollution created by firms in the course of profit-maximization is a hackneyed but none the less central example. I can see no incompatibility between the politics of red and green; on the contrary, socialism seems to me to provide the essential intellectual framework for environmental concerns. It should be conceded that one of the most arrogant, obstructive, and unconscionable polluters in Britain is the Central Electricity Generating Board. But all that shows is the inappropriateness of this kind of public corporation as a socialist instrument.

Pollution by producers is a form of market failure in that there is no way in which the market can incorporate into its calculations the economic costs, aesthetic damage, and threats to health and life itself created by pollution. The citizens must, acting through the instrumentality of the state, step in to curb the pursuit of profit—and let me emphasize that this is equally true whether the producers are privately owned firms, public corporations charged with acting commercially, or workers' co-operatives.

The evil is generated by the logic of the market mechanism itself. To the degree that it works in the way postulated by the elementary textbooks, that is to say to the degree that it is genuinely competitive, it forces firms on pain of bankruptcy to do whatever is legal (or more precisely whatever is cost-effective, taking into account the probability and cost of conviction) in the pursuit of profit—however injurious this may be to the labour-force, to those living in the neighbourhood, or indeed to the purchasers of their products.

There are more subtle forms of market failure, which again illustrate the way in which uncoordinated individual decisions may add up to outcomes that are not desired. There is no way in which a market can register the willingness to pay for having a service available. Many of us attach a good deal of importance to having public telephones disseminated over the country in case we are stranded and need them, yet it may well be that a large number of these public telephones do not get enough use to 'pay for themselves'. Acting according to a commercial criterion here would be failing to provide people with what they want and are willing to pay for. A fanatical marketeer could, presumably, suggest that everyone should adopt a telephone kiosk in some remote village and drive out periodically to it with a sackful of coins to make long telephone calls to Australia. I need not insult your intelligence by pointing out what is wrong with this proposal.

There are also, of course, distributive arguments in favour of retaining a dense network of public telephones, and the same mix of collective benefit and distributive considerations can be invoked in many other areas, of which public transport is probably the most important: here again, the value of public transport is not adequately measured by the fares that are collected because its very existence has a value. Even someone who always drives derives a benefit from public transport in the form of insurance against a breakdown.

In these examples, the market can be shown to fail in its own terms: it does not manage to come up with the goods that we want in our capacity as consumers. But the market can also fail in ways that take us beyond the limited perspective of consumerism. If we want to see some beautiful stretch of coastline protected for ever against development, or the ancient quarter of some city saved from demolition, the reason may indeed be that we want to preserve the option of going and looking at it ourselves some day. Here, the state has to step in to provide us with a certain form of 'consumption' that can be enjoyed only if private preferences for buying and selling are overridden by the preference for a public good. But we may instead step outside our role as consumers altogether, and support preservation simply because we think that it is good and right for the country to be one in which natural beauty and artefacts of historical interest or aesthetic value are preserved.

Another very significant illustration of the potential clash between market forces and the wishes we have as citizens is this. In very many countries, and sometimes localities within countries, people feel an intense sense of discomfort if more than a certain proportion of the real estate and productive capacity fall into the hands of non-nationals. As individuals they may be quite willing to sell to the highest bidder but as citizens they may at the same time vote to set a limit to the proportion of total assets that can be held in foreign hands. The socialist principle is that what people want as citizens should prevail over what they want as private buyers or sellers.

The distribution of income and wealth in a society can be analysed with the same apparatus. According to the by now notorious argument of Robert Nozick,[6] if a large number of people voluntarily pay, say, 50 pence to watch some star performer, they can obviously have no valid objection to whatever distribution of income arises from it, even if the result of this set of transactions and innumerable other sets of transactions like it is to create a grossly unequal distribution. The argument, if such it can be called, is obviously a variant on Locke's suggestion that by 'consenting to the use of money' people consent to whatever distribution of income and wealth comes about. You might as well say that every time we turn on a light we consent to nuclear reactors and acid rain, or that by not—between us—putting some arbitrary amount of money per year into a public call box somewhere on the Yorkshire moors, we consent to its being carted away.

All that can be deduced here is that a lot of people, taking independent decisions, preferred paying 50 pence to missing the star's performance. We cannot say that they approved of the resulting distribution of income, because that was not a choice on offer. The distribution of income is an aggregate outcome, and can be chosen only by a collective decision. We have already seen how we may choose collectively to modify the outcomes we would bring about individually—preventing development that our decisions as consumers would make profitable or barring sales to foreigners that would pay us as individual sellers. And so here too we may for a whole variety of reasons—distribution of power, concern for the quality of social relationships, as well as considerations of equality—wish to change by collective action the outcome of a mass of individual decisions.

IV

I said in my opening remarks that the present government has opened up conflicts of principle where before there was consensus, and this is nowhere better illustrated than in relation to schooling. I am not concerned here with the details of the government's policies but with the underlying principle, which is very plainly the individualistic one of turning decisions over to the operation of a market or quasi-market. What I want to do quite briefly is to show how the socialist critique of individualism applies here.

[6] Robert Nozick, *Anarchy, State, and Utopia* (New York: Basic Books, 1974), 160–4. This is usually referred to as the Wilt Chamberlain example, since it is built around the case of a well-known American basketball player.

Let us simplify the analysis by contrasting two ideal types of educational system. In one, children are allocated to schools so that each school will be representative of the social class and ethnic mix of the district—say the area of the local authority. In the other, parents either have educational vouchers which can be used at any school or have the right to apply for their children's admission to any school in the appropriate age-range run by the local authority. The schools in turn can select children from among the applicants.

We may now look at the operation of the second system. The result of all the decisions by parents and schools will be some pattern of allocation which nobody chose and perhaps nobody wants. Typically, it will be one in which there is a pecking order of schools. Even if all the schools in an area have equally good facilities and equally good teachers, all that is needed to create a hierarchy is a preference by parents for schools with more rather than fewer children of high academic attainment and selection by schools among applicants on the basis of academic attainment.

From a consumer point of view, this may be a quite unattractive outcome. If there are five schools and everyone wants to get into one of them, four-fifths of the parents are going to be disappointed. Freedom of choice is really no more than freedom to apply: the only school that can be chosen unconditionally is the one at the bottom of the heap—precisely because few choose it. There is no way in which it can be shown a priori that parents or children will be more satisfied on average with such a system of so-called parental choice than with one in which each child is allocated to a school whose composition is similar to that of the others in the area.

Suppose, however, that parents were happy enough to have their children educated in schools that were relatively homogeneous with respect to social class and ethnicity. The system of parental choice could then count as a success from the consumer point of view. But we should still have to ask how this system should be regarded from the point of view of the citizens—those with children currently in the school system and those without. I think the answer is that it should be looked on with misgivings. We live in a society where racial and ethnic tensions have already given rise to large-scale riots. We live in a society where the frustration and resentment of losers leads to vandalism and violence. Does it make sense to perpetuate the divisions of class and ethnic group in the schools? If we leave the composition of the schools to parental choice that is what we shall be doing even though the choice will not be made explicitly.

The relevance of socialism is here, as in my other examples, to insist that an outcome is not saved from critical assessment by its origin in individual choices. The overall result of a lot of choices made by parents and schools has to be compared with what can be achieved by allocating children to schools with the object of creating a microcosm of the area in each school, and then trying, by precept and practice, to encourage equal respect and understanding among children of different backgrounds.

Miracles are not to be expected from schools: they cannot themselves compensate for everything else that is wrong in a society. But what must be emphasized is that, whether by default or by explicit action, every society chooses either to perpetuate and intensify its divisions in its schools or to make some effort to overcome them.

v

The core of socialism, as I have presented it, is that people should act collectively through central and local government to attain ends that cannot be achieved by individual effort. Needless to say, collective action for shared ends can also be undertaken by people outside the framework of government. Trade unions are an excellent example: though not in themselves socialist, because they pursue a partial interest, they provide a model of socialism in action. Hence their importance in the history of socialism.

The trade union model of collective self-help is also of great significance for social welfare policy because trade unions all over Europe in the course of the nineteenth century developed schemes of insurance as a natural extension of their other activities in pursuit of the collective benefit of their members. Now in most continental European countries (the Scandinavian ones taking the lead) these mutual benefit societies were first subsidized and rationalized by the state and then finally more or less completely absorbed in schemes of universal social insurance. The usual way in which these schemes operate is that both contributions and benefits are roughly proportional to income, subject to some minimum level of benefit. There is, therefore, not a great deal of transfer between income strata, and this has the implication that those with higher incomes have no self-interested reason to resist a generous level of provision. The question people in each stratum are invited to ask themselves is: what level of benefits do I want to pay for? And the answer has turned out to be: a lot. It is a commonplace that, in the last forty years, the scale of transfer payments in Western Europe outside this country has grown phenomenally, so that costs now run at between a fifth and a quarter of the national income in most countries.

Meanwhile, the British experience has been strikingly different from that of the rest of Western Europe. Starting in the immediate post-war period with one of the best-funded systems, Britain has by now slipped below most of the others in the proportion of its gross national product that goes on income maintenance. Why is this? One possible explanation is that in the same period Britain has slipped from having the highest income per head in Western Europe to having one of the lowest, and therefore cannot 'afford' as much as the others. But why should relative poverty produce a lower *proportional* expenditure? One might think that if anything insurance would be relatively more important the less well off people are.

We should I think look for an answer in the mind-set that thinks in terms of 'what the country can afford' instead of 'what coverage people want to pay for'. Abstracting from their variations, let us say that the continental systems exhibit the 'insurance model'. How then shall we describe the underlying ethos of the British system, as it has developed over the course of this century? I suggest that it should be called the 'needs model'. By this I understand the following guiding idea: that payments should be made only to those who are in need, and should be set at a level sufficient to get them above some defined poverty level.

I shall not stop to belabour all the differences between a pure insurance model and a pure need model, but it is I hope evident that they are opposed at every turn. The most striking contrast between them is that the needs model entails means-testing for all benefits, whereas the insurance model in its pure form has no room for means-testing at all. Thus, under the insurance model people who are sick or unemployed will automatically receive, say, three-quarters of their previous income, while under a needs model they may receive nothing if they have too much money in the bank or a continuing source of family income. From the insurance point of view, this is as bad as an insurance company's refusing to compensate for a burglary on the grounds that the policyholder can perfectly well afford to replace the stolen items out of his or her own pocket. Conversely, from the needs point of view, paying out a lot of money to someone who is already well off is a 'waste' of resources that could be better 'targeted' on the 'needy'.

Life never makes things completely easy for the makers of models.

Although the bulk of the money disbursed within the continental systems falls under the insurance model, each country also has some kind of means-tested assistance for people who fall between the cracks. Conversely, the British system is some way from exemplifying the needs model exclusively. Formally, the system is one of social insurance with flat-rate benefits. There are, however, two observations to be made. The first is that flat-rate benefits, the legacy of the wartime Beveridge Report, violate the insurance concept, which is one of income replacement. A flat-rate scheme is like a system of fire insurance in which every houseowner gets just enough to rebuild a minimal house whatever the size of the one that has burnt down. It is clear that, in spite of its insurance trappings, a flat-rate system is best seen as a way of meeting needs—something that Beveridge himself acknowledged.

The second point to make is that, in any case, Beveridge's flat-rate benefits have never been set at a level above the official poverty line. The result has been that at no time since the war have there been fewer than millions of people on means-tested supplementary benefits. If the insurance-related benefits have to be topped up in this way, it seems fair to say that the system as a whole conforms primarily to the needs model.

As a further support for this view of the matter, I can adduce the fact that the surviving elements of the insurance model are seen as anomalies. Why, it is asked recurrently by some wiseacre, should 'we' be paying good money to people who do not need it? The solution, which is constantly being independently discovered, is a negative income tax which would put all benefits on a means-tested basis. (The change in name to negative taxation is thought for some reason to solve all the existing problems of means-tested benefits.)

On the face of it, the needs model is rather attractive: those who can afford it give, and those who need it receive. It is noteworthy that with almost no exceptions Anglophone philosophers who have written about the foundations of the 'Welfare State' have seen the task as one of defending the claims of need. The needs model is Good Samaritanism writ large, and indeed arguments in favour of it often start by appealing to cases where one person can save another from some situation of dire need. The basis of Good Samaritanism is that the aid is given without any expectation of return. The Samaritan may, of course, hope that somebody will do the same for him if the occasion ever arises, but there is no link between his present altruistic act and what may or may not happen to him in some like contingency in the future.

I expect that what I have just said will already have reminded a number of you of Richard Titmuss's argument in *The Gift Relationship*.[7] In that book voluntary blood donation, an act of unconditional altruism, was advanced as a paradigm for social policy generally. Now blood donation is significantly different from other areas of collective provision precisely in that it is voluntary: no supporter of a general scheme of transfer payments is going to suggest that the wherewithal should come from voluntary contributions. The relevance of blood donation is, however, taken to be this. Blood donation may be regarded as an expression of social solidarity, which we may understand as the generalization of Good Samaritanism. And social policy might then be seen as an expression of social solidarity too, here understood as universal and compulsory Good Samaritanism. Concretely, this would entail those who can afford it voting out of a sense of empathy to pay taxes to support those in need.

Titmuss believed that the moral basis of the post-war Welfare State was laid in the experience of the Second World War and in particular the sense of common vulnerability and interdependence generated by the blitz. There is much plausibility in this.[8] That disasters, natural or man-made, stimulate social solidarity is one of the best-documented findings in social science. But what is equally well established is that after things return to normal solidarity gradually diminishes, and Britain in the post-war period also illustrates this.

What happens when a system founded on an assumption of a high level of social solidarity has to exist in a society where that assumption has failed to be true? The answer is, I suggest: what has actually happened in this country over the past forty years. The system becomes meaner and meaner as time goes on. Where does this leave us? Fortunately, it leaves us still in a good position. The insurance model is, I wish to say, the implementation of the socialist principle with regard to social security. Insurance by its very nature requires a lot of people to get together, and the best insurance occurs when everyone is in it, with the power of the fisc as the ultimate underwriter. The reasons for state insurance are as strong now as they were when the mutual benefit societies were absorbed on the continent of Europe. Unemployment, for example, has never been satisfactorily

---

[7] R. M. Titmuss, *The Gift Relationship: From Human Blood to Social Policy* (London: George Allen and Unwin, 1970).

[8] See for support of this view Robert E. Goodin and John Dryzek, 'Risk sharing and Social Justice: The Motivational Foundations of the Post-War Welfare State', in Robert E. Goodin and Julian Le Grand, *Not Only the Poor: The Middle Classes and the Welfare State* (London: Allen and Unwin, 1977), 37–73.

insured against in the private market. And it is inevitable that private sickness pay insurance—like medical insurance—will charge higher premiums to those who are poorer health risks, or even refuse to insure them altogether. (We can see this phenomenon at work in the distasteful but entirely logical efforts of insurance companies to exclude from life insurance coverage those whom they regard as being at risk from AIDS.)

What I have just said should bring out an important point about social insurance. It is not the object of social insurance simply to ape the workings of private insurance, but to provide coverage for everybody without discriminating against bad risks. This is one of the ways in which social insurance is better than private insurance. The point of insurance is to provide protection against misfortunes, but no private scheme will provide protection against the misfortune of being a bad risk in the first place. Social insurance can and does.

Now it is of course true that, as a result of this, some very fortunate people would be better off in a hypothetical private market than under a social insurance scheme—though we should not forget the very high overheads of private insurance, overheads that are inherent in the attempt to keep out poor prospects. It is often suggested that, because of this, social insurance is not really insurance at all. The suggestion is obtuse in presupposing that private insurance is the only kind of insurance. Social insurance is a different and better kind of insurance because it is, as the cliché has it, 'from the cradle to the grave' (or 'from womb to tomb') and membership in it is not voluntary.

Because membership is compulsory, there is no necessity to treat bad risks less well than good ones. Moreover, those who are severely disabled from birth, so that they have no prospects of ever earning enough to pay insurance contributions, can be included by a simple and obvious extension of the insurance idea: that, of all the things we would wish to insure against if we could, being severely disabled at birth must surely head the list.

It is apparent that social insurance calls upon a certain degree of solidarity in that, for example, people of voting age know whether or not they are severely disabled, and the great majority are not. It is, however, in the nature of all public goods that some people get more out of them than others, and the disproportion between contribution and expected benefit is probably less for a system of social insurance than for almost any other public good. And I think that, if once people see the logic of social insurance, they should be able to see that it would be an anomaly to discriminate against or exclude the bad or hopeless risks.

VI

It is time to draw these remarks to a close. The fundamental argument for socialism, as I hope I have illustrated in my various examples, is simply that it is the only way of satisfying a lot of important desires. Undeniably, the antithesis of socialism—capitalism or individualism —gives us some of what we want. But it forces all aspirations into the one narrow channel of making and spending money. There is nothing about socialism that is incompatible with making and spending money, but, as I have tried to show, the object of socialism is to provide us with options in our capacity as citizens as well as in our capacity as individual consumers.

Acting through the market, we can do nothing to change a grotesquely unjust distribution of income, to create an adequate system of income-maintenance, to prevent industries from polluting and farmers from destroying the countryside, or to provide ourselves with properly funded public services of all kinds. Only in our capacity as citizens can we, acting collectively through local and national governments, bring about the outcomes that we want.

But do we really want them? I think it must be conceded that it is possible to create a society in which the response to market failure is not a swing to socialism, but an exacerbation of individual efforts to stay ahead by making and spending yet more money. Does the public health service have long waiting lists and inadequate facilities? Buy private insurance. Has public transport broken down? Buy a car for each member of the family above driving age. Has the countryside been built over or the footpaths eradicated? Buy some elaborate exercise machinery and work out at home. Is air pollution intolerable? Buy an air-filtering unit and stay indoors. Is what comes out of the tap foul to the taste and chock-full of carcinogens? Buy bottled water. And so on. We know it can all happen because it has: I have been doing little more than describing Southern California.

Now it is worth noticing two things about the private substitutes that I have described. The first is that in the aggregate they are probably much more expensive than would be the implementation of the appropriate public policy. The second is that they are extremely poor replacements for the missing outcomes of good public policy.

Nevertheless, it is plain that the members of a society can become so alienated from one another, so mistrustful of any form of collective action, that they prefer to go it alone.

We need not feel too sorry for the inhabitants of Southern California. Most of them have enough money to carry out the project of extreme privatization in style—and anyway there is all that sunshine. What is much less of a joke is the prospect of the same thing in a country with a third of the income and even less than a third of the sunshine.

Can it happen here? The object of the present government is undoubtedly to create the conditions for its happening. By systematically reducing the quality of public services of all kinds, it hopes to turn people away from them and encourage them to seek solutions individually. There is, it seems to me, no guarantee that this strategy will fail. As I said before, I do not regard socialism as coming with built-in prophecies. Perhaps, however perverse it may be, most people will get locked into pursuing private solutions to public deficiencies. But I hope not, because this would result in all of us living more limited and impoverished lives.

INDEX

1555